DIARY OF A RELUCTANT DREAMER

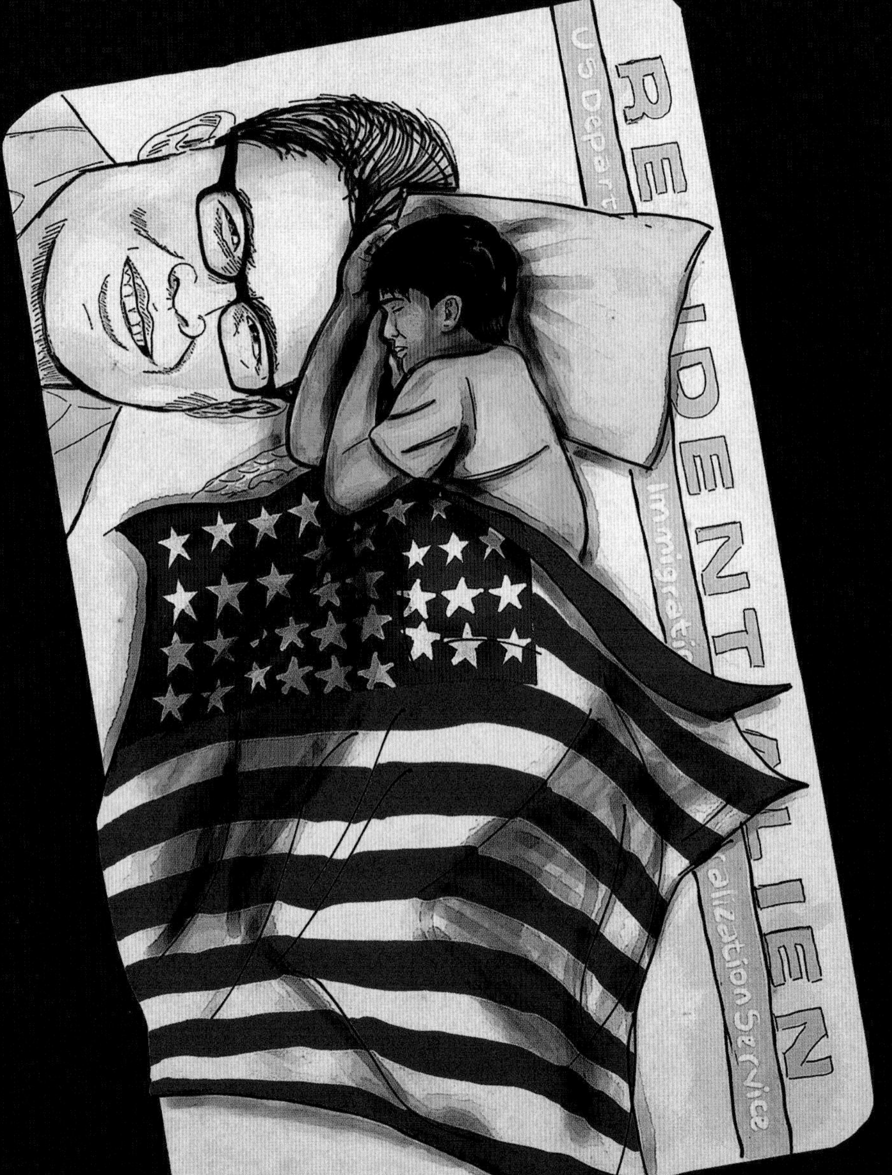

RE
IDENT
LIEN
US Depart
Immigrati
ralization Service

DIARY *of a* RELUCTANT DREAMER

Undocumented Vignettes from a Pre-American Life

ALBERTO LEDESMA

MAD CREEK BOOKS, AN IMPRINT OF THE OHIO STATE UNIVERSITY PRESS | COLUMBUS

Mad Creek Books, an imprint of The Ohio State University Press.

Library of Congress Cataloging-in-Publication Data
Names: Ledesma, Alberto, 1965– author.
Title: Diary of a reluctant dreamer : undocumented vignettes from a pre-American life / Alberto Ledesma.
Description: Columbus : Mad Creek Books, an imprint of The Ohio State University Press, [2017] | Series: Latinographix: The Ohio State Latinx comics series
Identifiers: LCCN 2017010341 | ISBN 9780814254400 (pbk. ; alk. paper) | ISBN 0814254403 (pbk. ; alk. paper)
Subjects: LCSH: Ledesma, Alberto, 1965—Comic books, strips, etc. | Illegal aliens—California—Oakland—Biography—Comic books, strips, etc. | Mexican Americans—California—Oakland—Biography—Comic books, strips, etc. | United States—Emigration and immigration—Social aspects—Comic books, strips, etc.
Classification: LCC PN6727.L379 Z46 2017 | DDC 741.5/973 [B]—dc23
LC record available at https://lccn.loc.gov/2017010341

Cover design by Lindsay Starr
Text design by Alberto Ledesma
Type set in Frank the Architect
Printed in China

∞ The paper used in this publication meets the minimum requirements of the American National Standard for Information Sciences—Permanence of Paper for Printed Library Materials. ANSI Z39.48-1992.

This is dedicated to my parents, Josefina and Adalberto, and my wife and daughter, Leticia and Sofia. This is also dedicated to all those generous friends who have contributed to making this humble project a reality. All of you are fellow travellers on this difficult but propitious journey.

Thank you for your tenderness and steadfast support.

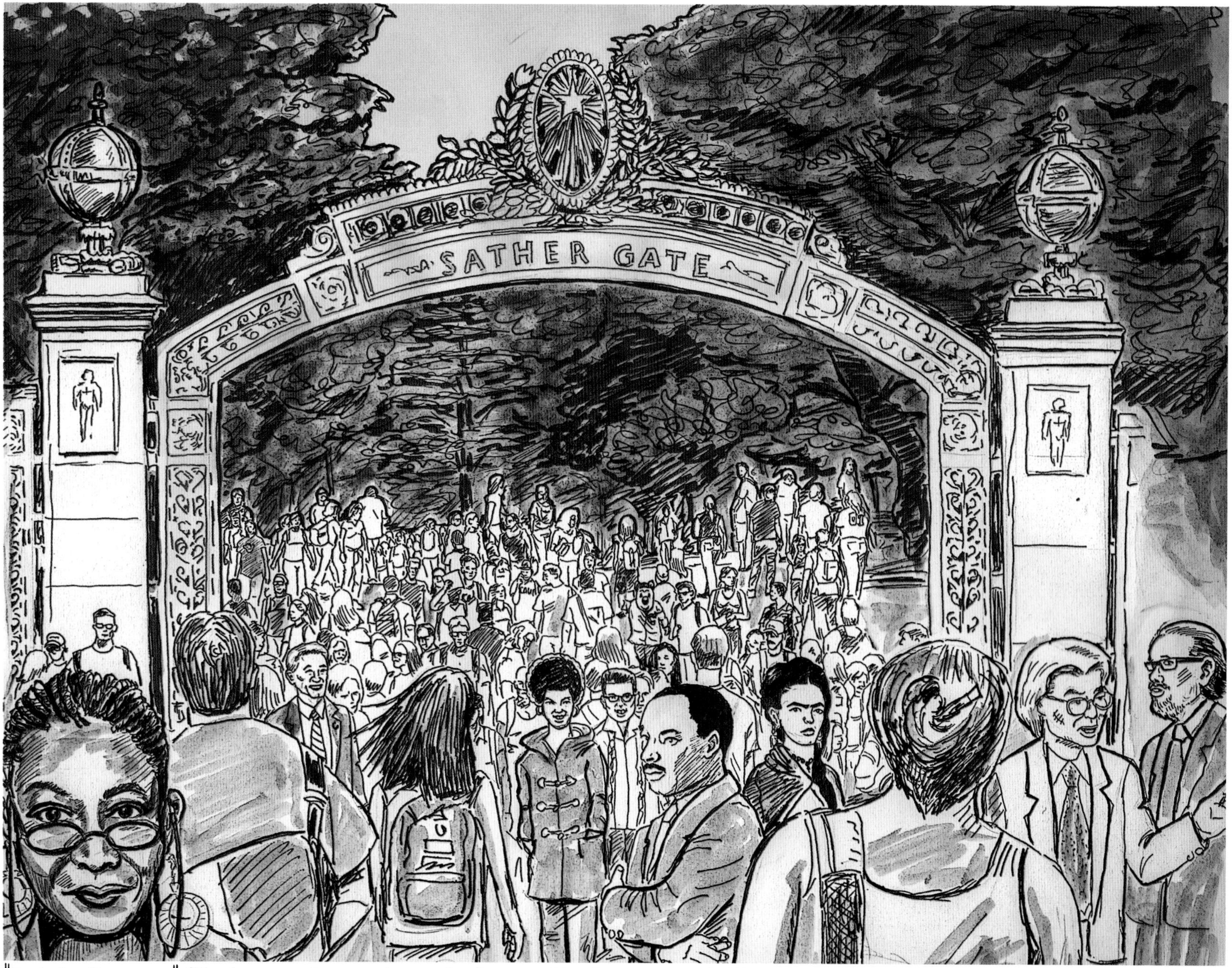
SATHER GATE

"Berkeley Dreamers," (Fountain pen, Copic marker, and gel pen on Strathmore paper, 2013)

Contents

Introduction   1

Doodling as Activism   3

Lunchtime Sketches   11

The First Years   17

Embracing My Undocumented Immigrant Identity   39

Assisting the Reluctant Dreamer   49

On Being an (Ex)Undocumented Immigrant Father   59

The Undocumented Alphabet   75

On the Need for Self-Amnesty   101

Deconstructing the Dreamer   109

Enter Trump   113

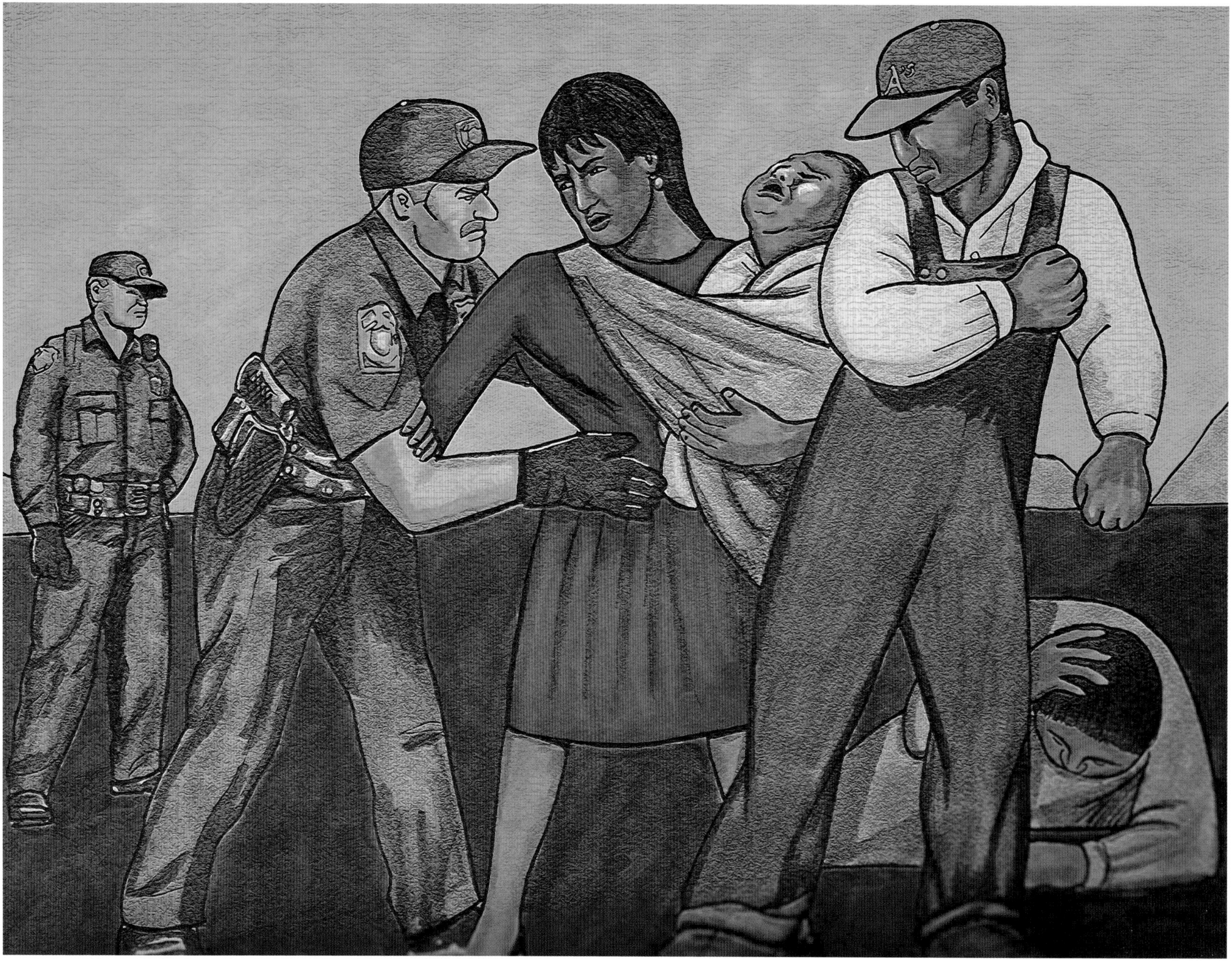

"There is no back of the line," A new take on a Diego Rivera Mural. (Fountain pen, Copic marker, and gel pen on Strathmore paper, 2014)

Diary of a Reluctant Dreamer:
AN INTRODUCTION

More than fifteen years before the immigration judge had asked me to raise my right hand to swear my allegiance to the United States, in one of those funky hot East Oakland nights in July, I had already decided that I would become "un Americano." It had happened around our small kitchen table, after mamá had cleared the dinner dishes to make way for our café con leche—that's when papá announced that we would soon be heading back to Guadalajara. There was no choice.

The piston foundry where papá had worked for ten years, the place that had given him the good job he had relied on to keep us in "el Norte," was relocating to Las Vegas, Nevada. Without that job we would not be able to survive in the US; and, he added, the factory in Las Vegas would not be opening for another year. We had to move.

But what exactly would we be moving back to? After so many years of living as an undocumented immigrant family in the *Yunaite Estais*, going back meant that my sisters and I would have to repeat years of elementary school. We would also need to reestablish friends and mourn relationships left behind. That night, after papá told us we had to leave the US, I decided to do everything in my power to stay.

In the following pages you will find a chronicle of all that I did as I transitioned from being a nervous undocumented immigrant kid to, a few decades later, a university professor and administrator. These doodles represent a sort of therapy that helped me grapple with my shifting identities. In the process, what I found was a way to help those who are still undocumented and who are afflicted, as I was, by a profound ambivalence about our Americanness. I hope that you enjoy these musings and learn from them as much as I did.

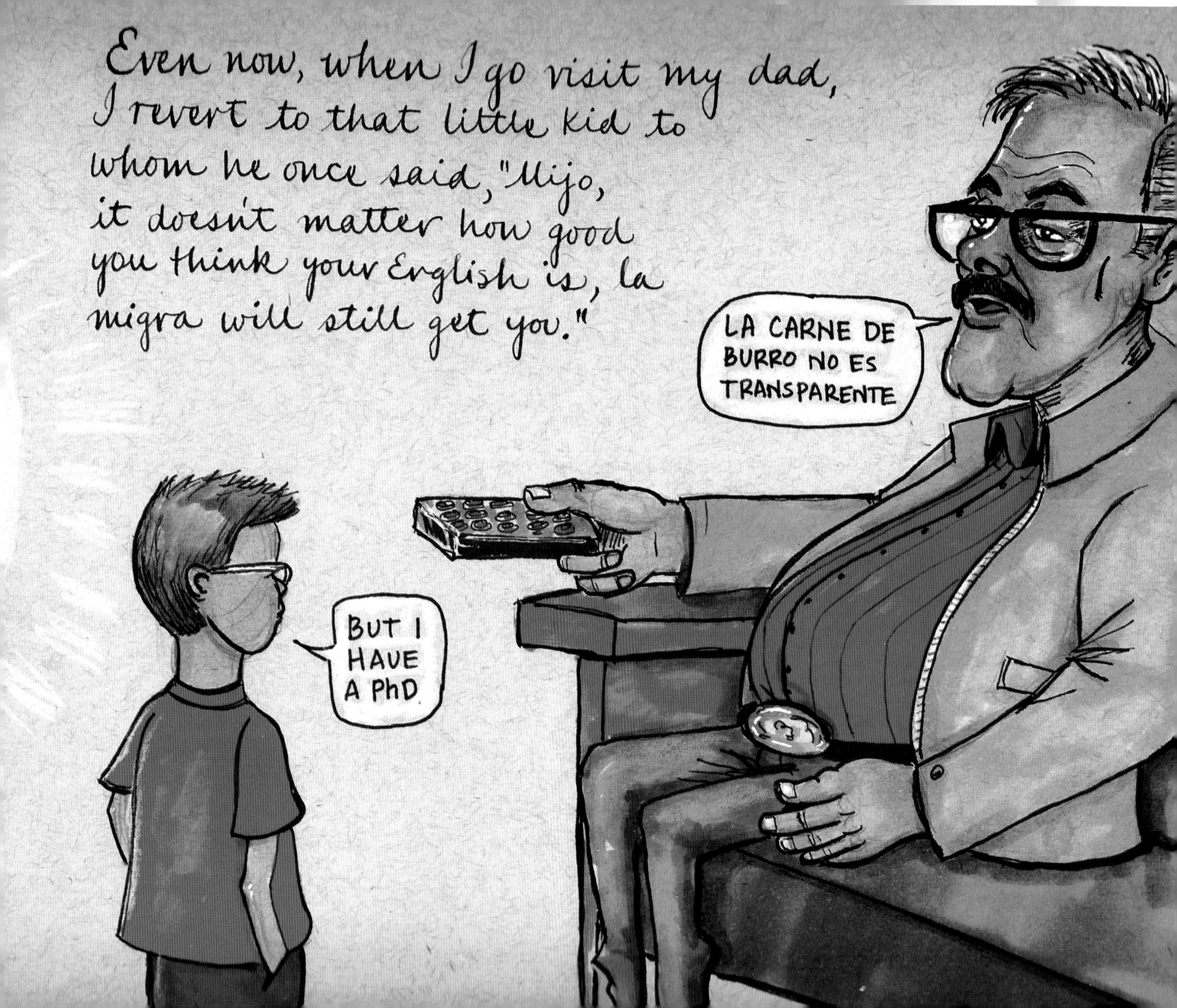
Even now, when I go visit my dad, I revert to that little kid to whom he once said, "Mijo, it doesn't matter how good you think your English is, la migra will still get you."
LA CARNE DE BURRO NO ES TRANSPARENTE
BUT I HAVE A PhD

CHAPTER 1

DOODLING AS ACTIVISM

Actually, when I was a little kid, if you would have asked me if I thought that I would ever be able to attend UC Berkeley in any capacity, I would have said "No."

I grew up in East Oakland, California, as an undocumented immigrant kid. At first, when we arrived in 1974, I thought that we would only be visiting for the summer, that the most time we would spend in the US would be a few months. To this day, almost forty years later, I have not been back to my hometown in Mexico.

The twelve years that I spent living in the heart of East Oakland as an undocumented immigrant conditioned me in a profound way, and it deeply affected how I behaved as a student, an academic, and now, as a Berkeley staff member.

Being undocumented, as I'm sure you can imagine, meant that we always lived with the fear of being caught, that any misstep we took could endanger the entire family. Though my dad worked tirelessly, though he made sure that we did well at school and always figured out honest ways to provide food and shelter even when he was between jobs, being undocumented meant that we always had to act with "cuidado," that we had to be careful when we were out and about.

In 1986, my family and I were able to legalize our status through the amnesty program that was part of the Immigration Reform and Control Act passed by Congress and signed by President Reagan. But though we were now "legal," those twelve years of conditioning did not disappear.

I have often wondered why, even to this day, we haven't heard more stories about what it meant to live as undocumented immigrants in the early 1980s. After all, more than three million people normalized their status through Reagan's amnesty. A large number of these amnestied undocumented immigrants, almost 40%, went on to become citizens. Why is it that we have not heard more stories about their experiences? Of course, what I have come to understand is that, though amnesty made it easy for a generation of undocumented immigrants to come out of the shadows, it did not remove the cultural taboo that still exists regarding that experience.

After amnesty, I thrived as a college student. Without the specter of a possible deportation, I felt that there were no limits to what I could do. Recently, I have learned that that desire to show that we are more than our legal status is what drives so many undocumented students to excel academically, to become "hyperdocumented," as Professor Aurora Chang puts it, to accumulate degree after degree, academic award after award.

After amnesty, I pursued a doctoral degree in which I studied the representation of undocumented immigrants in Mexican American narratives. What I discovered was that even there, in Mexican American fiction, you had a hierarchy of representation where usually, and particularly during the early stages of the Chicano literary expansion, immigrant subjects were discussed implicitly, in code, usually as part of the background and not as protagonists.

The taboo around discussing undocumented immigrant experience always mystified me. I strongly believed that it was a kind of American experience. In fact, I tried to write essays, critical and personal, and poetry about it in order to initiate a dialogue about what being undocumented meant. What I found in the mid-1990s were few people who responded to the dialogue I was attempting to initiate. Particularly when I was doing research, several of my colleagues expressed interest in what I was trying to do. In fact, when I attended profes-

On the Metaphysics of being undocumented

Just because you only value my arms and my back, it does not mean that I lack a mind with which to reflect on my condition. The truth is that I could write tomes about the ways that exploitation sharpens a worker's ability to see how society really works. But the kind of literacy I possess is not one you value; my voice is not one you can hear. Someday, it will be my children who will translate my experience in a fashion you will find hard to ignore.

"On the Metaphysics of Being Undocumented," 2014. I drew this image on parchment soon after finishing a stint as part of the VONA (Voices of Our Nation's Artists) Writing Program. During the program my instructors asked me to "get into the shoes" of the undocumented characters I was trying to write about. This is what I came up with.

sional conferences, I noticed a growing interest in my analysis of inter-ethnic immigrant narratives. But the field of undocumented immigrant studies was still in its nascent stages; there were not as many colleagues doing research about undocumented immigrant epistemology as there are now.

The fact is that I became impatient about initiating a public dialogue regarding undocumented immigration, even within the Mexican American community. I waited for those three million others who had gone through the IRCA normalization process with me to share their experiences. But, for the most part, there was just silence.

I waited for these stories because I needed them; I yearned for that sense of community that comes when you know that others have gone through the same things you have gone through. For me, dealing with being undocumented was difficult, stressful. I felt guilty, angry, and upset. But I kept it all in. It was a solitary experience, an ordeal that one dealt with on one's own, even within our families. Nobody really seemed to want to talk about it.

So, what happens to all these stories that remain repressed out of fear or a sense that one does not have the language to articulate them? What happens to all the tragic, heroic, and often funny accounts of close calls and challenges overcomed? Didn't amnesty mean that we were now free to talk about what we had experienced? This is what I have tried to understand all these many years. I knew that there was a deep well of compelling stories that could be shared with others, that could be understood for their universal truths—because I had lived them.

This has always been my project. For a while, as a professor, I gave it my all. I taught classes on the immigrant experience. submitted journal articles, and sat on literary panels. And then, when my baby daughter, Sofia, was born, everything changed.

I became a staff member at UC Berkeley. At that time, Leticia, my wife, was finishing medical school in San Francisco, and we quickly realized that if we each kept doing what we were doing, given the nature of our work, we would spend less time directly raising our daughter than the amount of time she would spend at daycare. It would also mean that Sofia would spend little time with her grandparents, all of whom still lived in East Oakland.

The solution was simple: I requested to take a couple of years of sabbatical at California State University, Monterey Bay so that Leticia would be able to work locally and so that I would take care of Sofia, let her spend as much time as possible with her grandparents and as little at childcare.

Of course, I also rationalized this decision because I thought it gave me the chance to write the next great Mexican American novel. At that point I thought that the time for telling my story was ripe; I had been studying the subject for many years, and I now felt prepared to relate it. Since then, the task has proven harder than I thought.

In the meantime, I found a position at Berkeley as a staff member. I eventually became a Writing Program Co-coordinator at the Student Learning Center. The job proved to be ideal because it focused on writing and teaching. I worked with students at all levels, and I got to study and discuss what effective writing techniques students might use. From time to time, I even got to work with students who came from East Oakland and who were undocumented.

One of the best parts of the job at the Student Learning Center was that I got to teach lecture-based courses in the summer as part of the Summer Bridge Program. Thus it happened that in the summer of 2011 I was giving a midterm in my Summer Bridge Chicano History course. We only had a couple

Often, when people ask me about my past life as a professor, I tell them that I left academe when my daughter was born so that I could spend more time with her. It was partially true.

THIS IS THE IMAGE I TRIED TO PROJECT OF MYSELF AS A PROFESSOR. BUT, YOU SHOULD ASK YOURSELF, WAS HE EVER THAT STUDIOUS OR THAT THIN?

While I did not want my daughter to grow up away from her grandparents if she followed me to the university where I was working, the truth is that I had grown increasingly fearful of what I was researching.

I had chosen to study Mexican American writers, to see the way they represented the undocumented immigrant experience—my experience.
What I found out was that too frequently undocumented immigrants were writen as stereotypes; they were merely shadows in the background, with no authentic voice of their own.
Then, when I presented my findings in a literary conference, I realized that I, too, was essentializing immigrants. The only way I could render authentic stories was to write them myself, I finally concluded.

YES, I'VE ALWAYS THOUGHT OF MYSELF AS A SHADOWED SCHOLAR.

But writing "authentic stories" has proven difficult without betraying the trust my parents put in me when they allowed me to go to school in the first place. I've always felt guilty about the path I chose. And yet, I have always also been driven by the need to show that the undocumented are thinking subjects, locked away like Antonio Gramsci in a prison with only their thoughts for company, hoping to find true liberation someday.

I DON'T UNDERSTAND MOST OF THE STUFF HE'S SAYING.

I THINK THAT WE LET HIM READ TOO MUCH. QUICK, GIVE HIM THE TV REMOTE!

This is an actual page from my Molskine "Diary of a Dreamer," page 51. I drew it with fountain pen and Prismacolor gray marker in 2012. Misspellings retained.

6

of weeks left in the class, and I wanted to add a discussion of the Dream Act and the unprecedented activism by undocumented immigrant students that was erupting throughout the nation. But I did not want to give my students any more reading; they had already been complaining about having too much of it and we were running out of time. I felt stuck: How would I introduce the subject and contextualize it within the course without giving them too much reading?

As my students took their midterm, I tried to grapple with the question of how to teach them about what was happening with undocumented immigrant activists—"dreamers," as they called themselves. And so I grabbed a scratch piece of paper from the stack that I had brought for the class and began doodling a quick cartoon of what I wanted them to consider: "A Day in the Life of a Dream Act Student."

Sketching the image was fun: I tried to show different aspects of an undocumented student's daily struggle—the challenge of financing an education when there was no financial aid. Then, when I noticed how often students lingered to see what I was working on after they had turned in their midterm, it hit me; why couldn't I use this doodle to introduce the topic?

"How is the current Undocumented Immigrant Student Movement similar in genesis to the Chicano Student Movement of the 1960s?" I asked at the start of my next lecture. "They are both about the material struggles of students who find themselves in institutions that are not necessarily designed for them." Then I projected my doodle on a Powerpoint slide and focused on various parts of the image. "Here's what an AB540 student has to contend with on an everyday basis."

Sure enough, the students became interested in the subject immediately. In fact, many of them became so curious that they took it upon themselves to research the topic even more intensely. Inspired by the way my students had reacted, I then shared the cartoon on Facebook, and that response that I had been looking to get from my academic writing, that dialogue that I had been looking to start for all those years, all of a sudden, I got that response from my cartoon. Of course, now that I think about it, a lot of the responses that I generated were due to the form in which I relayed my message. As the saying goes—"a picture is worth a thousand words."

Here I was rendering figurative essays with the cartoons that I was drawing. My students were also used to looking at political cartoons that had complex messages, so they were able to decode difficult concepts rather quickly.

Ironically, that goal that I had of "illustrating" what the undocumented immigrant experience was like when I was a young scholar, of showing how undocumented immigration is another kind of American experience, I was suddenly able to do that with the cartoons.

I discovered that my cartoons were particularly effective because they are flexible in the way they shift our perspective. The fourth wall is pliable; you can have an omniscient and first-person narrator at the same time. Now what I had forgotten is that I had learned this lesson on perspective already, back when I was in high school. But, because of all those years of training I had received in graduate school, I thought that the only option I had for sharing my critical view of the world was through literary narrative. Though I had skill in it, critical cartooning was not what I had been officially trained in. So, I totally neglected this talent.

In high school I had a teacher, Mrs. Wolfe, who thought I had some potential, and so she nominated me for a scholarship

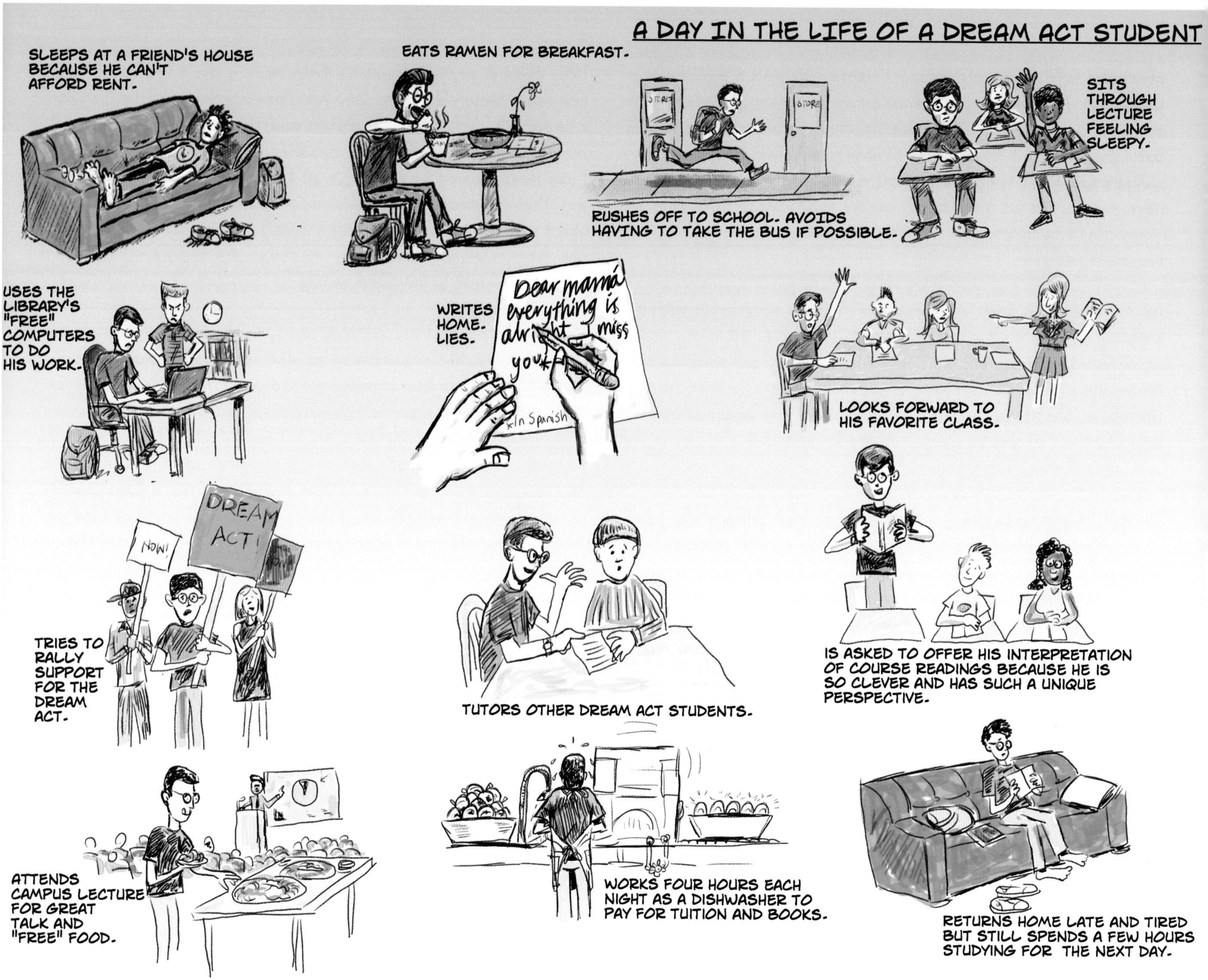
A DAY IN THE LIFE OF A DREAM ACT STUDENT
SLEEPS AT A FRIEND'S HOUSE BECAUSE HE CAN'T AFFORD RENT.
EATS RAMEN FOR BREAKFAST.
RUSHES OFF TO SCHOOL. AVOIDS HAVING TO TAKE THE BUS IF POSSIBLE.
SITS THROUGH LECTURE FEELING SLEEPY.
USES THE LIBRARY'S "FREE" COMPUTERS TO DO HIS WORK.
WRITES HOME. LIES.
Dear mamá everything is alright I miss you*
*In Spanish
LOOKS FORWARD TO HIS FAVORITE CLASS.
DREAM ACT
NOW!
TRIES TO RALLY SUPPORT FOR THE DREAM ACT.
TUTORS OTHER DREAM ACT STUDENTS.
IS ASKED TO OFFER HIS INTERPRETATION OF COURSE READINGS BECAUSE HE IS SO CLEVER AND HAS SUCH A UNIQUE PERSPECTIVE.
ATTENDS CAMPUS LECTURE FOR GREAT TALK AND "FREE" FOOD.
WORKS FOUR HOURS EACH NIGHT AS A DISHWASHER TO PAY FOR TUITION AND BOOKS.
RETURNS HOME LATE AND TIRED BUT STILL SPENDS A FEW HOURS STUDYING FOR THE NEXT DAY.

competition without me knowing it. Had I known it, I would have certainly not applied for this scholarship at all—it was a scholarship to go to Washington, DC, as a Latino student representative from East Oakland. I felt honored and did not want to disappoint Mrs. Wolfe; but, because I was undocumented, I also recognized the danger.

I was invited to an interview along with other candidates. And it was there that I decided that the best way to avoid the danger was by tanking the interview, but I wanted to do it in such a way that Mrs. Wolfe might hear good things about my effort. Whenever I was asked questions, I took the Cantinflas approach—that technique pioneered by the brilliant Mexican comic of answering questions without really answering them, of responding with non-sensical gibbersih, without offering any substance.

I was naïve. I did not realize that what the interview committee was looking for was someone who was diplomatic, someone who was polite and would not ruffle any feathers with the politicians in Washington. I ended up winning something I wanted to lose or losing something I wanted to win. So, I ended up going to Washington, DC. It was an extremely stressful experience. We ended up going to the White House, the Capitol Building, the Smithsonian, and the Supreme Court. But one particular place that we went to that caused the most stress was the FBI Building.

In the cartoon I drew about it, you can see the sources of my anxiety: the crowd, the guards. It had been just a little bit of time since Reagan had been shot. There were metal detectors everywhere. And there were guards checking people. So here I am in the Federal Bureau of Investigation. I thought that if I were going to be caught anywhere in Washington, it would surely be there, in the home of the best detectives on Earth.

So here I was undocumented, about to take the FBI Building tour, sweating like a pig. And all of a sudden, I notice people pointing at me as I moved. Other students, guards, men and women in suits and briefcases, all staring at me and grinning.

And, just as I'm about to go through the metal detector, the boy from Indiana who was my roommate at the hotel walks up to me with a grin on his face. I almost wanted to beat him to the punch. To tell him that "yes" I was undocumented and that I had had enough, that I just wanted to go home. He leaned close to my ear and told me that my pants zipper had been unzipped for most of the day. I looked down and, sure enough, the cheap zipper on the black, pinstripe suit that my father had bought me at the Eastmont Mall in East Oakland, so that I could "blend in" according to papá, had busted.

I tried to pull up my zipper so fast that I actually broke it. But, I did not care. The boy had said nothing about my immigration status. I felt relieved.

I realized in that moment that that fear I had about being undocumented and being caught, that most of that fear mostly existed in my head. And that I was not permitting myself to be myself because of that fear. And, after many years, the truth is that I had forgotten that lesson. I had seen cartooning as antithetical to my academic goals; that was the only perspective I valued. It was a skill that I couldn't seriously engage because it was on the other side of the disciplinary border.

Well, here it is. I have embraced my cartooning as much as I have my undocumented past. This is who I am.

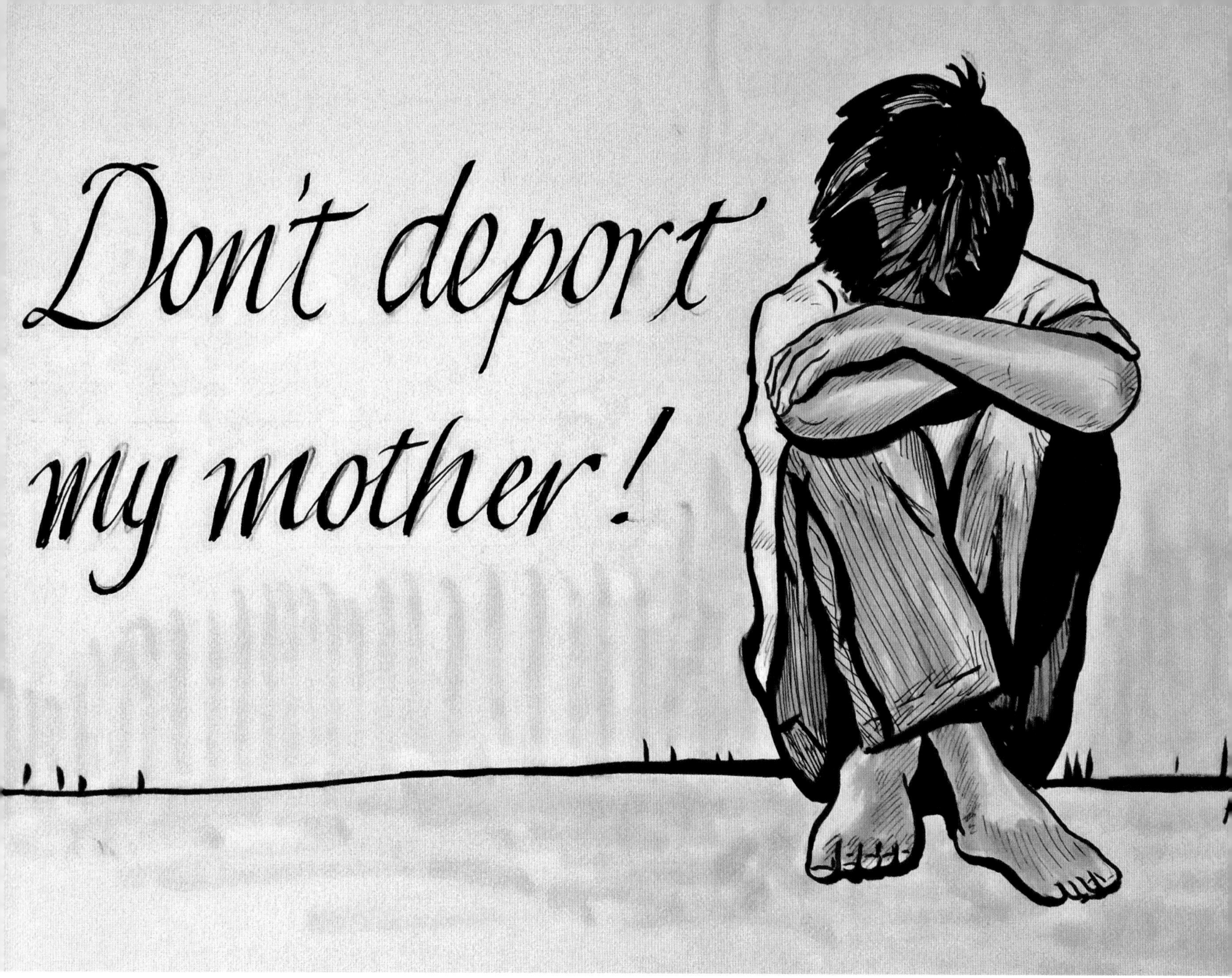
Don't deport
my mother!

I drew this illustration on July 12, 2016, after the Supreme Court rejected President Barack Obama's DAPA (Deferred Action for Parents of Americans) Executive Action.

CHAPTER 2

LUNCHTIME SKETCHES

The truth is that the illustrations collected in this ongoing "Diary of a Reluctant Dreamer" did not start out in such a fully-realized fashion. For months, before I began packing soft-lead pencils, gum erasers, and Prismacolor markers into my bag, the only things I drew were impressionistic sketches of my life as a UC Berkeley administrator who had once been an undocumented immigrant. It usually took me less than 30 minutes, after I had walked from my office in Barrows Hall to a restaurant near Telegraph Avenue. After I had my lunch, as the remains of a Diet Coke announced that I had indeed obtained my meal from that particular establishment, I hurried to render images that captured something about my undocumented past. Doing these sketches was like doing freewrites before writing a personal essay. Usually, it was during my walk from my office door to the restaurant table that I would come up with the theme for the day. As I ate my food—chicken flautas at the Durant Cafe, a BLT at Cafe Milano, a chicken sandwich at Smart Alec's—I would refine my idea as to what I would draw. Of course, in busy Berkeley, not all of the owners whose restaurants I visited seemed to enjoy my artistic filibusters during their rush hours. After some time, I learned that there were certain places, usually farther away from campus, that would tolerate me sitting, sketching in my notebook, long after my food was gone. My art, then, developed haphazardly, crafted around used packages of ketchup and balled-up brown napkins. But these sketches nourished my growth more than all the bento boxes, ham sandwiches, and carne asada tacos I ate. Here, in this section, is a sampling of what I did when I first got started.

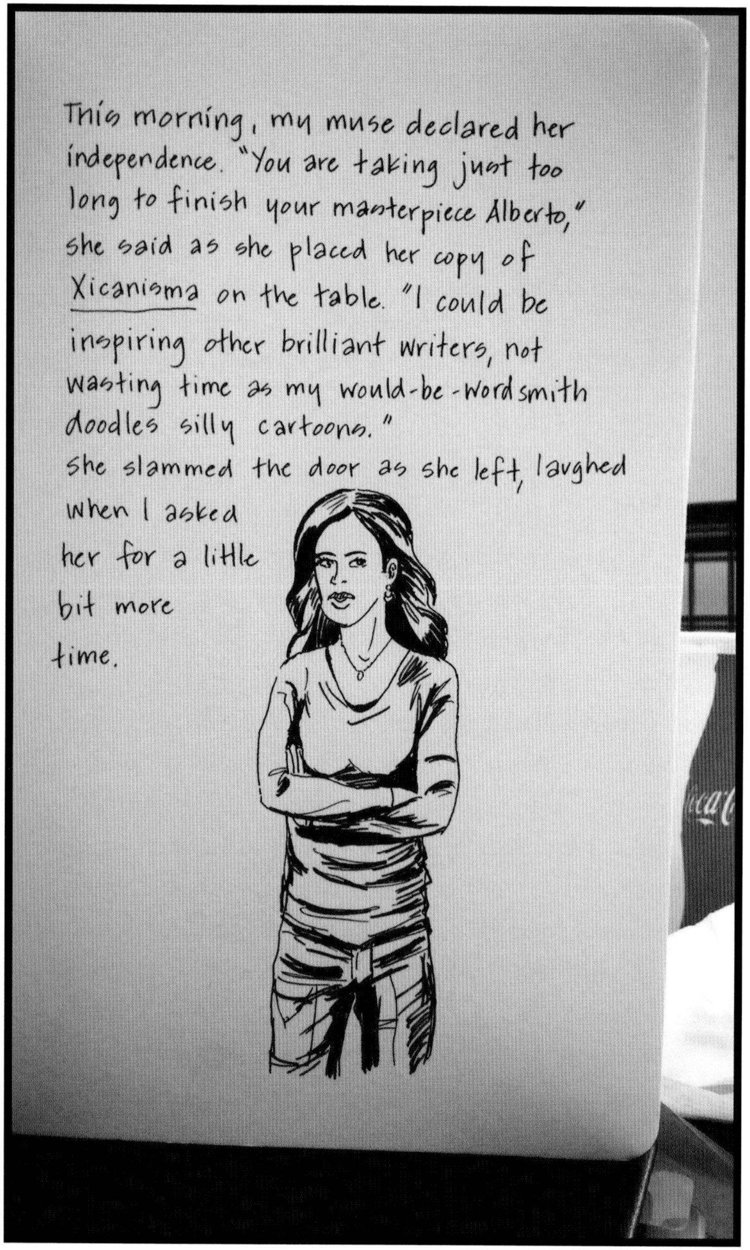
This morning, my muse declared her independence. "You are taking just too long to finish your masterpiece Alberto," she said as she placed her copy of Xicanisma on the table. "I could be inspiring other brilliant writers, not wasting time as my would-be-wordsmith doodles silly cartoons."
She slammed the door as she left, laughed when I asked her for a little bit more time.

"Mourning the loss of discipline." July 24, 2012.

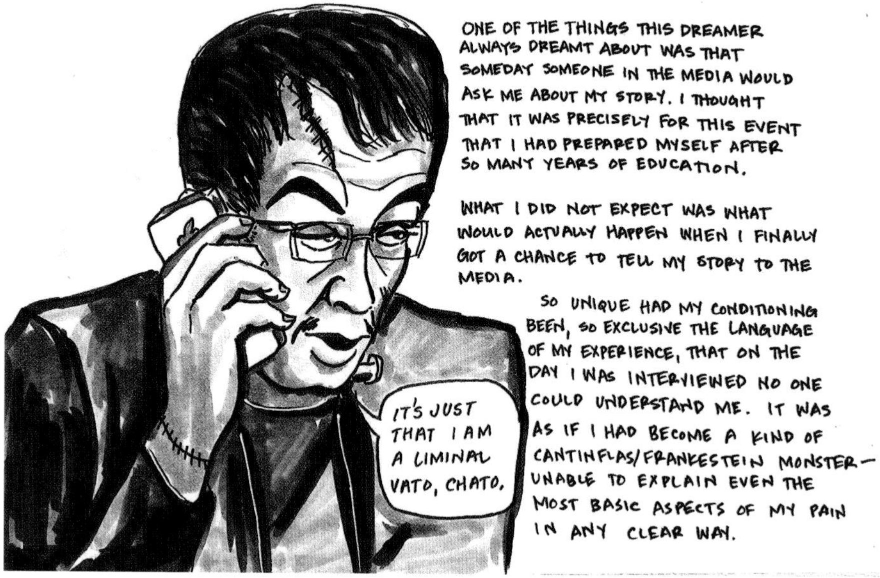
ONE OF THE THINGS THIS DREAMER ALWAYS DREAMT ABOUT WAS THAT SOMEDAY SOMEONE IN THE MEDIA WOULD ASK ME ABOUT MY STORY. I THOUGHT THAT IT WAS PRECISELY FOR THIS EVENT THAT I HAD PREPARED MYSELF AFTER SO MANY YEARS OF EDUCATION.
WHAT I DID NOT EXPECT WAS WHAT WOULD ACTUALLY HAPPEN WHEN I FINALLY GOT A CHANCE TO TELL MY STORY TO THE MEDIA.
SO UNIQUE HAD MY CONDITIONING BEEN, SO EXCLUSIVE THE LANGUAGE OF MY EXPERIENCE, THAT ON THE DAY I WAS INTERVIEWED NO ONE COULD UNDERSTAND ME. IT WAS AS IF I HAD BECOME A KIND OF CANTINFLAS/FRANKESTEIN MONSTER— UNABLE TO EXPLAIN EVEN THE MOST BASIC ASPECTS OF MY PAIN IN ANY CLEAR WAY.
IT'S JUST THAT I AM A LIMINAL VATO, CHATO.

"Frantinflas, the undocumented Prometheus." January 13, 2014.

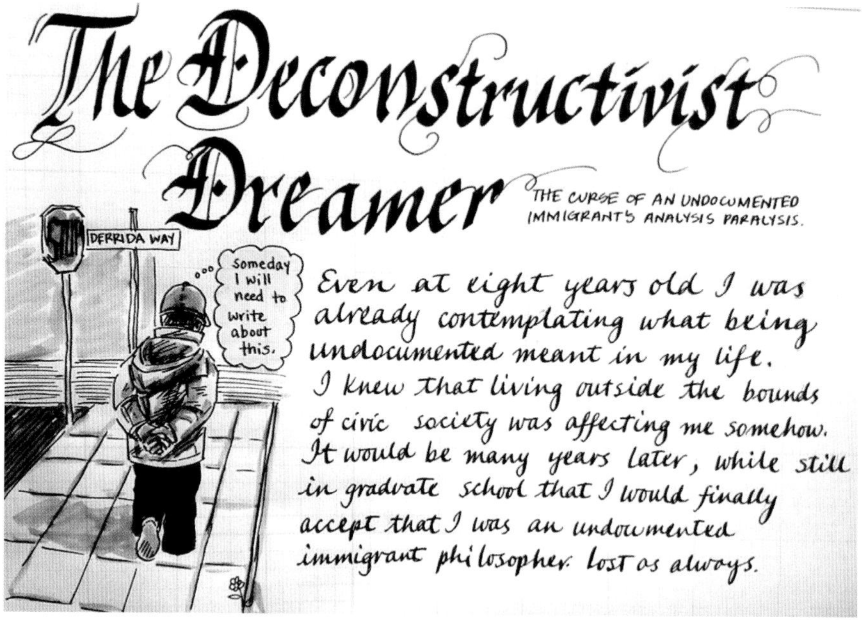
The Deconstructivist Dreamer
THE CURSE OF AN UNDOCUMENTED IMMIGRANT'S ANALYSIS PARALYSIS.
DERRIDA WAY
STOP
Someday I will need to write about this.
Even at eight years old I was already contemplating what being undocumented meant in my life.
I knew that living outside the bounds of civic society was affecting me somehow.
It would be many years later, while still in gradvate school that I would finally accept that I was an undoumented immigrant philosopher. lost as always.

"The Deconstructivist Dreamer." March 16, 2013.

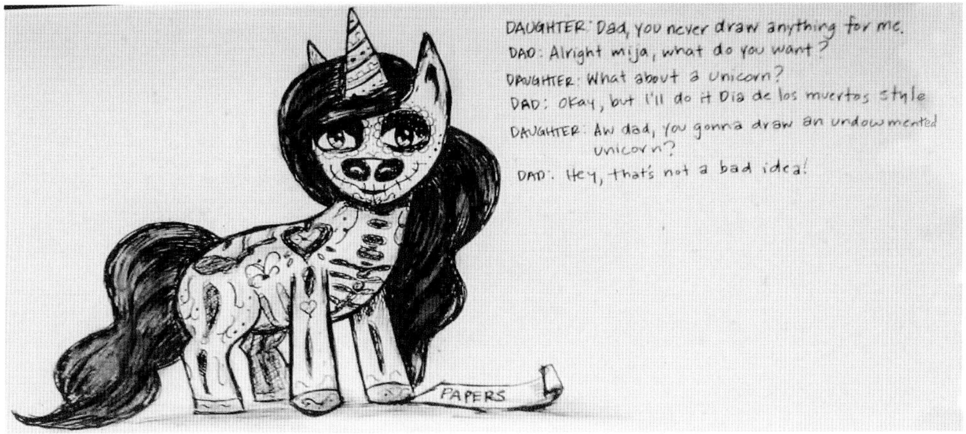
DAUGHTER: Dad, you never draw anything for me.
DAD: Alright mija, what do you want?
DAUGHTER: What about a unicorn?
DAD: Okay, but I'll do it Dia de los muertos style
DAUGHTER: Aw dad, you gonna draw an undocumented unicorn?
DAD: Hey, that's not a bad idea!
PAPERS

"An undocumented unicorn." October 26, 2013.

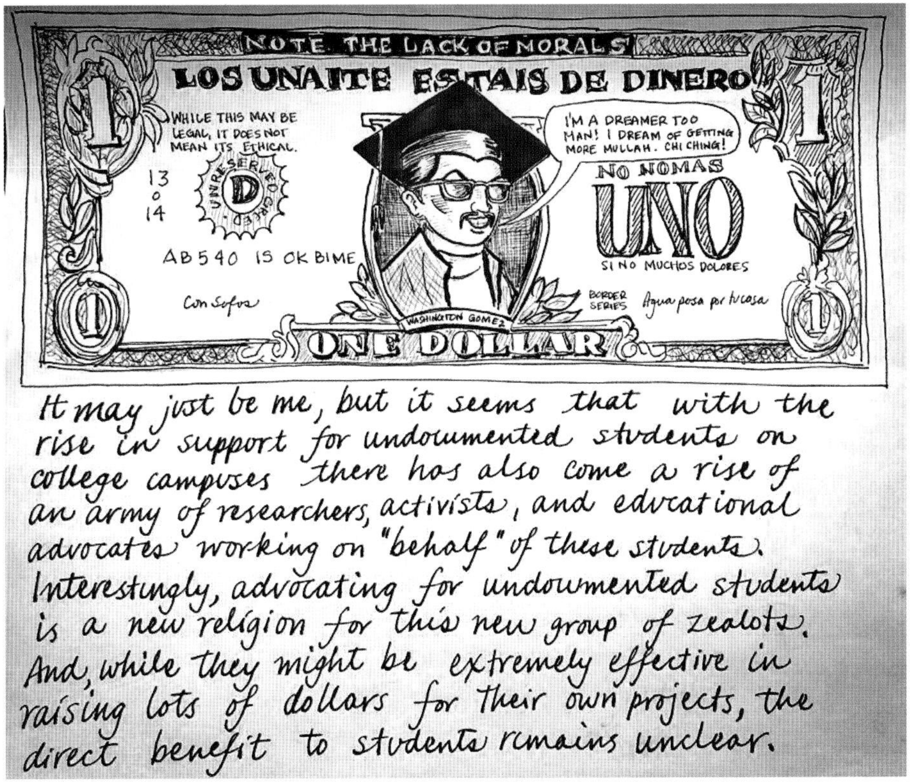
NOTE THE LACK OF MORALS
LOS UNAITE ESTAIS DE DINERO
WHILE THIS MAY BE LEGAL, IT DOES NOT MEAN ITS ETHICAL.
UNRESERVED GREED
D
13 o 14
AB540 IS OK BIME
Con Sofos
I'M A DREAMER TOO MAN! I DREAM OF GETTING MORE MULLAH. CHI CHING!
NO NOMAS
UNO
SI NO MUCHOS DOLORES
BORDER SERIES
Agua pasa por tu casa
WASHINGTON GOMEZ
ONE DOLLAR
It may just be me, but it seems that with the rise in support for undocumented students on college campuses there has also come a rise of an army of researchers, activists, and educational advocates working on "behalf" of these students. Interestingly, advocating for undocumented students is a new religion for this new group of zealots. And, while they might be extremely effective in raising lots of dollars for their own projects, the direct benefit to students remains unclear.

"Opportunism, a fistful of dolores." April 17, 2014.

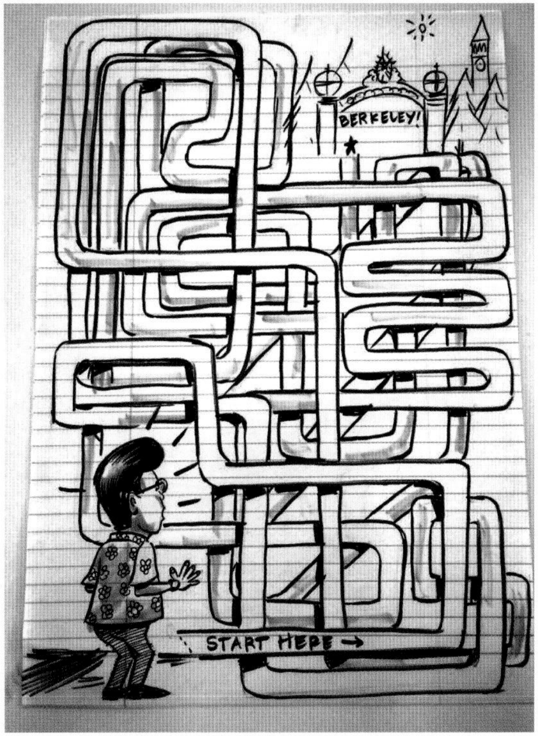
BERKELEY!
START HERE →

"Here's an easy guide." August 21, 2015.

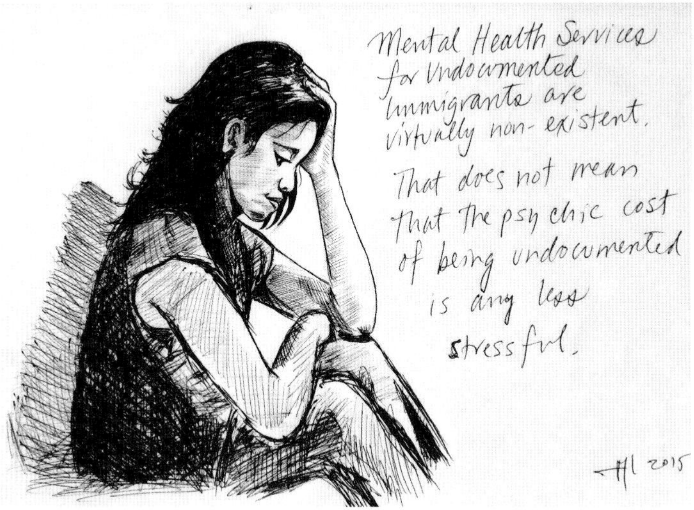
Mental Health Services for Undocumented Immigrants are virtually non-existent.
That does not mean that the psychic cost of being undocumented is any less stressful.

"The psychic cost." February 24, 2015.

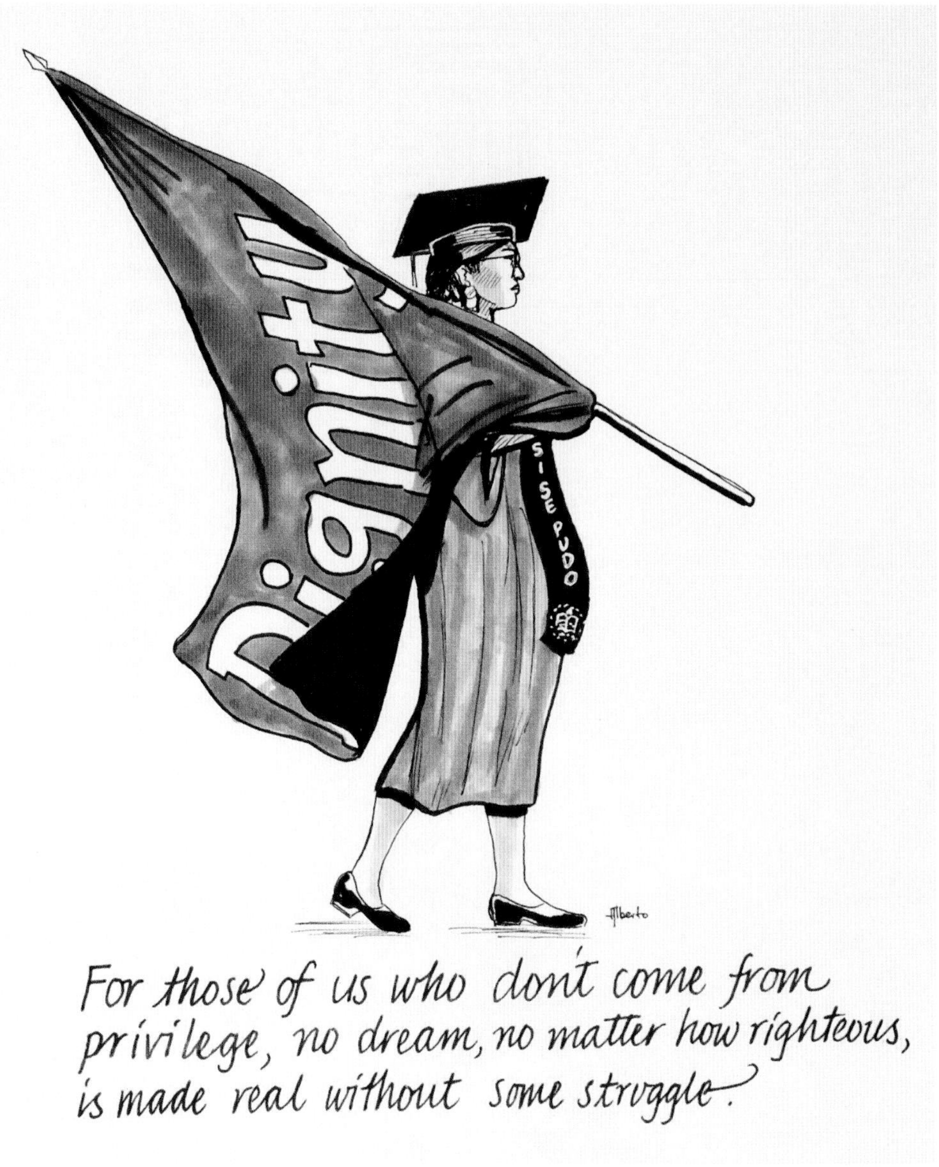
Dignity
SI SE PUDO
Alberto
For those of us who don't come from privilege, no dream, no matter how righteous, is made real without some struggle.

"Dignity." May 26, 2016.

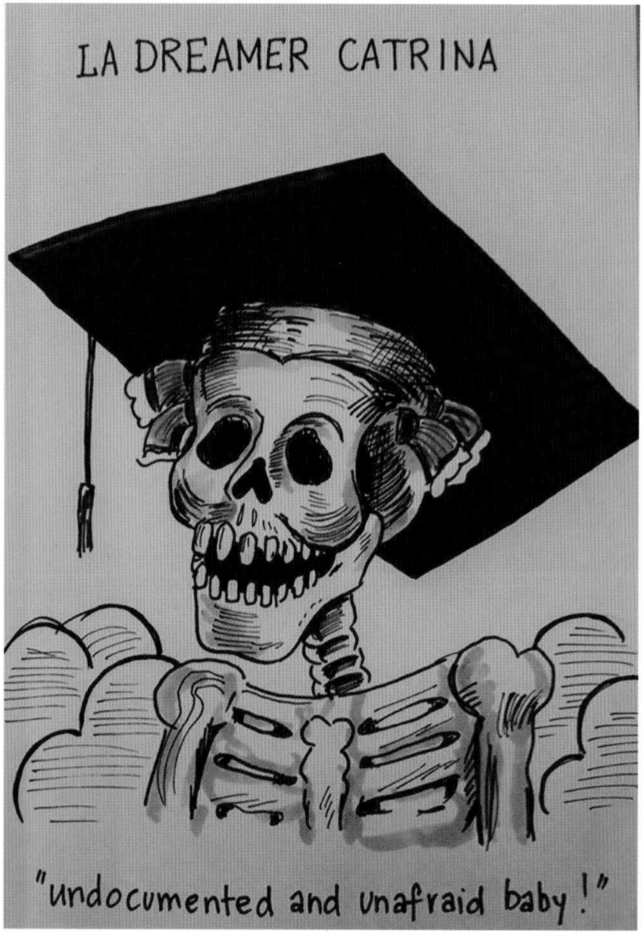
LA DREAMER CATRINA
"undocumented and unafraid baby!"

"La Dreamer Catrina." September 14, 2013.

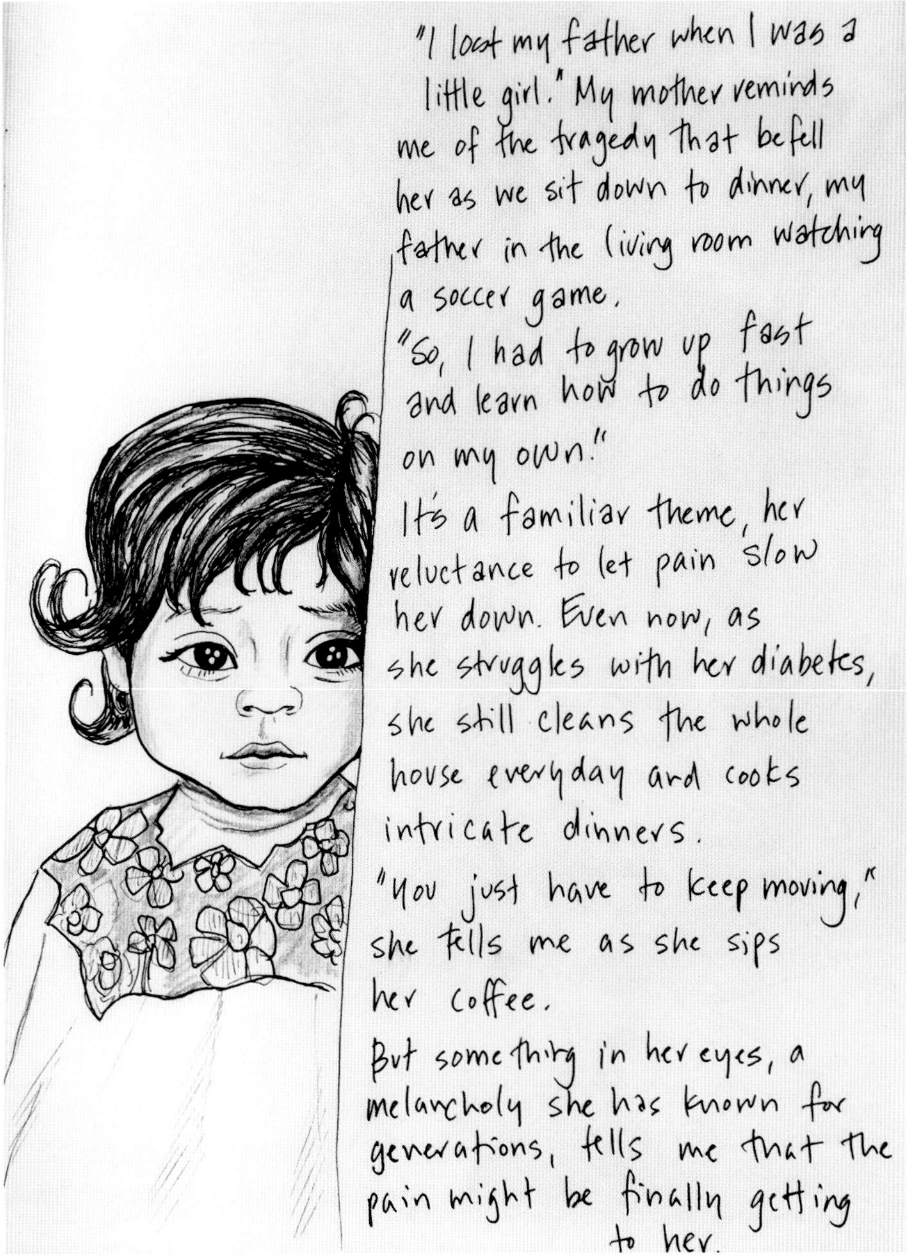
"I lost my father when I was a little girl." My mother reminds me of the tragedy that befell her as we sit down to dinner, my father in the living room watching a soccer game.
"So, I had to grow up fast and learn how to do things on my own."
It's a familiar theme, her reluctance to let pain slow her down. Even now, as she struggles with her diabetes, she still cleans the whole house everyday and cooks intricate dinners.
"You just have to keep moving," she tells me as she sips her coffee.
But something in her eyes, a melancholy she has known for generations, tells me that the pain might be finally getting to her.
"The melancholy in my mother's eyes." January 28, 2015.

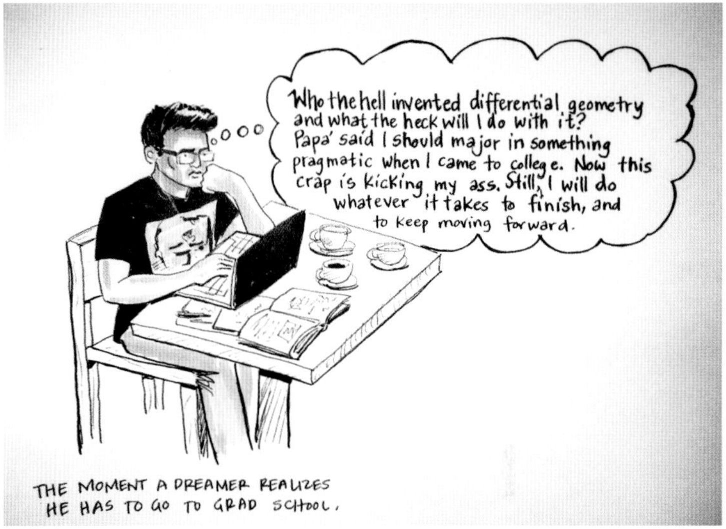
Who the hell invented differential geometry and what the heck will I do with it? Papa' said I should major in something pragmatic when I came to college. Now this crap is kicking my ass. Still, I will do whatever it takes to finish, and to keep moving forward.
THE MOMENT A DREAMER REALIZES HE HAS TO GO TO GRAD SCHOOL.
"Thinking of grad school." August 6, 2014.

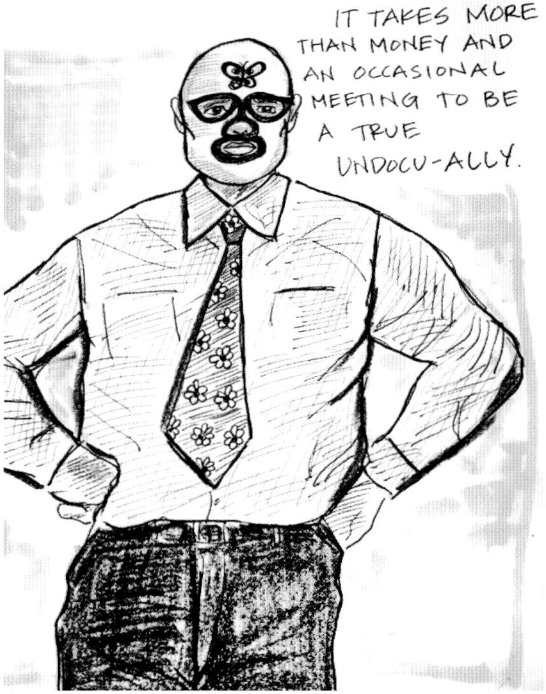
IT TAKES MORE THAN MONEY AND AN OCCASIONAL MEETING TO BE A TRUE UNDOCU-ALLY.
"A true undocu-ally." February 18, 2015.

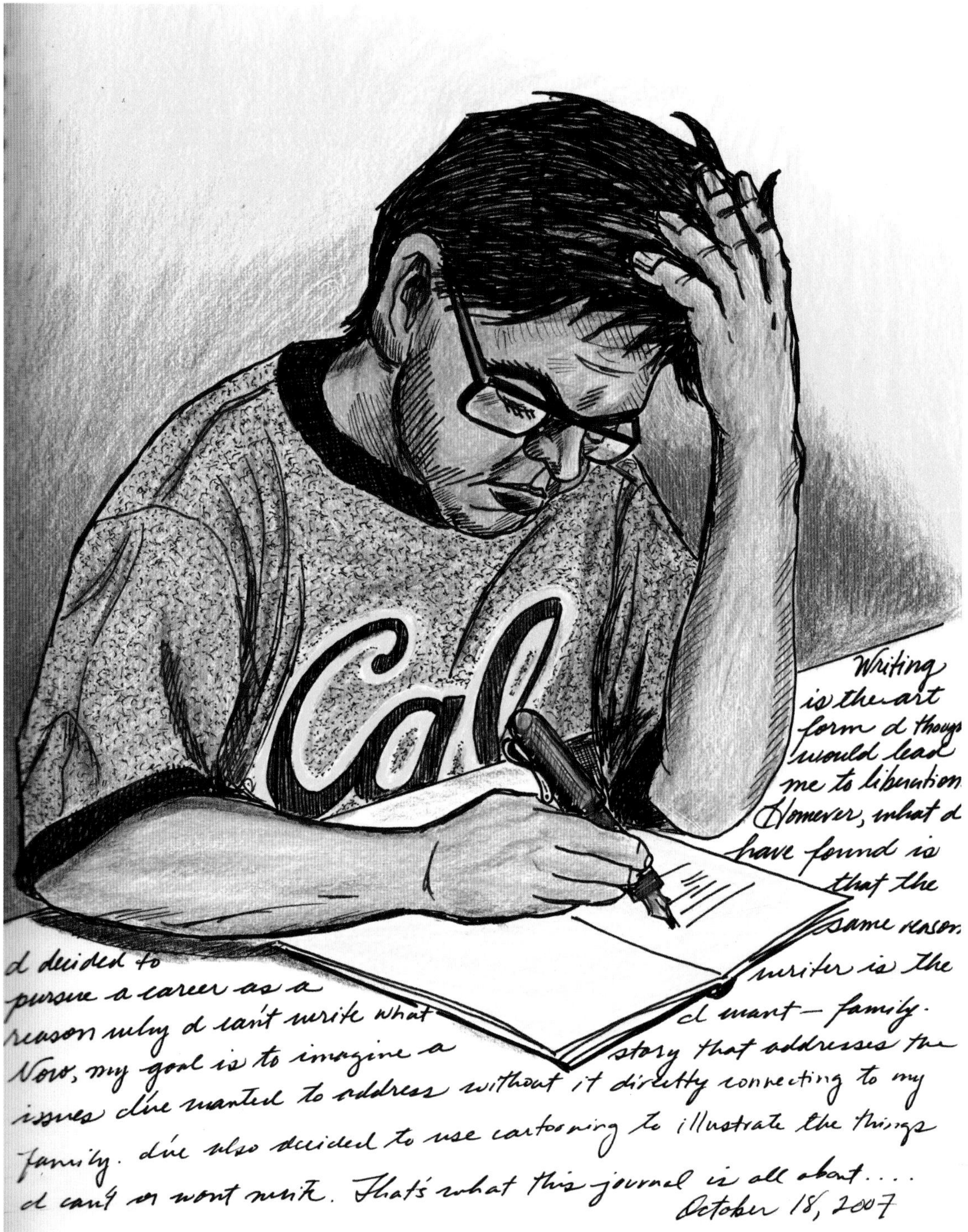
Writing
is the art
form I thought
would lead
me to liberation.
However, what I
have found is
that the
same reason
I decided to
pursue a career as a
writer is the
reason why I can't write what
I want—family.
Now, my goal is to imagine a
story that addresses the
issues I've wanted to address without it directly connecting to my
family. I've also decided to use cartooning to illustrate the things
I can't or won't write. That's what this journal is all about....
October 18, 2007

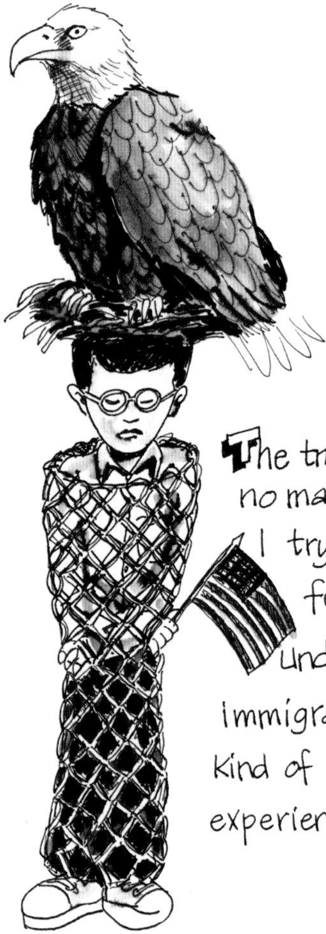

The truth is that
no matter how hard
I try to show them
few people consider
undocumented
immigration as a
kind of American
experience.

July 20, 2011.

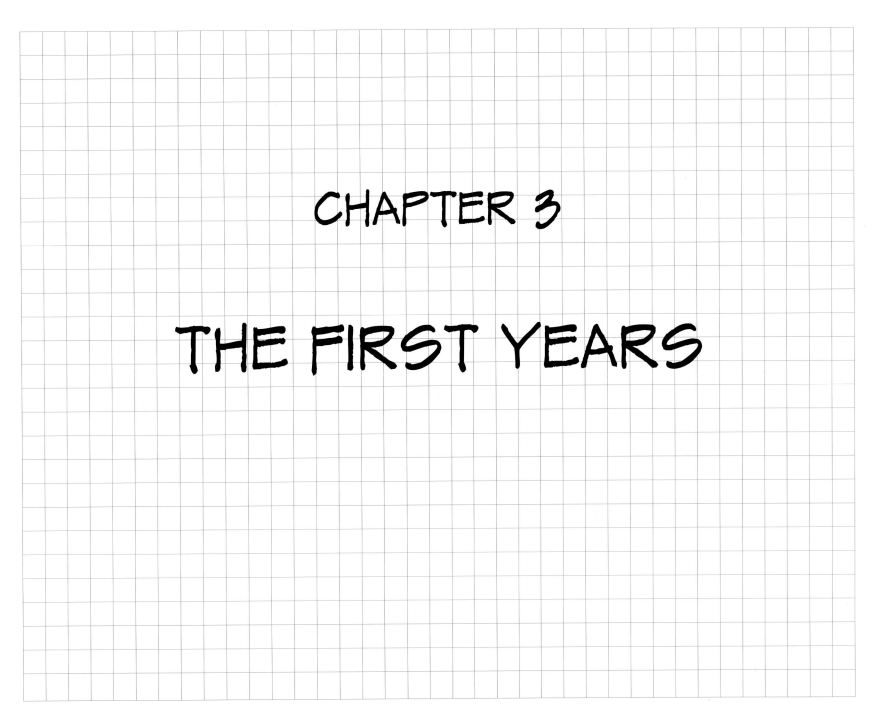

CHAPTER 3

THE FIRST YEARS

BERKELEY
UCLA
BERKELEY
HARVARD
BERKELEY
BERKELEY

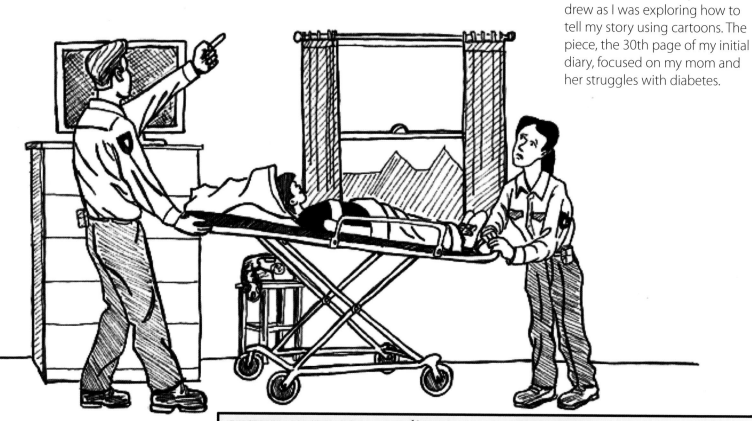

This is one of the first pieces I drew as I was exploring how to tell my story using cartoons. The piece, the 30th page of my initial diary, focused on my mom and her struggles with diabetes.

SEVERAL YEARS AGO, MAMÁ'S BLOOD SUGAR WENT SO LOW THAT WE HAD TO CALL THE AMBULANCE TO COME GET HER. AS THE PARAMEDICS WERE WHEELING HER OUT THE HOUSE, AS THEY WERE RUSHING TO GET HER TO THE HOSPITAL, ONE OF THEM NOTICED ALL THE COLLEGE DIPLOMAS MAMÁ HAD HUNG ON THE WALL OF HER BEDROOM. HE WAS STUNNED, AMAZED THAT IN A HOME AS HUMBLE AS MAMÁ'S EAST OAKLAND CASITA, SOMEONE WOULD HAVE SO MANY CERTIFICATES FROM SUCH PRESTIGIOUS COLLEGES. IN THAT BRIEF MOMENT, MAMÁ OPENED HER EYES AND SMILED.

September 11, 2011.

Starting my Diary of a Dreamer on Facebook was also the way that I learned how to draw the way I do today. At first, my renderings were unsophisticated doodles with little dimmension or texture. While I was an avid consumer of comic books as a kid and often liked to copy drawings of gargantuan superheroes, my experience with drawing the quotidian details of life as an undocumented immigrant was minimal. Still, I tried, focusing on representing the real drama I had experienced as an undocumented kid as best as I could.

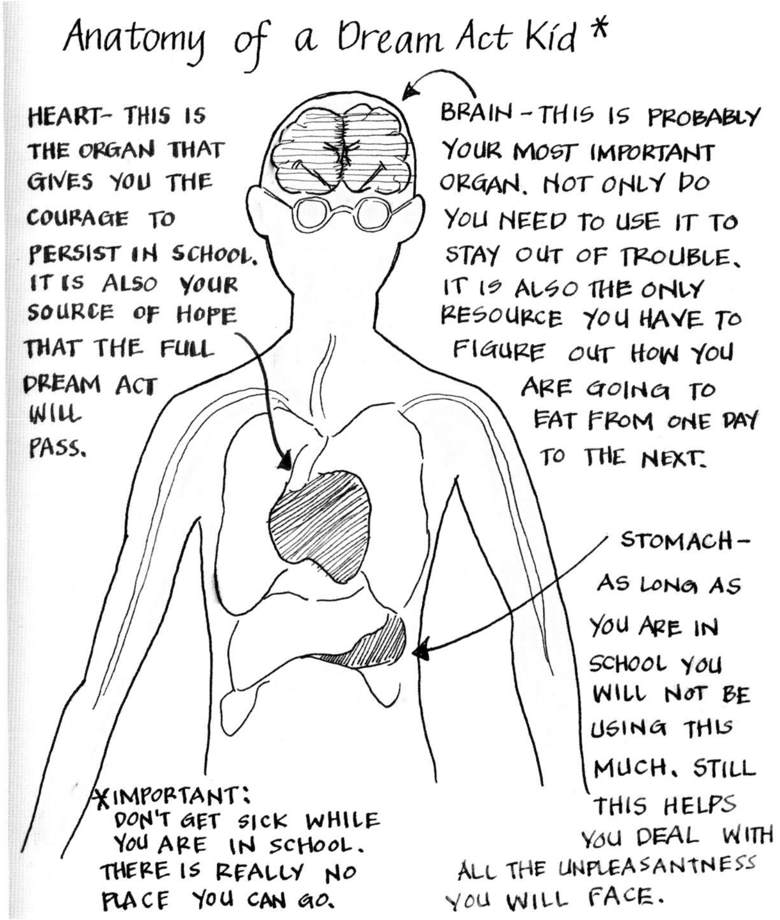

Anatomy of a Dream Act Kid *
HEART- THIS IS THE ORGAN THAT GIVES YOU THE COURAGE TO PERSIST IN SCHOOL. IT IS ALSO YOUR SOURCE OF HOPE THAT THE FULL DREAM ACT WILL PASS.
BRAIN - THIS IS PROBABLY YOUR MOST IMPORTANT ORGAN. NOT ONLY DO YOU NEED TO USE IT TO STAY OUT OF TROUBLE. IT IS ALSO THE ONLY RESOURCE YOU HAVE TO FIGURE OUT HOW YOU ARE GOING TO EAT FROM ONE DAY TO THE NEXT.
STOMACH- AS LONG AS YOU ARE IN SCHOOL YOU WILL NOT BE USING THIS MUCH. STILL THIS HELPS YOU DEAL WITH ALL THE UNPLEASANTNESS YOU WILL FACE.
*IMPORTANT: DON'T GET SICK WHILE YOU ARE IN SCHOOL. THERE IS REALLY NO PLACE YOU CAN GO.

July 30, 2011.

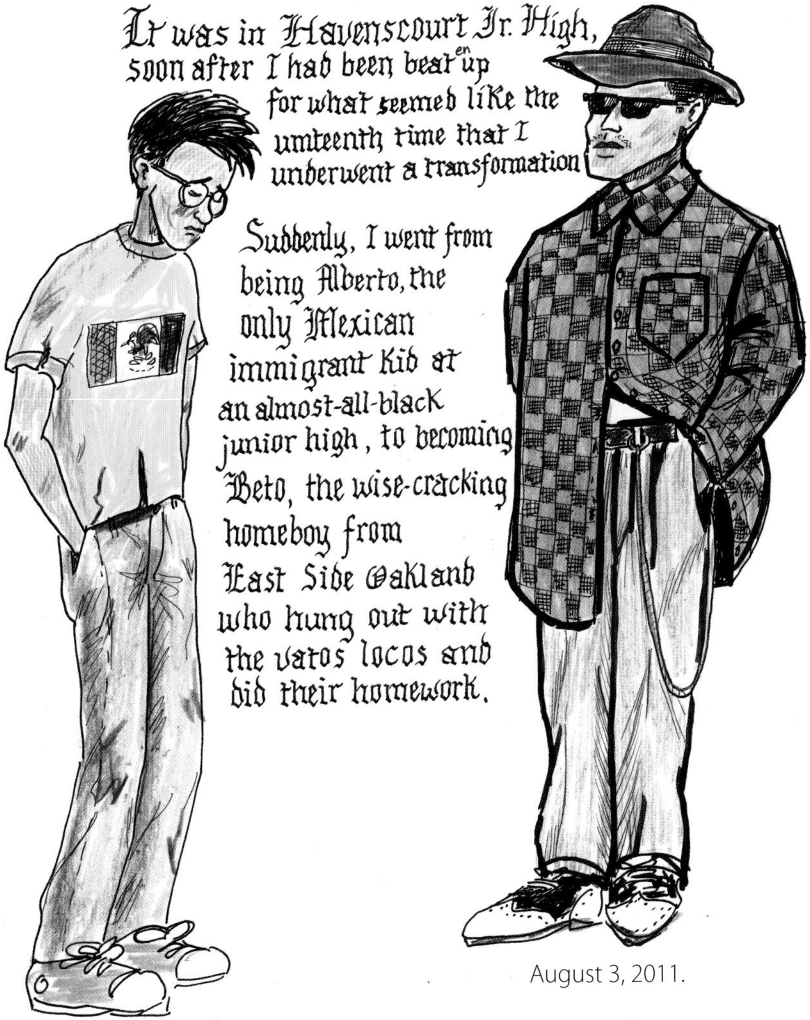

It was in Havenscourt Jr. High, soon after I had been beaten up for what seemed like the umteenth time that I underwent a transformation
Suddenly, I went from being Alberto, the only Mexican immigrant kid at an almost-all-black junior high, to becoming Beto, the wise-cracking homeboy from East Side Oakland who hung out with the vatos locos and did their homework.

August 3, 2011.

August 21, 2011.

MY FAMILY

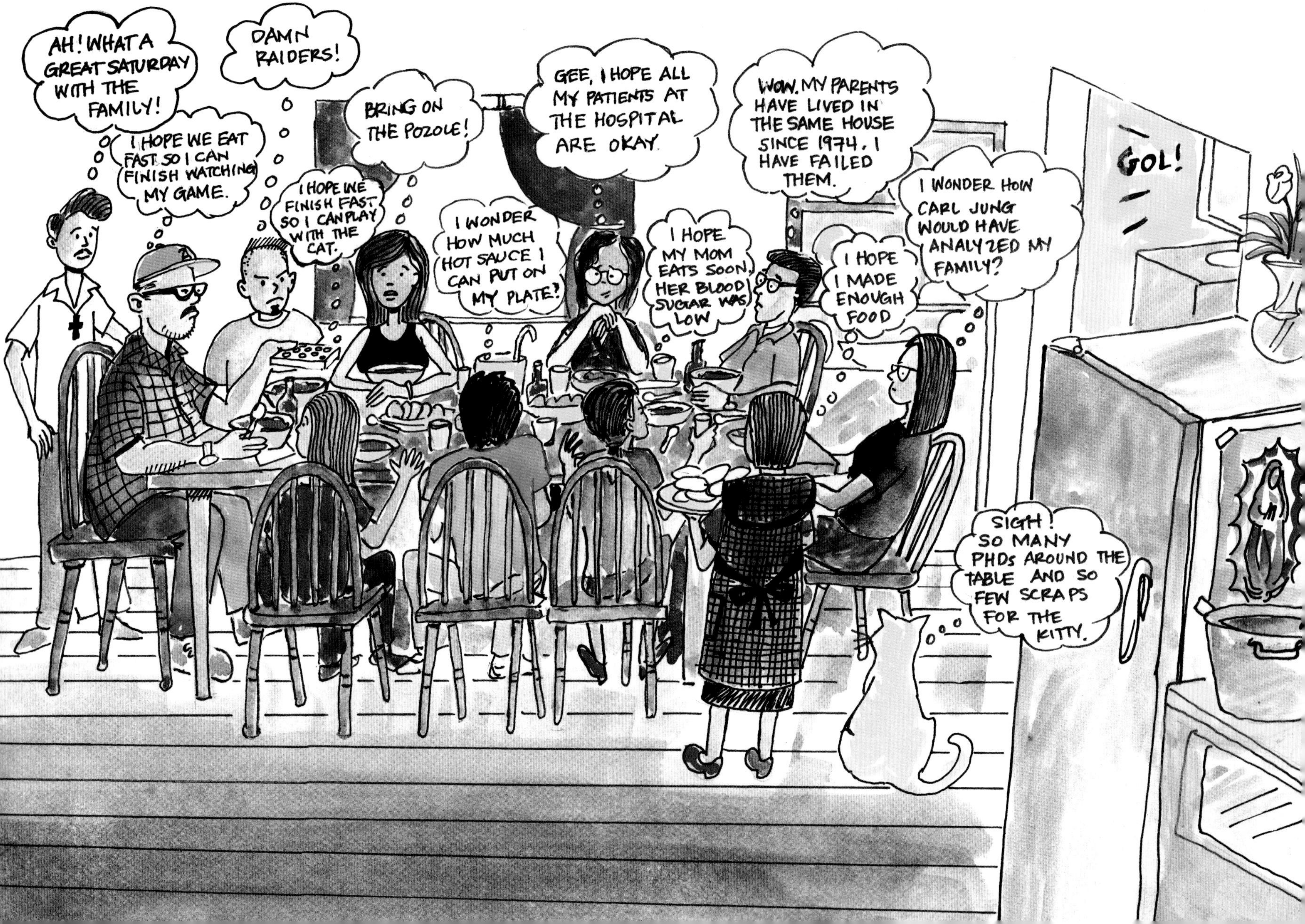

AH! WHAT A GREAT SATURDAY WITH THE FAMILY!
DAMN RAIDERS!
I HOPE WE EAT FAST SO I CAN FINISH WATCHING MY GAME.
BRING ON THE POZOLE!
I HOPE WE FINISH FAST SO I CAN PLAY WITH THE CAT.
GEE, I HOPE ALL MY PATIENTS AT THE HOSPITAL ARE OKAY.
I WONDER HOW MUCH HOT SAUCE I CAN PUT ON MY PLATE?
WOW. MY PARENTS HAVE LIVED IN THE SAME HOUSE SINCE 1974. I HAVE FAILED THEM.
I HOPE MY MOM EATS SOON, HER BLOOD SUGAR WAS LOW
I HOPE I MADE ENOUGH FOOD
I WONDER HOW CARL JUNG WOULD HAVE ANALYZED MY FAMILY?
GOL!
SIGH! SO MANY PHDs AROUND THE TABLE AND SO FEW SCRAPS FOR THE KITTY.

HIS (HIDDEN INSIDE THE CABINET): TEQUILA WHISKEY RUM

HERS

Ay Diosito, help me. Last night, after the lights went off, I heard the kitchen door open and I couldn't get up. I wanted to run to him when I heard his footsteps on the kitchen floor, to tell papá of the terrible day I'd had at school, but when I heard mamá telling him that he had gotten home drunk, I just pulled the covers over my head and held my breath.

It's happened so many times before, mamá waiting in the dark for papá to return from the pool hall or wherever he is. Sometimes, she has sat by the window sewing his work pants or hemming the curtains way into the night. Sometimes, she has stepped out into the darkened porch, following every white headlight passing in front of our house with her tired eyes. Last night I really needed to talk to him, but she seemed too angry with him.

"¡¿Porque llegaste borracho otra vez?!" She asked him I don't know how many times.

I wanted to get up, to run to the kitchen and hug papá around the waist so that he could help me.

Papá didn't say anything. I just heard the screeching of a chair's leg on our linoleum floor and mamá closing the door to her bedroom. Then I fell asleep.

I really thought I was going to be able to do it, to ask papá if he could come with me to school in the morning. But, when I woke up, mamá was already working in the kitchen and her bed was empty. I looked for papá in bathroom, searched for him in the living room and in the back where my sisters sleep. Then, I saw that the station wagon was gone.

October 16, 2011.

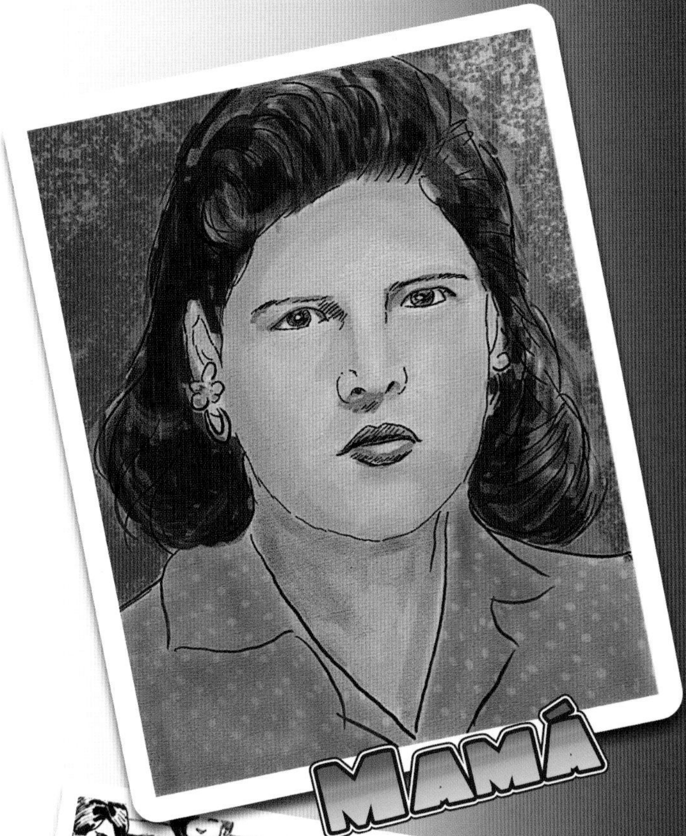
MAMÁ

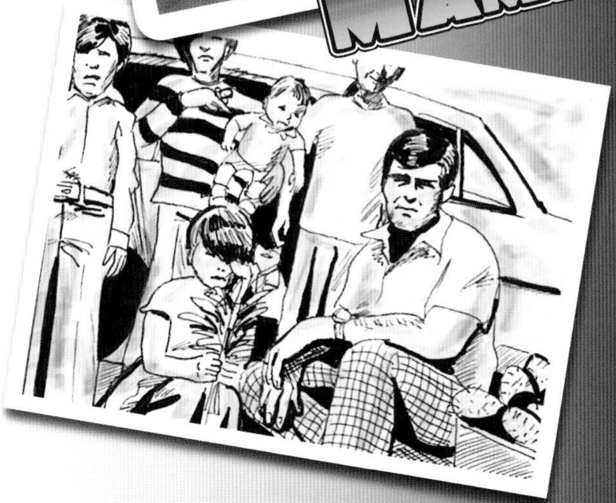

I called you this morning to see how you were doing. You said things were now fine, that you hadn't thrown up since last night, that your nausea was beginning to dissipate. You lied.

The traffic on 580 was horrendous. I was still half an hour away from work. You heard another car's horn and you told me to be careful.

You are now the quintessential, workaholic abuelita. My own madre sufrida. Except that your suffering has nothing to do with cultural stereotypes. It's diabetes and circumstantial tragedy that has made you into who you are today.

I think of your youth, your days as a girl growing up in Huisquilco. How idyllic life must have felt growing up in a family of singers, one of five sisters entertaining a town of pistoleros. I imagine you on the stage, alive in your ranchera soprano and pink crinoline.

But those pistoleros had already taken your father and would soon force your husband to flee northward.

Even after you moved to Guadalajara, after two brothers I would never know had passed away from a cold and a rusty nail, you still sang, your voice deep with the texture of all you have lived. You joined your husband in el norte, brought your kids along to learn a new kind of music. But it seemed so strange, so gray.

This morning, when I heard your voice, you tried to sing again, to tell me that everything was going to be alright.

Perhaps.

October 1, 2011.

WHEN I WAS IN HIGH SCHOOL, SERGIO DARED ME TO TRY OUT FOR THE WRESTLING TEAM. HE SAID THAT HE WOULD DO IT TOO. I WAS TOO SCARED TO SAY NO, SO I WENT WITH HIM TO THE GYM AFTER SCHOOL, WHERE MR. JEROME WAS HAVING TRY-OUTS. SERGIO ACCOMPANIED ME ONLY A FEW DAYS AFTER THAT. BUT, RATHER THAN FACE MR. JEROME TO TELL HIM THAT I, TOO, HAD CHANGED MY MIND, I STUCK WITH THE TEAM FOR TWO YEARS.

I STILL REMEMBER MY FIRST MATCH. IT WAS AT THE JUNIOR VARSITY TOURNAMENT HOSTED BY OAKLAND TECH. I WAS TO FIGHT ANOTHER IMMIGRANT KID WHO LOOKED AS SCARED AS I WAS. THE WHISTLE SOUNDED, I LUNGED FORWARD, AND HE FELL BACKWARDS. SUDDENLY, I WAS LAYING ON TOP OF HIM, A SEVEN-SECOND PIN! MY TEAM MATES FROM FREMONT HIGH HOOTED AND HOLLERED WHEN I RETURNED TO THE BENCH. AS EXPECTED, THE GLORY DID NOT LAST LONG. MY NEXT MATCH, THIS TIME WITH A ROUGH-LOOKING KID FROM MCCLYMONDS, ALSO RESULTED IN A RECORD. HE PINNED ME IN SIX SECONDS FLAT.

EL VALIENTE VIVE HASTA QUE EL COBARDE QUIERE.

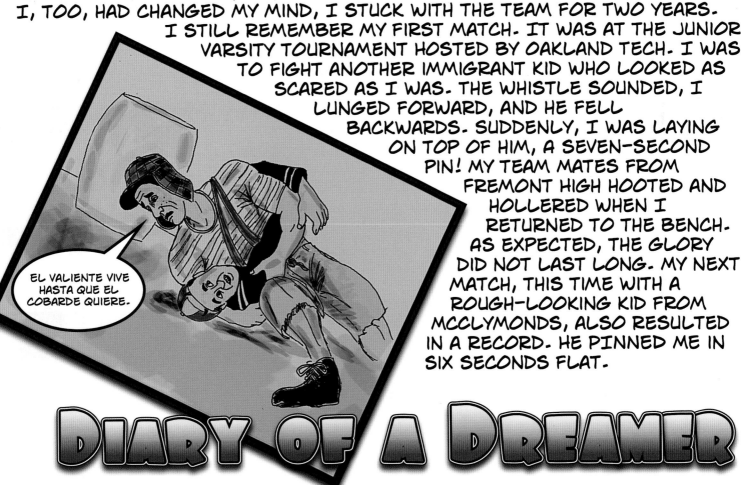

DIARY OF A DREAMER

October 8, 2011.

IT WASN'T UNTIL CLINTON WAS PRESIDENT THAT I DEVELOPED THE COURAGE TO TAKE MY CITIZENSHIP EXAM. IN CALIFORNIA, PETE WILSON WAS ALREADY PUSHING PROPOSITION 187 AND I WAS ABOUT TO FINISH MY DOCTORAL DEGREE IN ETHNIC STUDIES AT BERKELEY. I WAS LIVING IN LOS ANGELES, HAD MOVED THERE WHEN LETICIA HAD BEEN ACCEPTED TO THE USC SCHOOL OF MEDICINE. TOGETHER, SHE AND I WALKED INTO THE FEDERAL BUILDING, WAITED UNTIL OUR NAMES WERE CALLED, AND THEN STOOD IN FRONT OF A MAN WHO ASKED US TO DEMONSTRATE THAT WE KNEW BASIC AMERICAN HISTORY. I STILL REMEMBER THE FIRST QUESTION THE INS MAN ASKED ME AS I STOOD IN FRONT OF HIM IN HIS CUBICLE. "WHO WAS THE PRESIDENT WHO FREED THE SLAVES?" HE COCKED HIS HEAD TO THE SIDE AS HE WAITED FOR ME TO ANSWER. I THOUGHT OF RON TAKAKI'S *A DIFFERENT MIRROR*, OF ALL THE STATISTICS THAT CORRELATED RACE AND POVERTY IN THE US, OF HOW MANY BROWN AND BLACK MEN HAD BEEN SENT TO PRISON FOR CRIMES THAT WERE NORMALLY NO MORE THAN MISDEMEANORS IN WHITE NEIGHBORHOODS. "ABRAHAM LINCOLN," I FINALLY SAID AS BEADS OF SWEAT TRICKLED DOWN MY FACE.

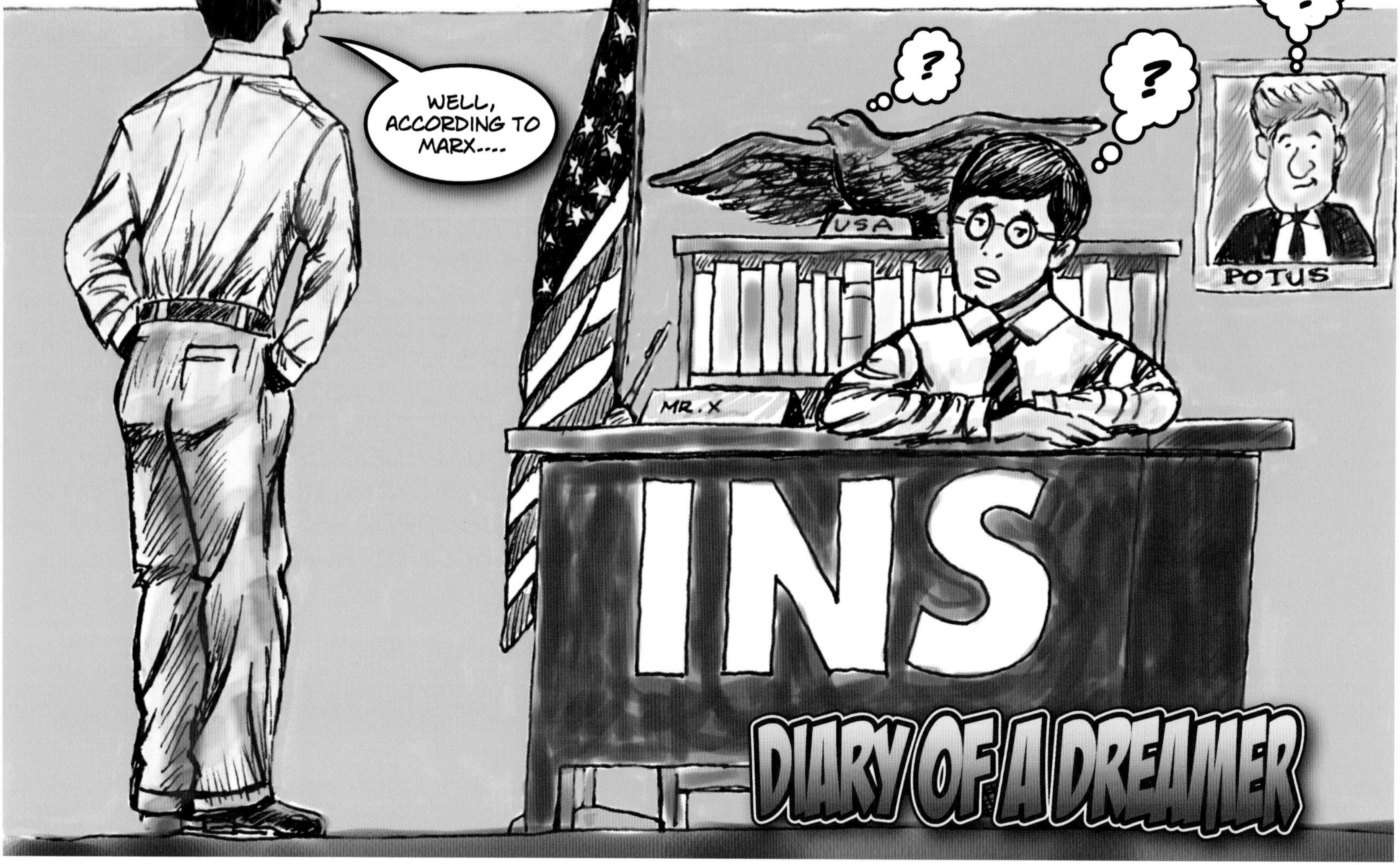
WELL, ACCORDING TO MARX....
?
?
?
USA
MR. X
POTUS
INS
DIARY OF A DREAMER

A GLOSSARY OF UNDOCUMENTED GRAMMATICAL TERMS

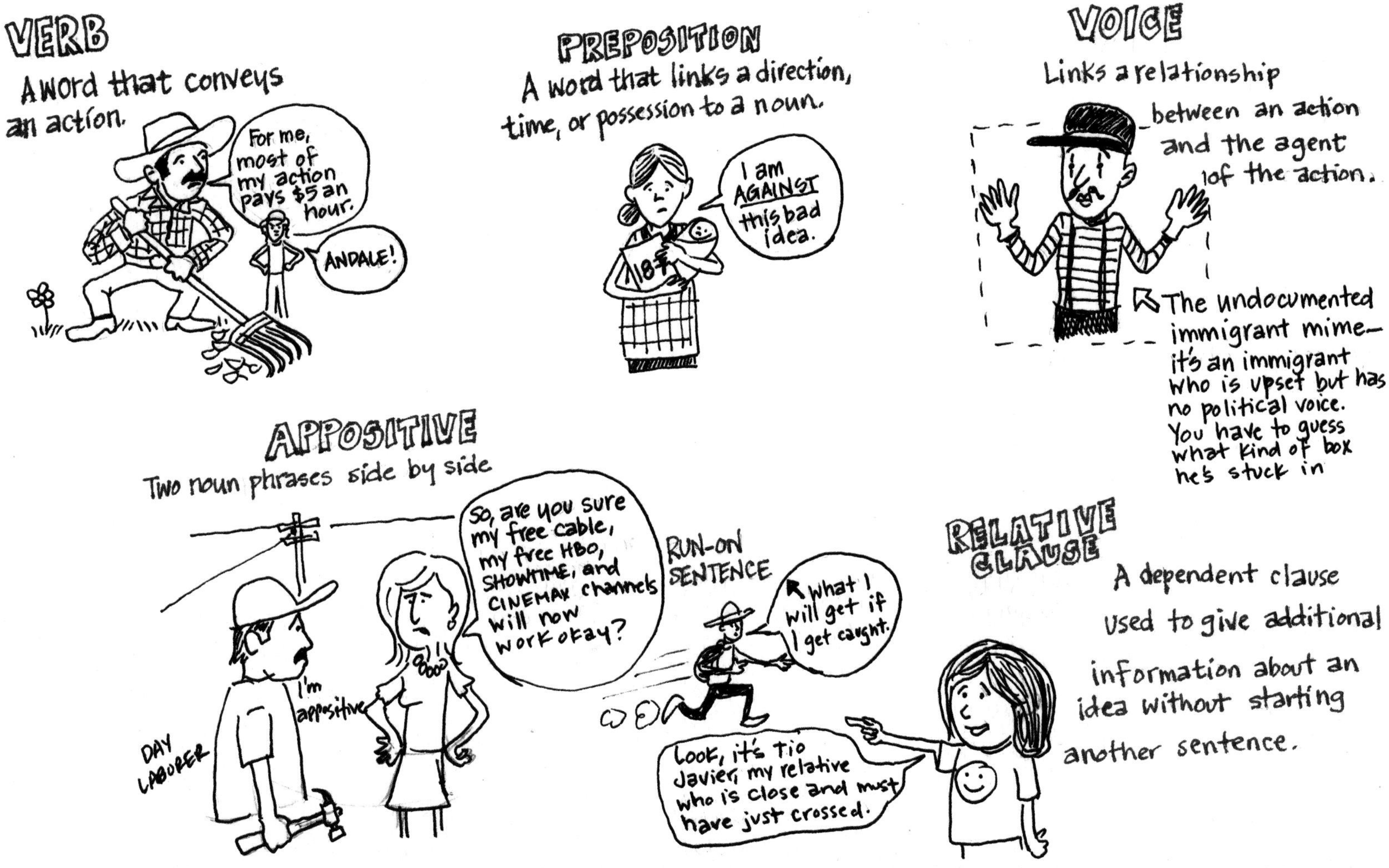
VERB
A word that conveys an action.
For me, most of my action pays $5 an hour.
ANDALE!
PREPOSITION
A word that links a direction, time, or possession to a noun.
I am AGAINST this bad idea.
18
VOICE
Links a relationship between an action and the agent of the action.
The undocumented immigrant mime— it's an immigrant who is upset but has no political voice. You have to guess what kind of box he's stuck in
APPOSITIVE
Two noun phrases side by side
So, are you sure my free cable, my free HBO, SHOWTIME, and CINEMAX channels will now work okay?
I'm appositive
DAY LABORER
RUN-ON SENTENCE
What I will get if I get caught.
RELATIVE CLAUSE
A dependent clause used to give additional information about an idea without starting another sentence.
Look, it's Tio Javier, my relative who is close and must have just crossed.

November 29, 2011.

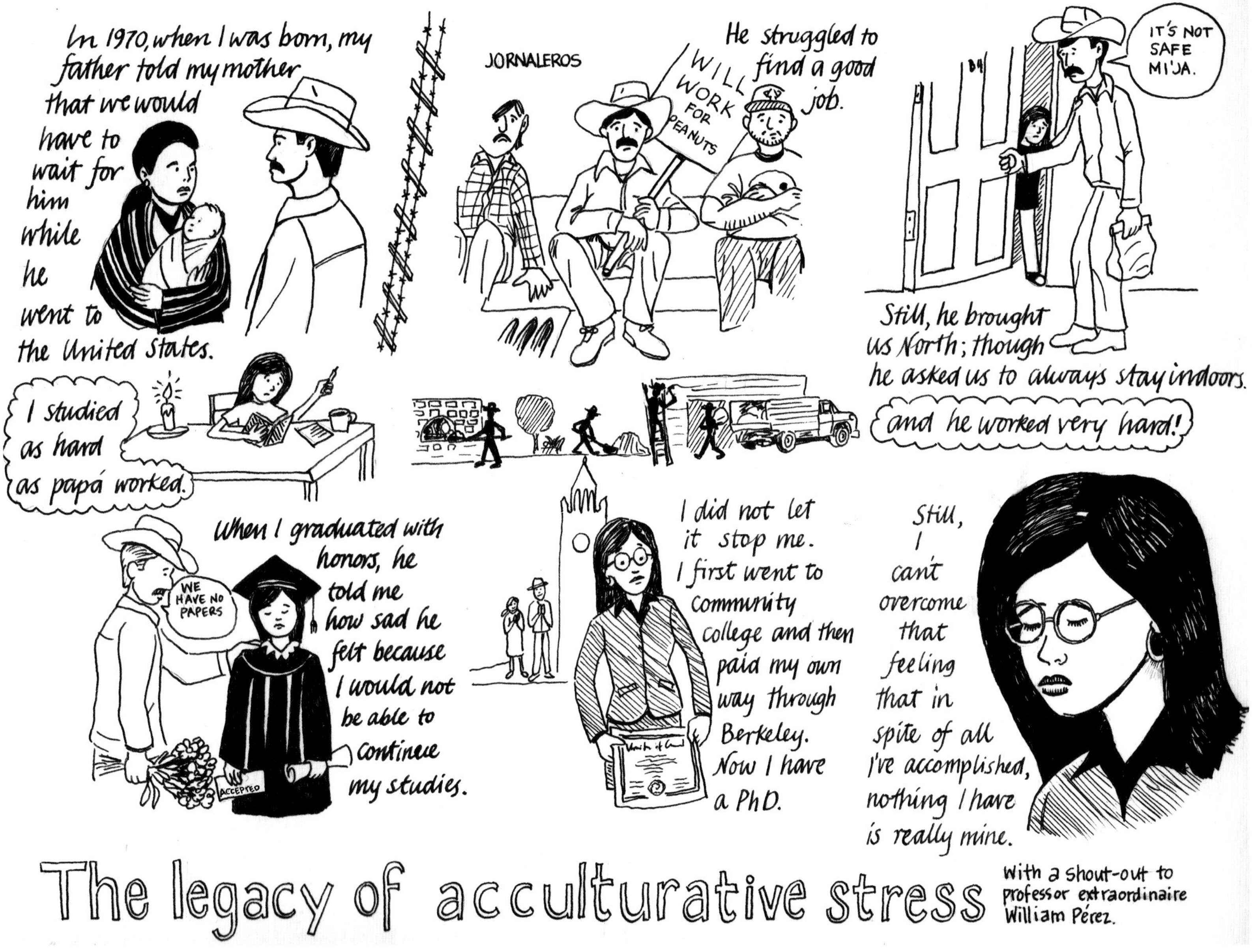
In 1970, when I was born, my father told my mother that we would have to wait for him while he went to the United States.
JORNALEROS
WILL WORK FOR PEANUTS
He struggled to find a good job.
IT'S NOT SAFE MI'JA.
Still, he brought us North; though he asked us to always stay indoors.
I studied as hard as papá worked.
and he worked very hard!
When I graduated with honors, he told me how sad he felt because I would not be able to continue my studies.
WE HAVE NO PAPERS
ACCEPTED
I did not let it stop me. I first went to community college and then paid my own way through Berkeley. Now I have a PhD.
Still, I can't overcome that feeling that in spite of all I've accomplished, nothing I have is really mine.
The legacy of acculturative stress
With a shout-out to professor extraordinaire William Pérez.

December 30, 2011.

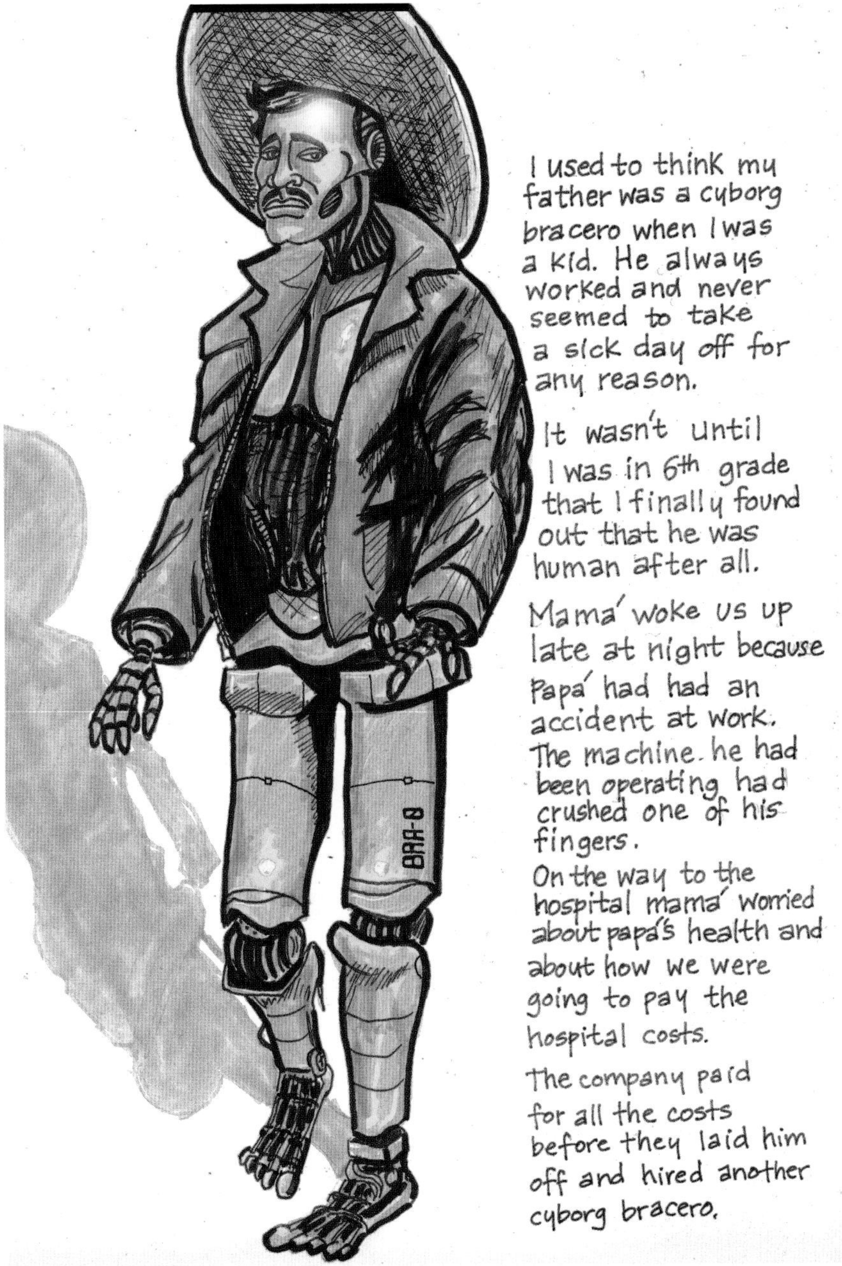
I used to think my father was a cyborg bracero when I was a kid. He always worked and never seemed to take a sick day off for any reason.
It wasn't until I was in 6th grade that I finally found out that he was human after all.
Mamá woke us up late at night because Papá had had an accident at work. The machine he had been operating had crushed one of his fingers.
On the way to the hospital mamá worried about papá's health and about how we were going to pay the hospital costs.
The company paid for all the costs before they laid him off and hired another cyborg bracero.
BRA-0

February 11, 2012.

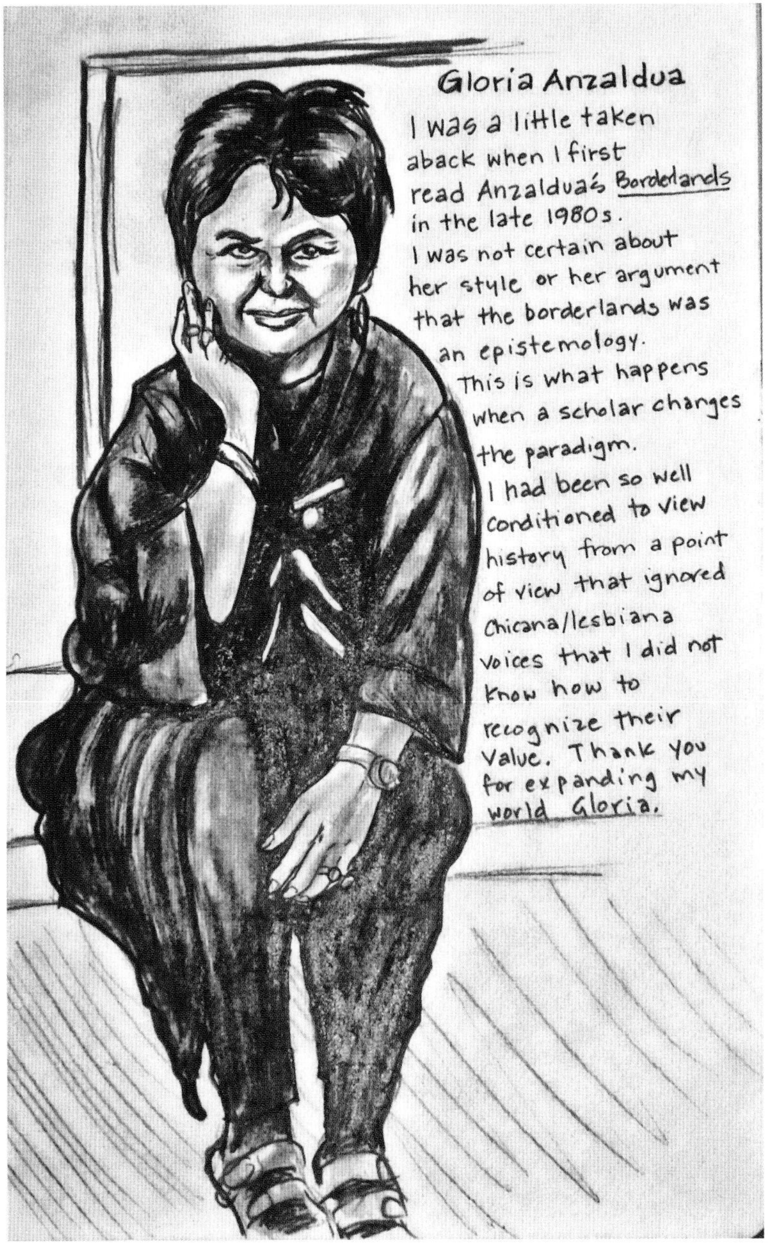
Gloria Anzaldua
I was a little taken aback when I first read Anzaldua's Borderlands in the late 1980s. I was not certain about her style or her argument that the borderlands was an epistemology. This is what happens when a scholar changes the paradigm. I had been so well conditioned to view history from a point of view that ignored Chicana/lesbiana voices that I did not know how to recognize their value. Thank you for expanding my world Gloria.

February 19, 2012.

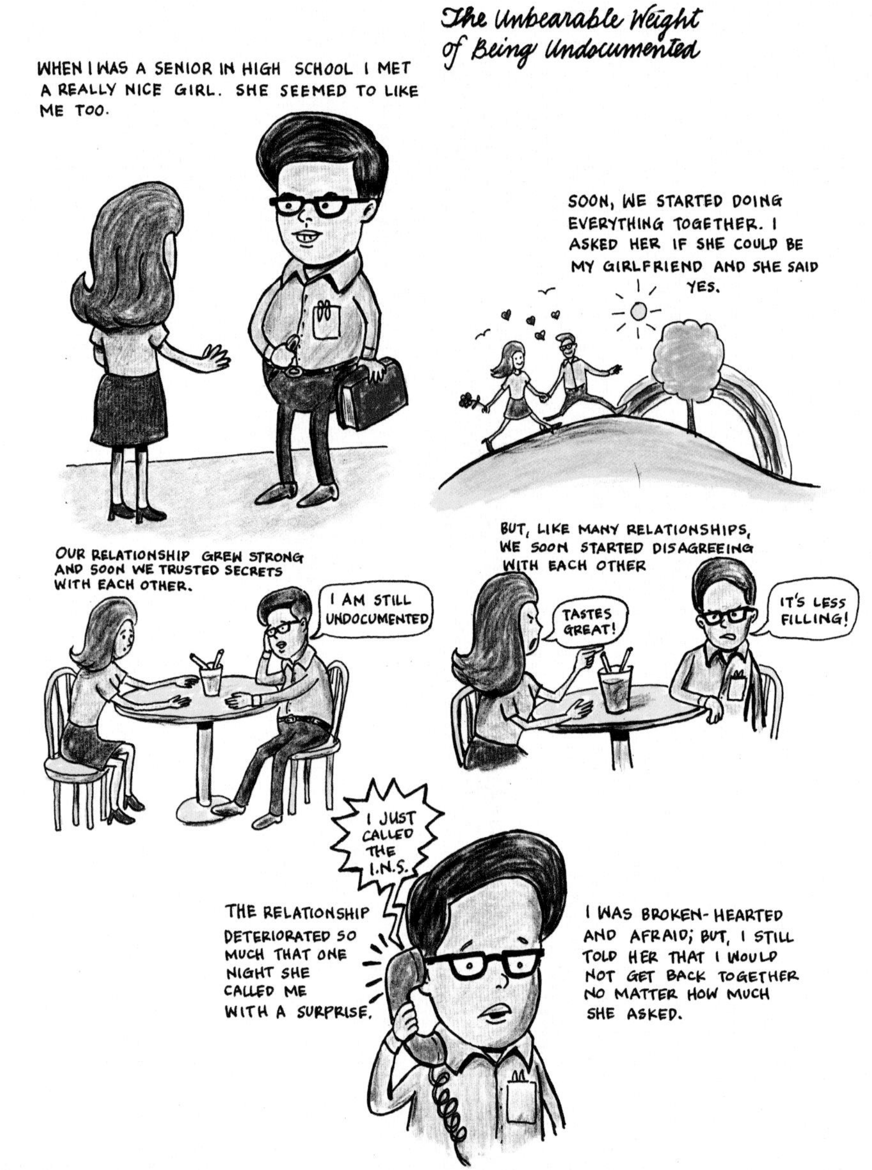
The Unbearable Weight of Being Undocumented
WHEN I WAS A SENIOR IN HIGH SCHOOL I MET A REALLY NICE GIRL. SHE SEEMED TO LIKE ME TOO.
SOON, WE STARTED DOING EVERYTHING TOGETHER. I ASKED HER IF SHE COULD BE MY GIRLFRIEND AND SHE SAID YES.
OUR RELATIONSHIP GREW STRONG AND SOON WE TRUSTED SECRETS WITH EACH OTHER.
I AM STILL UNDOCUMENTED
BUT, LIKE MANY RELATIONSHIPS, WE SOON STARTED DISAGREEING WITH EACH OTHER
TASTES GREAT!
IT'S LESS FILLING!
THE RELATIONSHIP DETERIORATED SO MUCH THAT ONE NIGHT SHE CALLED ME WITH A SURPRISE.
I JUST CALLED THE I.N.S.
I WAS BROKEN-HEARTED AND AFRAID; BUT, I STILL TOLD HER THAT I WOULD NOT GET BACK TOGETHER NO MATTER HOW MUCH SHE ASKED.

March 3, 2012.

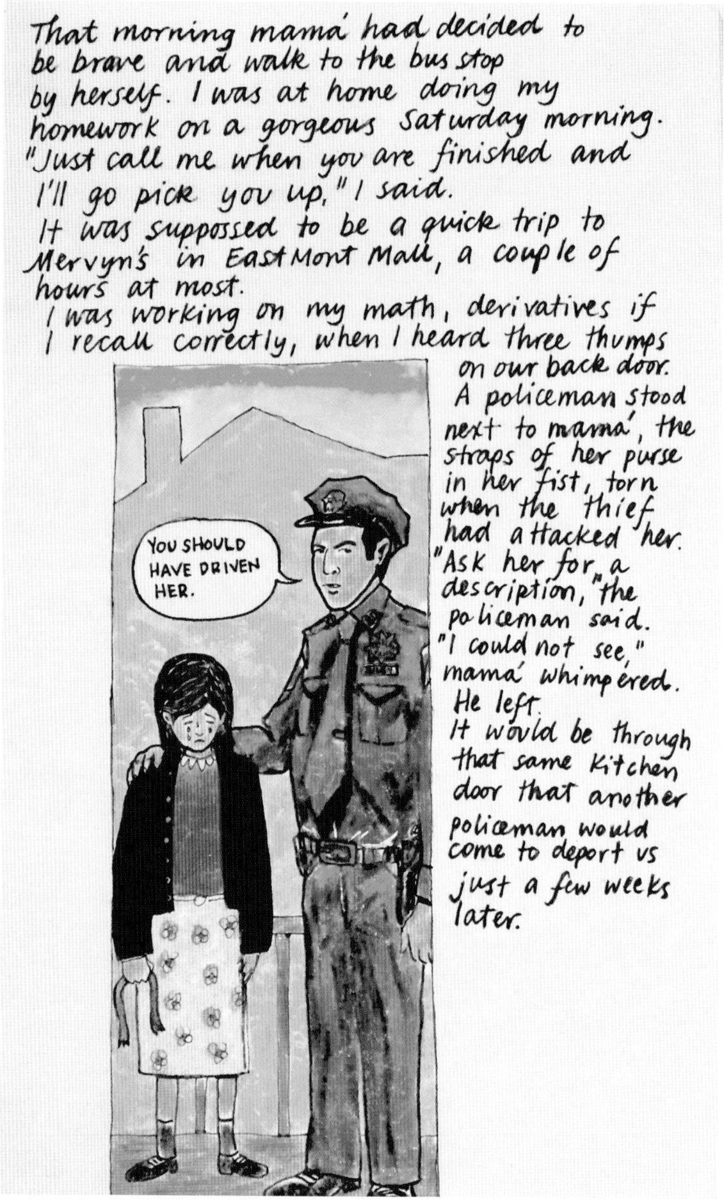
That morning mamá had decided to be brave and walk to the bus stop by herself. I was at home doing my homework on a gorgeous Saturday morning. "Just call me when you are finished and I'll go pick you up," I said.
It was suppossed to be a quick trip to Mervyn's in EastMont Mall, a couple of hours at most.
I was working on my math, derivatives if I recall correctly, when I heard three thumps on our back door.
A policeman stood next to mamá, the straps of her purse in her fist, torn when the thief had attacked her.
"Ask her for a description," the policeman said.
"I could not see," mamá whimpered.
He left.
It would be through that same kitchen door that another policeman would come to deport us just a few weeks later.
YOU SHOULD HAVE DRIVEN HER.

March 9, 2012.

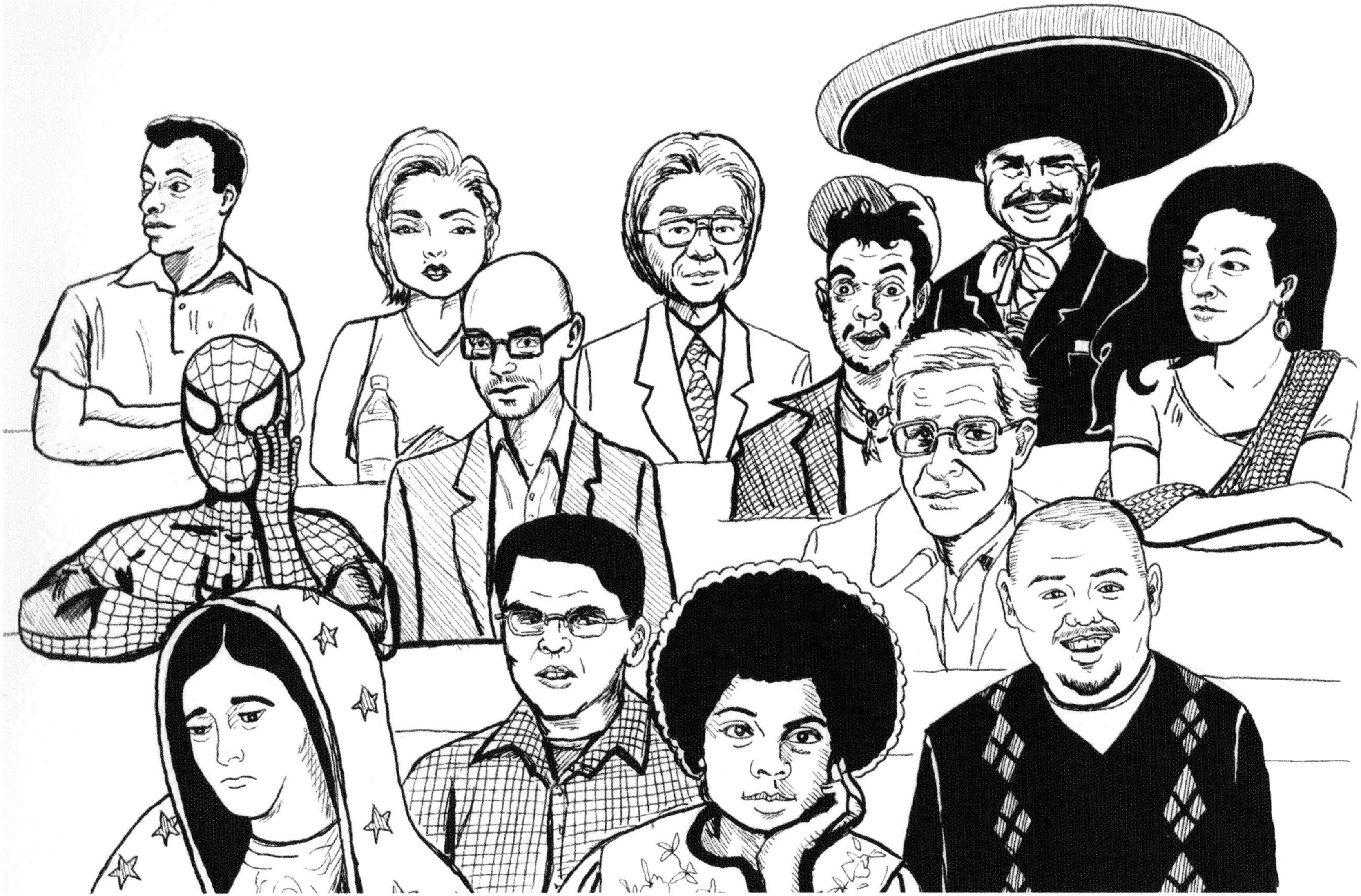

"My Influences." December 28, 2012.

WE ARE WITH YOU ERIKA

The irony of being a Dreamer Activist is that it involves so much grassroots work. That's the paradox of being a Dreamer; rather than waiting for an illusion to materialize, you have to work your butt off and organize to raise consciousness among those who believe the status quo is alright.

Fighting for compassionate immigration reform is not just a matter of self-interest. It is another civil rights cause that those who have not experienced what it's like to live without papers often obfuscate with false moralisms about decontextualized legalities.

This is something Erika Andiola has always understood. Even in the midst of uncertainty she has always been willing to fight for a chance to be heard, to advocate for those who have already given in to the onslaught of relentless oppression.

Suddenly her family gets targeted for deportation and one suspects that the coincidence is too much. It is as if the very powers that Erika has been seeking to transform have reared their lesser natures and pushed back against the giddy multitude.

But what is happening to Erika is not just affecting her. It is an effort to silence more than just one dream.

January 11, 2013.

30

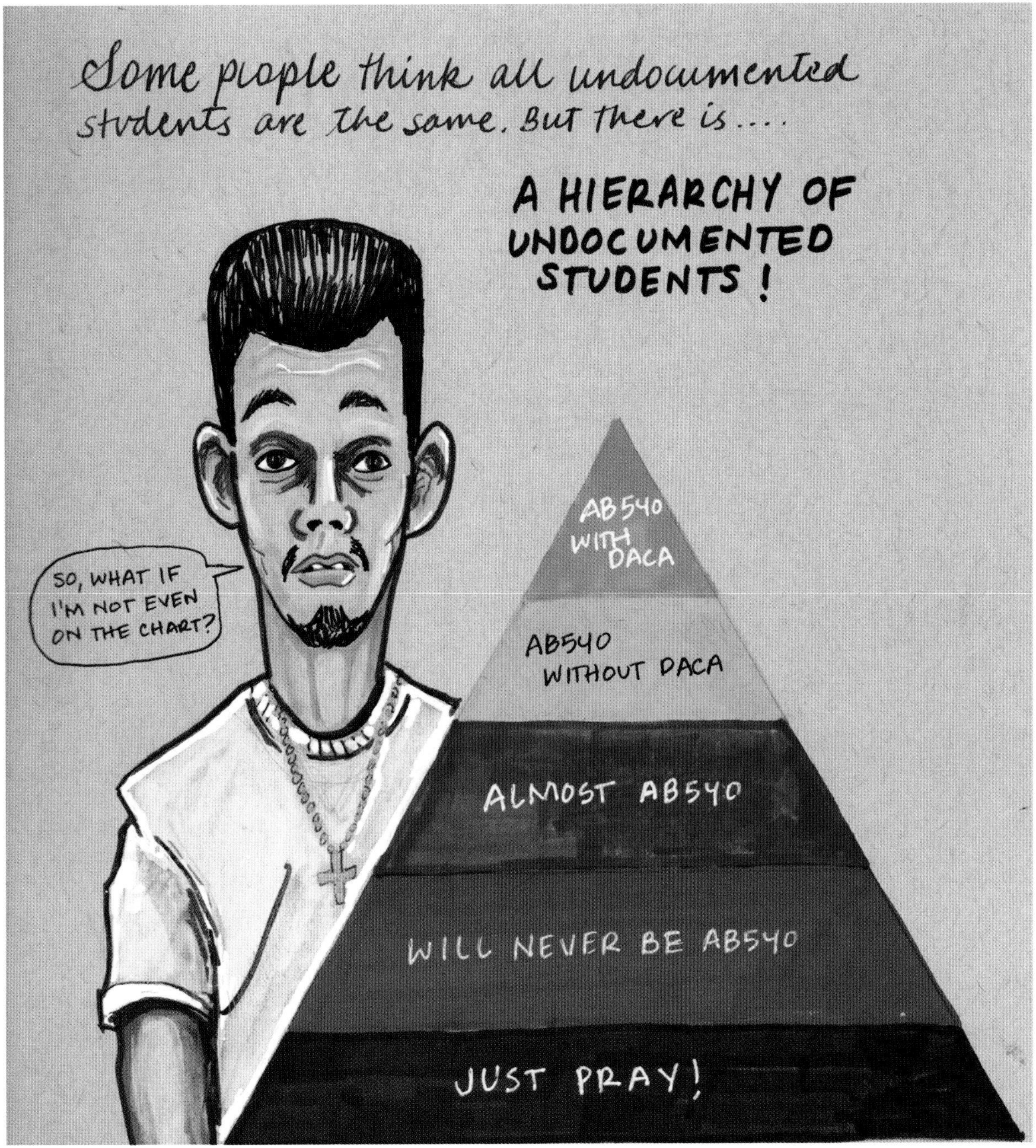
Some people think all undocumented students are the same. But there is....
A HIERARCHY OF UNDOCUMENTED STUDENTS!
SO, WHAT IF I'M NOT EVEN ON THE CHART?
AB540 WITH DACA
AB540 WITHOUT DACA
ALMOST AB540
WILL NEVER BE AB540
JUST PRAY!

March 23, 2013.

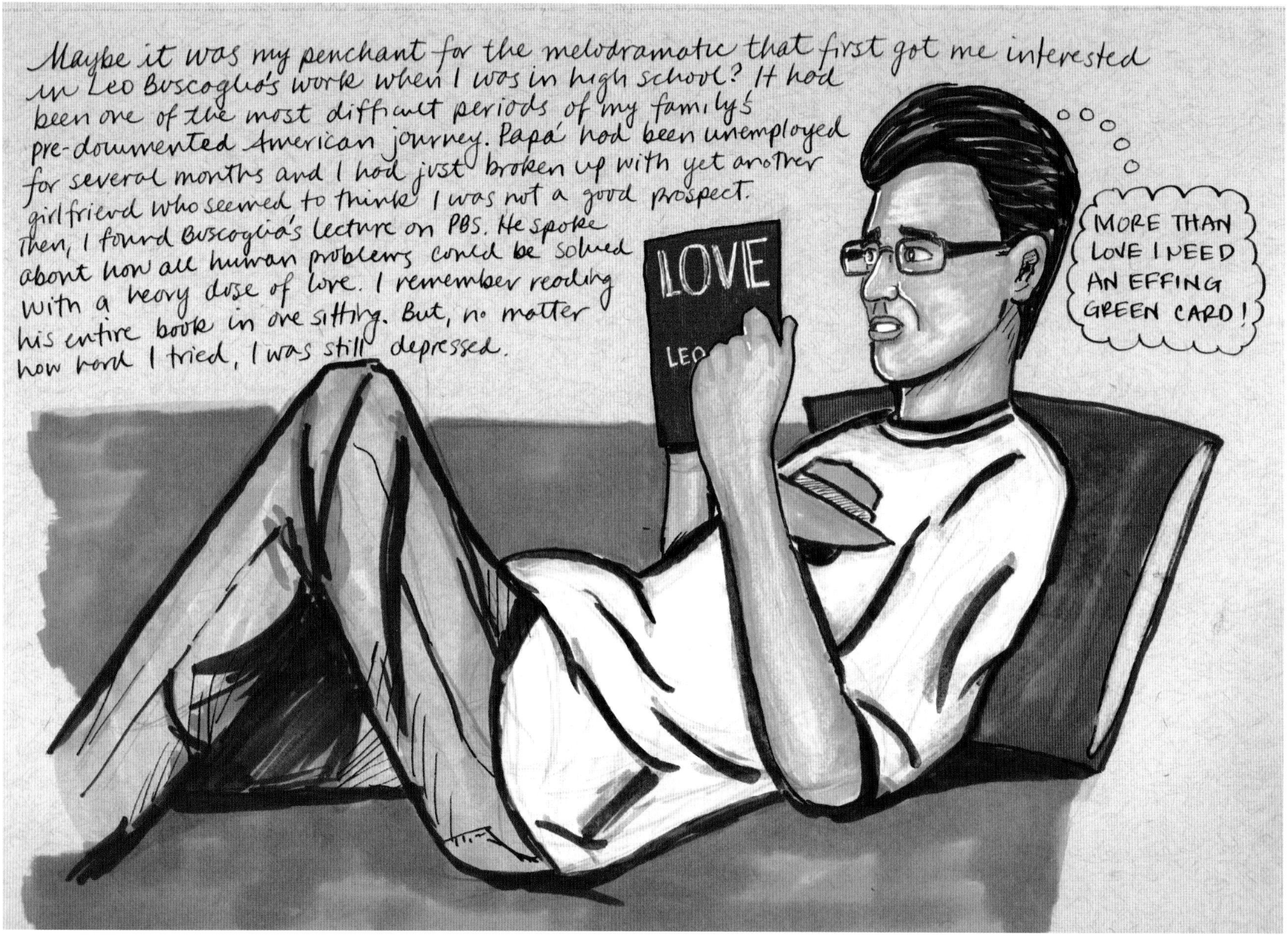

Maybe it was my penchant for the melodramatic that first got me interested in Leo Buscoglia's work when I was in high school? It had been one of the most difficult periods of my family's pre-doumented American journey. Papá had been unemployed for several months and I had just broken up with yet another girlfriend who seemed to think I was not a good prospect. Then, I found Buscoglia's lecture on PBS. He spoke about how all human problems could be solved with a heavy dose of love. I remember reading his entire book in one sitting. But, no matter how hard I tried, I was still depressed.
LOVE
LEO
MORE THAN LOVE I NEED AN EFFING GREEN CARD!

May 15, 2013. Misspellings retained.

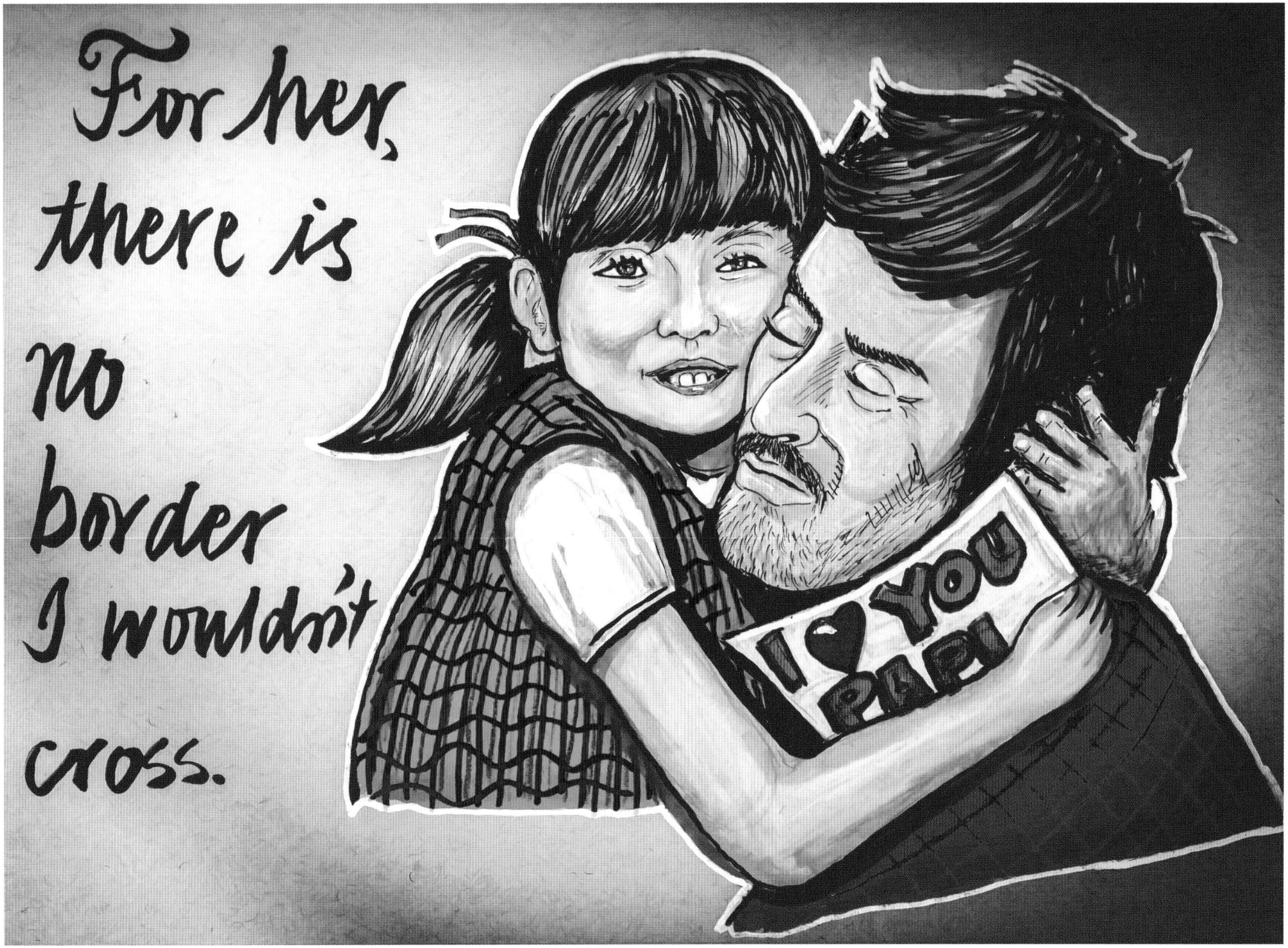
For her,
there is
no
border
I wouldn't
cross.
I ♥ YOU
PAPI

May 26, 2013.

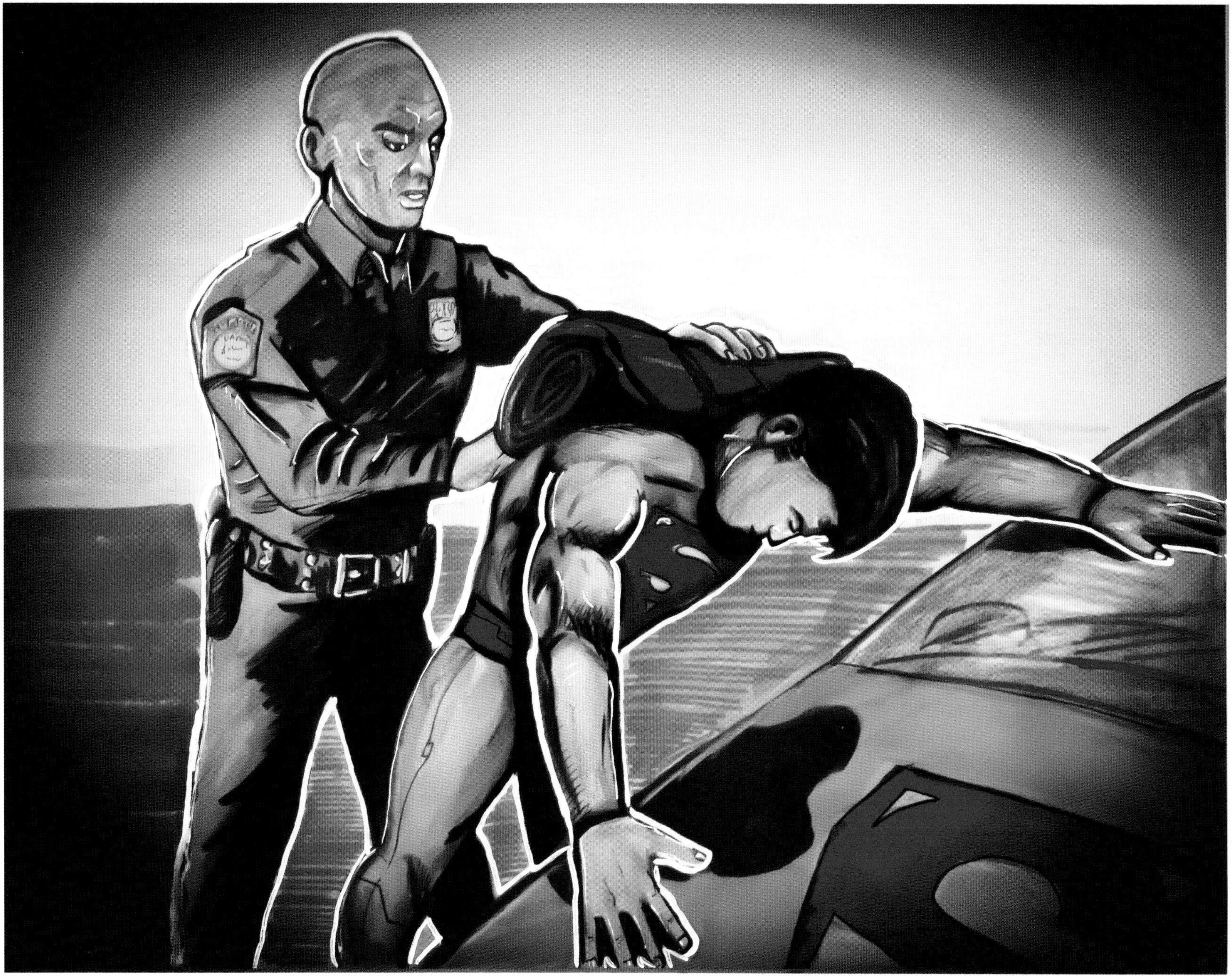

July 6, 2013.

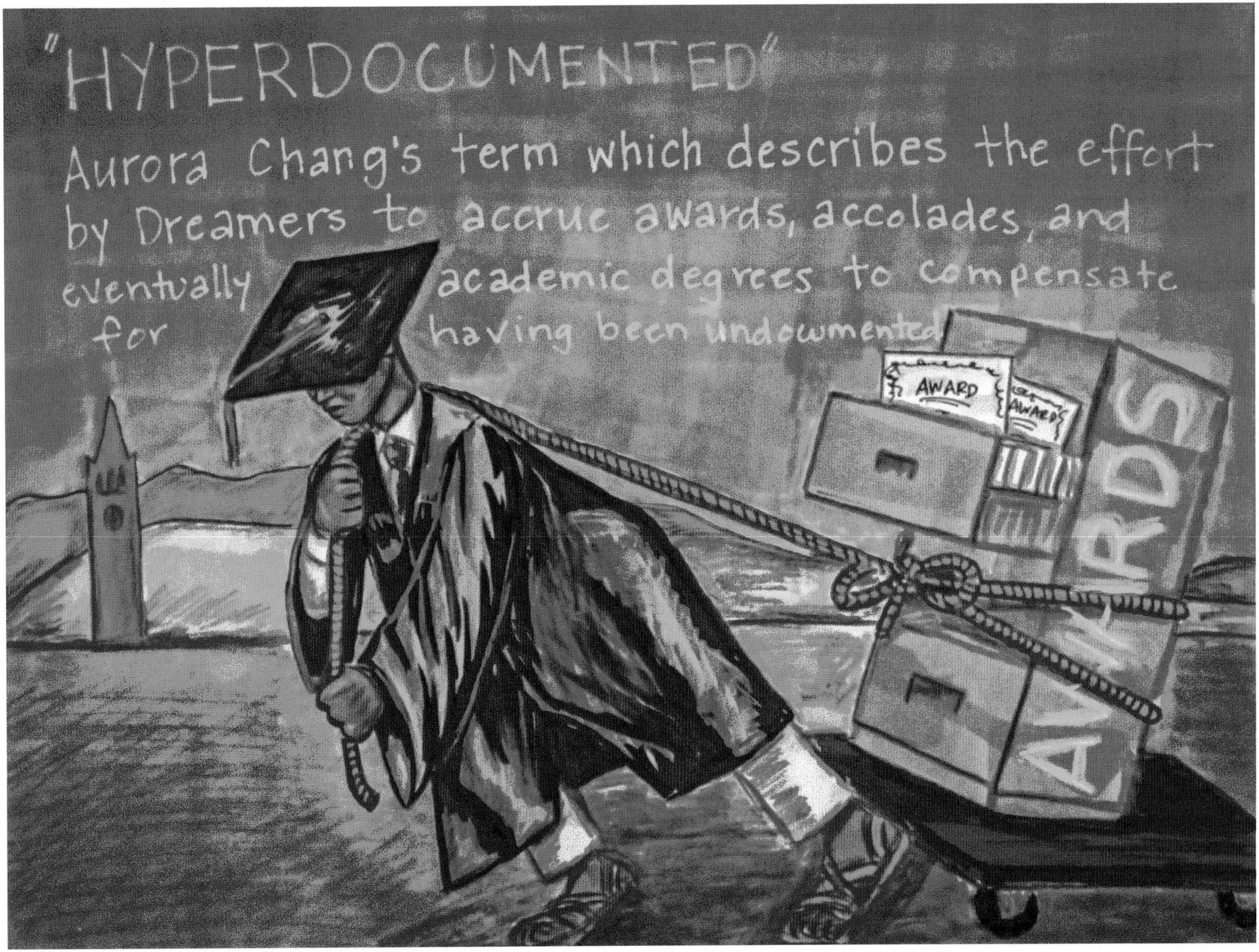
"HYPERDOCUMENTED"
Aurora Chang's term which describes the effort by Dreamers to accrue awards, accolades, and eventually academic degrees to compensate for having been undowmented
AWARD
AWARDS

August 16, 2013.

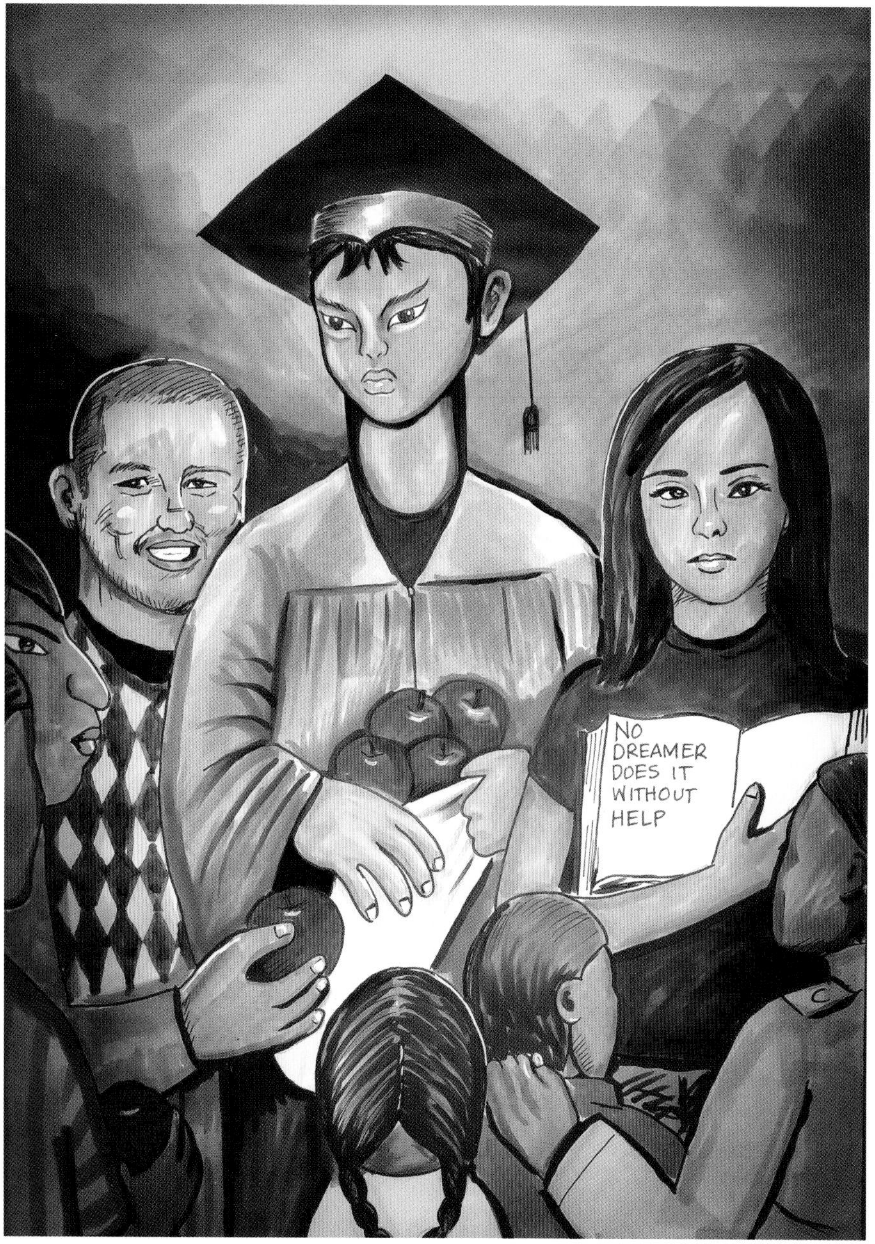
NO
DREAMER
DOES IT
WITHOUT
HELP

September 1, 2013.

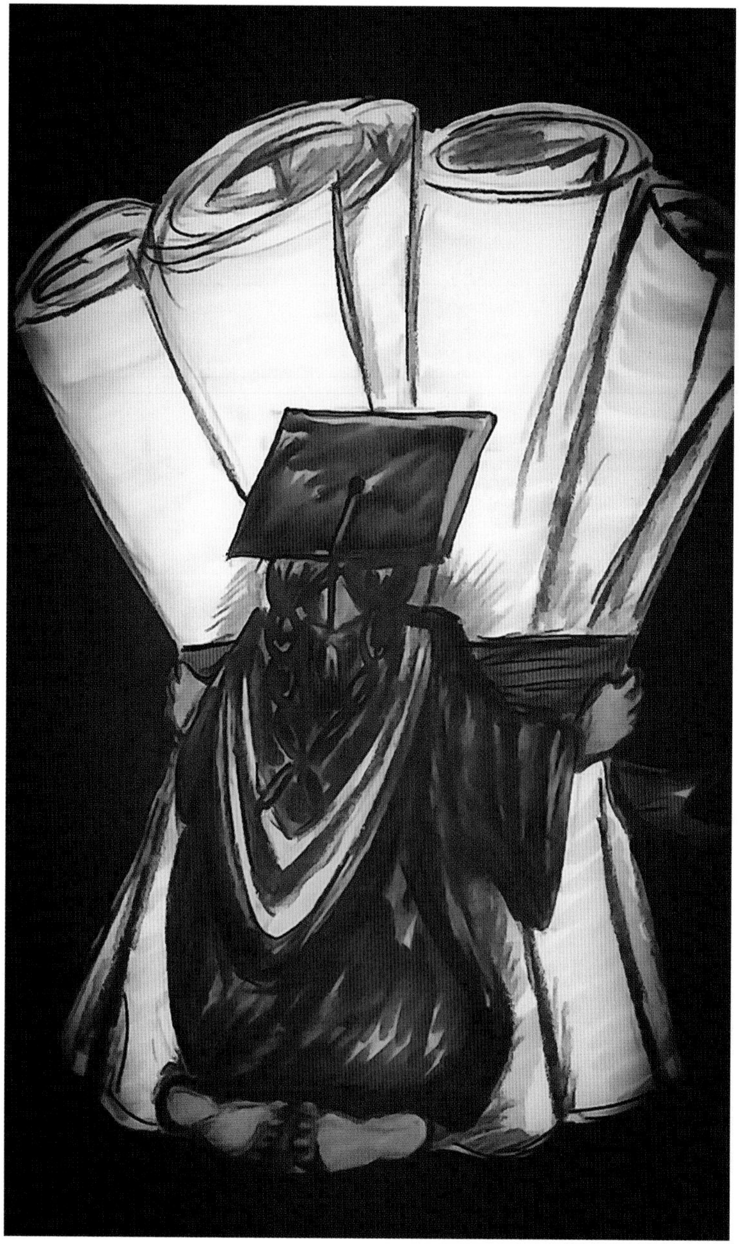

August 29, 2013.

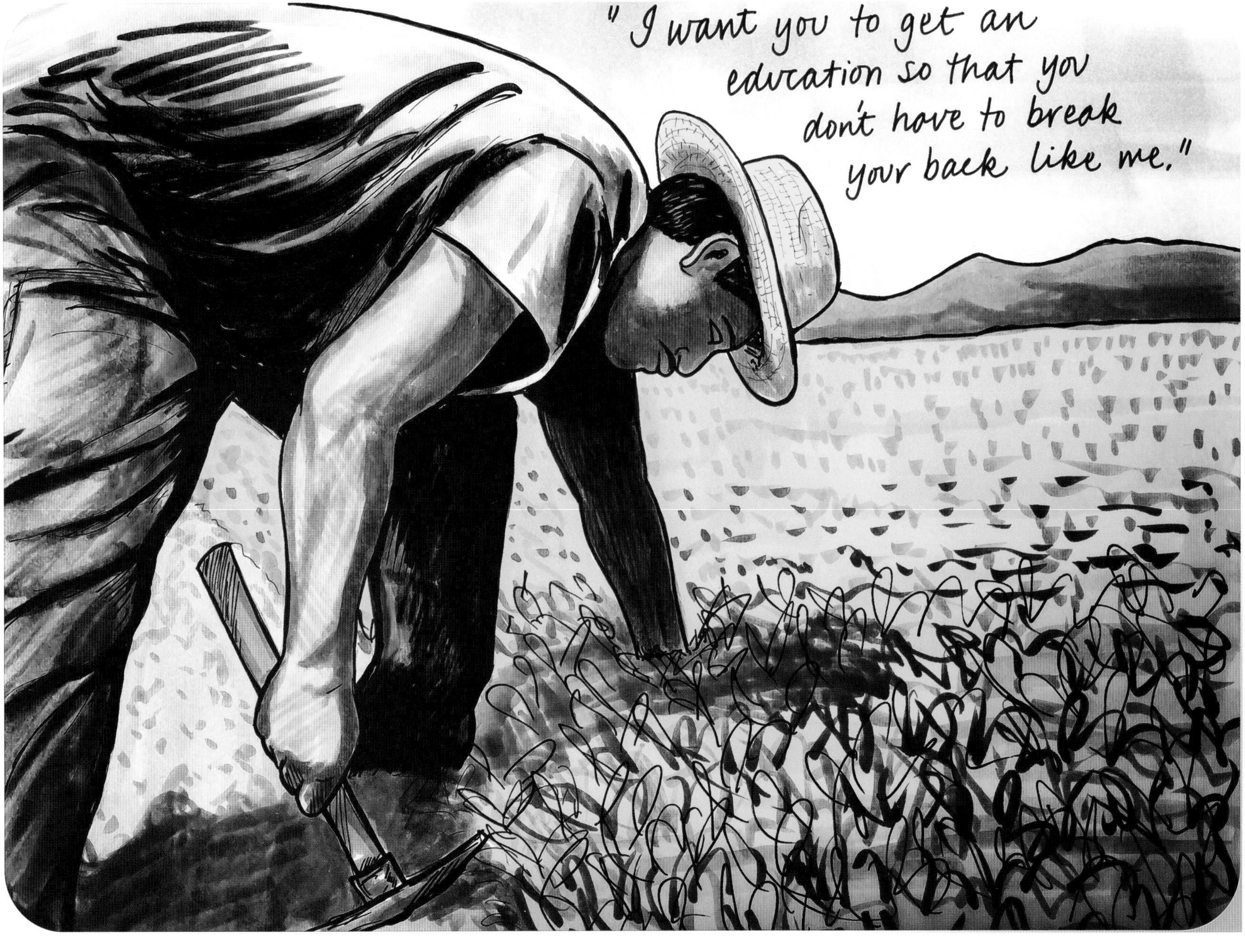
"I want you to get an education so that you don't have to break your back like me."

"Genesis of a Dream." September 28, 2013.

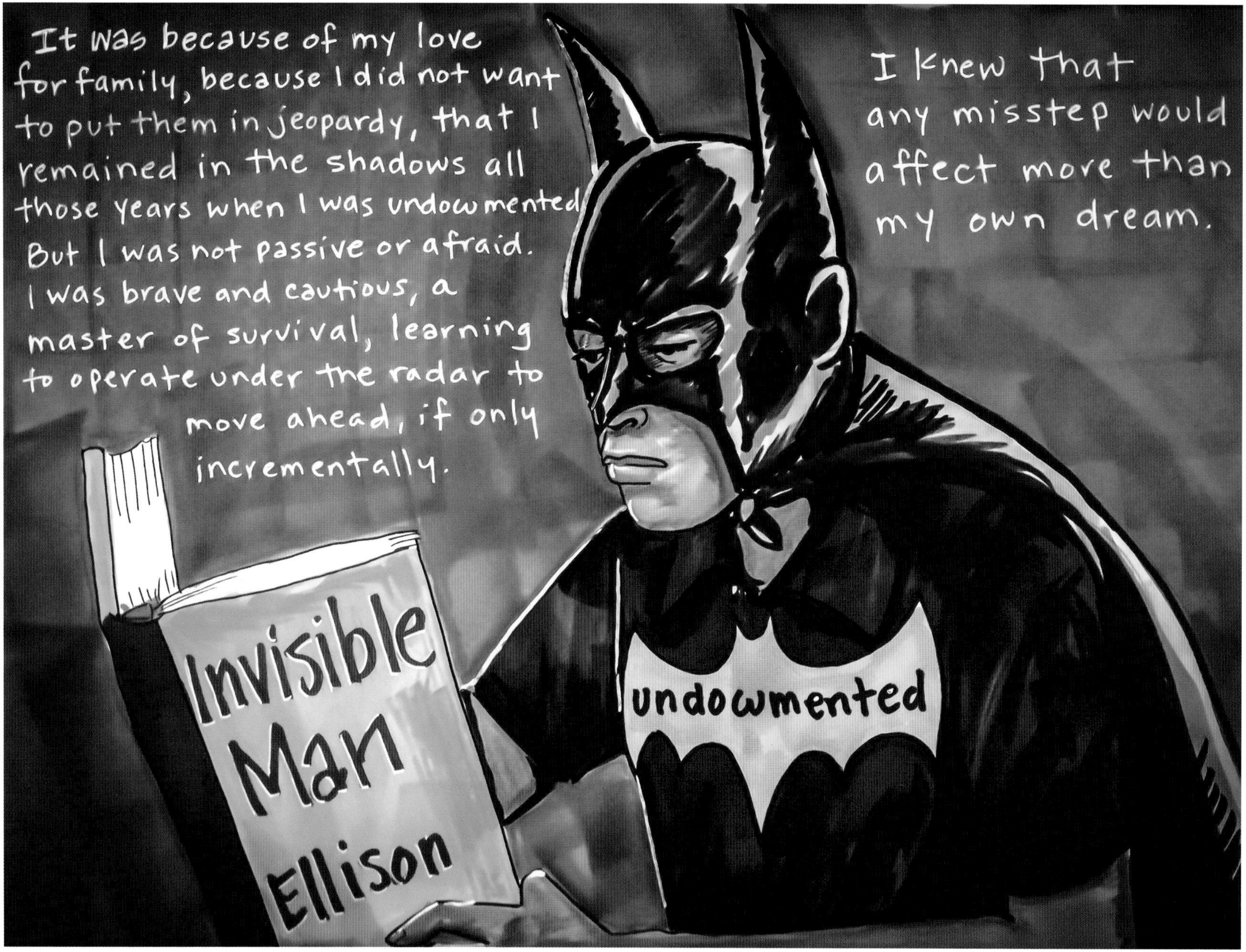
It was because of my love for family, because I did not want to put them in jeopardy, that I remained in the shadows all those years when I was undowmented. But I was not passive or afraid. I was brave and cautious, a master of survival, learning to operate under the radar to move ahead, if only incrementally.
I knew that any misstep would affect more than my own dream.
Invisible Man
Ellison
undowmented

August 27, 2013.

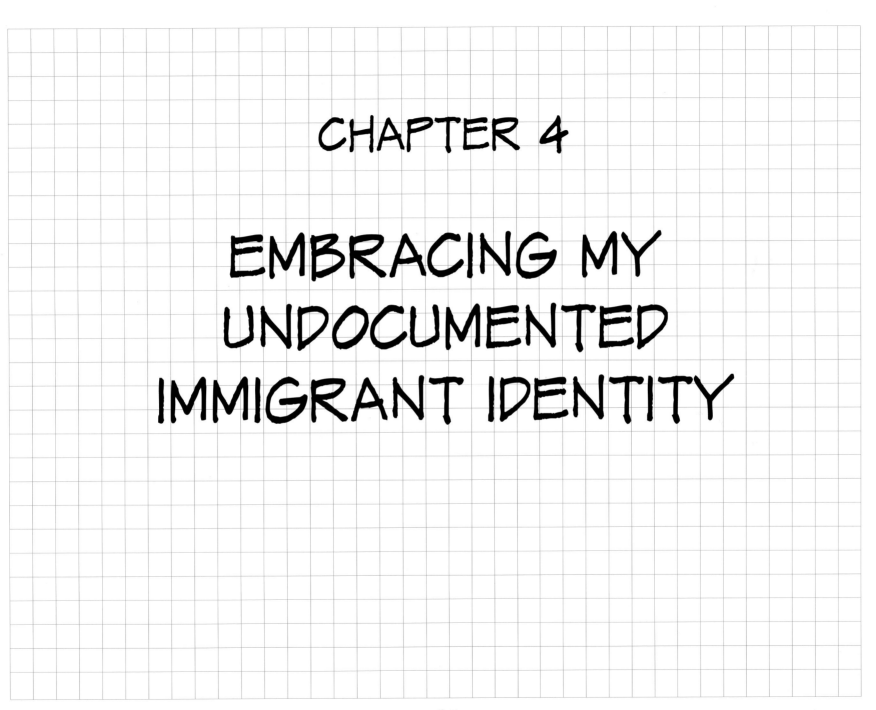

CHAPTER 4

EMBRACING MY UNDOCUMENTED IMMIGRANT IDENTITY

We'll call him Jim—Jim Garcia. Before this night in late May 2009, I had never met him. He stood about five foot seven in his Crocs—my height, but he was about 40 pounds heavier. He wore rimless glasses, but unlike me he sported a scruffy beard and a buzz haircut. We were assembled at a Holiday Inn bar in Albuquerque, where we were all attending a Latino writers' conference. I'd been told that he was a children's book writer, that he had just won some award in Texas for his first picture book, and that he was funny. All I noticed at first was that I liked how he giggled.

The other two writers sitting at our table I knew from a past conference. To protect their privacy I've changed their names in this essay, but suffice it to say that all of us, it seemed, identified as Latino writers: Rafael the Nicaraguan, Andrew the Puerto Rican, and I the Mexican immigrant. As for Jim? I didn't know but assumed he was Latino. I would soon find out differently.

After a long day of seminars on how to write marketable fiction and the like, the four of us had sat down to unwind over a few drinks. By half past midnight, we had the bar to ourselves and were sitting at the far corner of the tiny place, while behind us, on a flat-screen above our heads, analysts discussed again the Lakers' lopsided win over Orlando and the bartender cleaned glasses.

We crowded around a table no larger than a Little Caesar's pizza box, its surface a cityscape of nacho platters, half-full schooners with remnant arcs of salt on their rims, a nearly empty third pitcher of margaritas, and four of those ridiculously small plates that make you realize just how impossible it is to scoop guacamole and Monterey Jack when someone offers a corn chip—at least not without dripping it on your shirt. I held my lemonade on my lap, grasping the cool glass with the fingertips of my right hand, taking sips as the minutes of conversation passed and the voices of my new friends began to slur. Having long ago made a commitment to avoid drinking, I smiled, still painfully sober in spite of the hour. I laughed when they laughed, happy to be in a community of writers like me. I listened as they spoke of their work and the places they'd been. After ten years of living there, Rafael still missed Spain. Andrew was happy that his new novel was getting so many positive reviews. Jim was thinking of a new idea for his second children's book. Some day soon, I thought, that would be me—recently published and still ambitious.

Someone raised a glass. "Here's to the writer's life!" And I, too, raised my lemonade. Then it happened. Jim sighed, downed the last of his margarita and leaned forward on his chair. "Don't get me started with these damned illegals," he said with a giggle. "I just think we ought to deport them all."

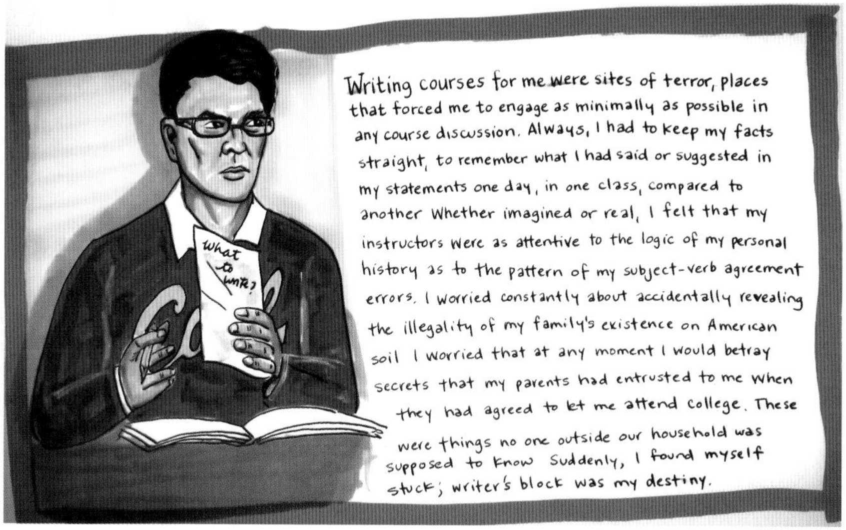
What to write?
Writing courses for me were sites of terror, places that forced me to engage as minimally as possible in any course discussion. Always, I had to keep my facts straight, to remember what I had said or suggested in my statements one day, in one class, compared to another Whether imagined or real, I felt that my instructors were as attentive to the logic of my personal history as to the pattern of my subject-verb agreement errors. I worried constantly about accidentally revealing the illegality of my family's existence on American soil I worried that at any moment I would betray secrets that my parents had entrusted to me when they had agreed to let me attend college. These were things no one outside our household was supposed to know Suddenly, I found myself stuck; writer's block was my destiny.

August 15, 2013.

The rest of us froze, then gazed at each other, as if each of us was waiting for the other to say something. Even the bartender stopped the flurry of his towel.

That pause, that moment while we waited to continue the conversation seemed to last forever. Now, the fatigue our eyes had betrayed just seconds before transformed to something different: anger, confusion, fascination.

My heartbeat quickened. I drank the rest of my lemonade in one gulp and placed the empty glass at the edge of the table. I took in a deep breath, slowly seeking to calm the beginning of convulsions in my asthmatic lungs. And I spoke.

"Excuse me. What exactly did you mean by that comment?"

His smile dissolved until his mouth was left agape. He looked at me, seemingly puzzled at first, and then he tilted his head, pensive as he weighed his approach to my question. He pushed his thick glasses up the bridge of his nose with his index finger.

"Look," he said, his once nasal, high-pitched voice now deeper and more serious. "I've spent my whole life living in Eastern Texas. My family has been there for generations. I am sick and tired of all these illegals coming over the border and making a mess of things for the rest of us. It's about time we do something about it."

There was no hesitation in his remarks, not even a hint of discomfort or of the irony of what he was saying and where. Here we all were, at a writers' conference by and for Latinos, most of us feeling optimistic about our growing demographic of readers, and even here there was an immigration debate.

I crossed my arms and massaged the stubble on my chin as he continued. He was not backing down. Instead, he looked at Rafael and Andrew and nodded as he commented about how much undocumented immigrants were costing our country. "Isn't that right?" he asked rhetorically.

Rafael and Andrew shrugged, their faces mirroring one another like identical Rorschach blots. Rafael took a drink from his nearly full margarita. Andrew looked away, towards one of the empty tables of the restaurant adjacent to the bar. Then Jim spoke again.

"Hispanics are never going to be accepted as true Americans so long as we condone the flood of illegals coming to this country. They have absolutely no respect for our laws."

*   *   *

In that moment, I felt the urge to tell Jim about my past—that for a decade my family and I had lived in the heart of East Oakland's African American ghetto as undocumented Mexican immigrants. That even now, 25 years after normalizing our status, I held my breath whenever a police cruiser pulled close. But my undocumented immigrant past is not something I can easily talk about. In fact, years after becoming a citizen, I avoided talking about it altogether, even when I felt the urge to do so. The more I suppressed the urge, the greater it grew.

For a while, I thought I could appease that restless desire to confess my undocumented immigrant past by pursuing an academic degree. I wrote a dissertation at the University of California at Berkeley that focused on the ways undocumented immigrants have been represented in Mexican American novels and stories. I was proud of my achievement, of documenting, as it were, the silences of undocumented immigrants who have been part of the Mexican American community for most of the last 100 years. I discovered that even in stories where authors did not intend to focus on undocumented immigrants, indocumentado experiences were chronicled as part of the setting. They were the aunts and uncles, the long-lost cousins, the nameless faces of passersby that have appeared here and there in many Chicano classics.

When I worked as a faculty member, I taught courses that compared Mexican undocumented immigrant experiences to those of previous immigrant generations from Asia and Europe. I also looked at the parallels between the exploitation of undocumented immigrant and African American labor. "Mexican undocumented immigration is another kind of American experience," I argued.

Still, I was not satisfied. It was my story I wanted to tell. The problem, however, was that I was scared, that I am still afraid that any disclosure of my family's undocumented immigrant past will come back to haunt me. Who in their right mind would embrace an illegal immigrant identity at a time of increased ICE raids and deportations? And, even if I were successful in publishing a memoir about my life as an undocumented immigrant, what would happen to my family? Would they be okay with it? Would they be okay that I wanted to confess what I thought was an unforgivable sin—that I actually resented my parents for bringing our family to the United States to suffer one humiliation after another?

But, there are so few trained writers, scholars with doctoral degrees, or educational activists who have actually experienced life in the United States as an undocumented immigrant. Is it not my responsibility to represent?

"Little Diego, Dreamer Boy." August 16, 2013.

42

The dirty little secret is that regardless of all the credentials I have accumulated, of all the books on law and argumentation that I've read, of all the impassioned speeches I have recorded and reviewed, talking about or writing stories about my undocumented immigrant past has not gotten easier.

In truth, it's only been a few years since I gave in and started calling myself a writer. Even now, I writhe in my seat whenever I have to confess to an old friend or new acquaintance that I've yet to publish something more than the poetry and critical essays I produced decades ago. Yes, I have a lot of material that I've sketched out in journals. What I lack is the courage to follow through, to finish editing my work so publishers seriously consider it.

Because I'm that afraid.

So I recognize the fear that compelled Jim's comments—a fear that, like mine, probably comes from shame. A fear that, similar to mine, is likely born out of the pain of being associated with what society tells us is repugnant. A fear that reminds us that others, particularly those who possess power over our lives, will see us solely as illegal and nothing else.

*   *   *

Maybe it was the lateness of the day. Maybe it was the thought that unless I spoke up I could never honestly belong to this or any community of writers. The fact is that there, in that tiny hotel bar in Albuquerque, I heard myself verbalizing a sequence of words with a speed, precision, and volume I had never experienced before.

"I don't understand how you can say these things when you are attending a Latino writers' conference. Do you seriously think that Mexican immigrant experiences have no business being included in this conference?"

The fire that had lighted Jim's eyes seemed to cool. He sat back, his glasses now perched near the tip of his nose. He held the padded armrests of his chair tightly, as if at any moment he would need to jump to his feet and walk away. Now, the lines across his forehead grew deeper, and tiny beads of sweat condensed everywhere on his brown skin, reflecting the bar's green-hued lamplights in a nervous glow.

"It, it, it's just that where I grew up near Waco...well, you know, everybody's a redneck, and illegals are really screwing things up." The more he leaned back, the more I leaned forward. The fainter his voice became, the more I felt my nostrils flaring and my top lip quivering. And the fainter his voice became, the louder my words sounded in the empty bar, until all that I could hear was the echo of an unknown voice emanating from my lips.

"But why do you even call the undocumented illegals?" I heard myself asking. "Are you an immigration judge? How many deportation trials have you adjudicated to determine if any of these immigrants is worthy of residency? Aren't people in the United States supposed to be innocent until proven guilty? If there is even one person who can convince a judge that she should not be deported, how can you deny any undocumented immigrant the opportunity to appeal their status?"

He said nothing. He looked at me as if he were the illegal and I the agent deporting him. Rafael and Andrew said nothing. The bartender walked to our table to tell us he was closing for the night. In unison, we turned to look up at him. In turn, he focused on Jim and me, apparently disgusted with one or both of us.

That night, as we walked across the pastel pink and turquoise carpet of the empty hotel lobby and headed towards the elevators, I realized Jim wasn't the person with whom I had been arguing most. It had been towards myself that I felt the most anger.

I thought back to a summer morning in 1974, when I was eight, in our little blue house in East Oakland. It was a few weeks after papá had arranged for mamá, me, and the rest of our family to be smuggled across the border at Tijuana. It was early—maybe six or so—and my parents were sitting at the kitchen table sharing a cup of coffee. That's when I overheard papá asking mamá why I was so miedoso.

"He's not scared," mamá had answered matter-of-factly. "It's just that this place is too new for him."

But I had been scared. Very scared. And because of it I grew up to become a man who was overly cautious, nauseatingly polite, always worried about offending others. I was the perpetually smiling, self-effacing immigrant Cantinflas, who deflected insults as if they were the most natural and innocent wisps of autumn air.

But that fear, that approach had failed me. Silence would not protect me from being caught.

Oddly enough, Jim stayed close to me that night. We waited several minutes for the elevator to come down, all of us staring at the flashing lights above the elevator doors until one of us remembered that no one had pushed the button. It was then that Jim pushed his glasses back up his nose and turned to me. "Look man, maybe I was wrong to have said that stuff. It's just that when you said you wrote stories about undocumented immigrants, well, I just snapped."

Earlier that night, long before Jim had blurted his comment, Andrew had asked me about my work. I had told him what I do, that I write stories about how a family of undocumented immigrants struggles to adjust to life in East Oakland and ends up having all of the kids graduating from UC Berkeley, two of them with doctorates.

It's my family's story.

When Rafael had asked if the agents at the conference had been interested in my work, I'd told him they had, especially if I wrote the work as non-fiction.

"So, are you?" he asked. I didn't respond.

*   *   *

Psychologists say that fear is an emotional response to real or imagined dangers. Humans react to threats by confronting, evading, or becoming paralyzed by them. The truth is that I don't really know what will happen to my family or me if I publish the details of my undocumented immigrant past.

What my confrontation with Jim made clear is that unless Americans of undocumented immigrant heritage break our silence about what it feels like to live undocumented, unless I publish this and other work, the notion that undocumented immigrants are brain-dead parasites incapable of intellectual and ethical reflections regarding their social, political, and historical condition in American society will persist. And, unless these ideas are challenged, undocumented immigrants will continue to be regarded solely as cheap rental equipment, machinery devoid of spiritual or intellectual worth.

But I know what I am worth. I am more than a label or my citizenship status. My parents are more than their third-grade education. And my Berkeley Ph.D. means nothing if I remain quiet in the face of anti-immigrant attacks.

*   *   *

When I was in high school I became obsessed
with buying a Chevy Impala lowrider. It was still
a few years before amensty and the border patrol was
doing raids locally, having already netted several of my
friends and their families. I THOUGHT THAT BY OWNING
A LOWRIDER AND PRETENDING TO BE A VATO LOCO I WOULD BE
SAFE, A MEXICAN AMERICAN PRACTICING MEXICAN AMERICAN
CULTURAL RITUALS

Little did I know
that in Huisquilco,
the town in Mexico
my parents had
left behind,
lowriders
we've already
cruising
the plaza.

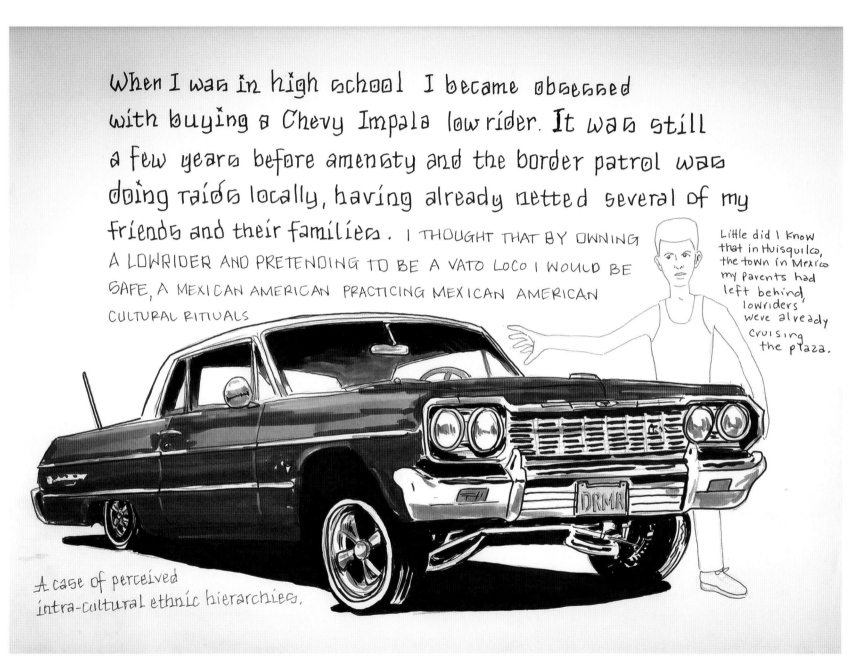

A case of perceived
intra-cultural ethnic hierarchies.

DRMR

September 7, 2013.

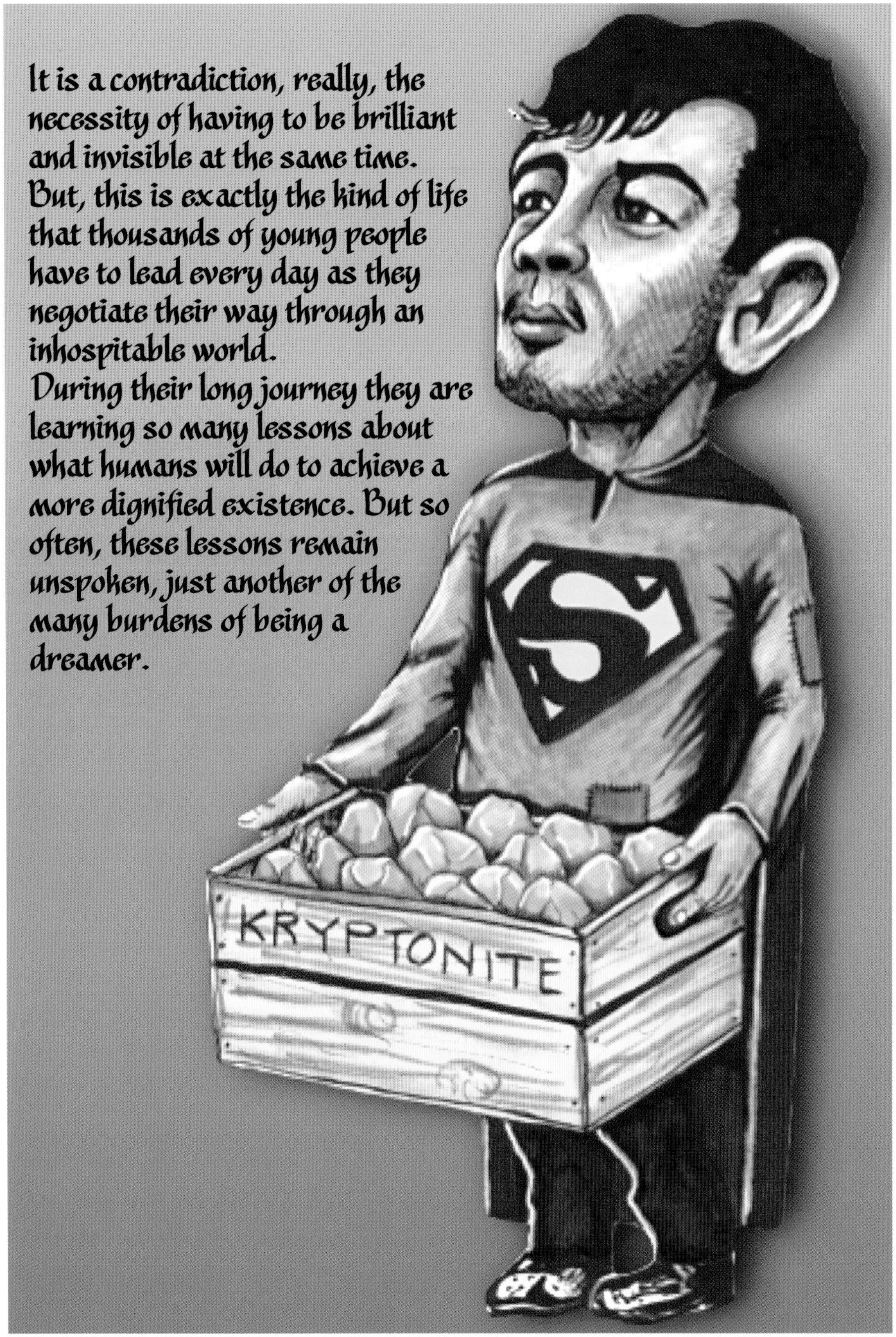
It is a contradiction, really, the necessity of having to be brilliant and invisible at the same time.
But, this is exactly the kind of life that thousands of young people have to lead every day as they negotiate their way through an inhospitable world.
During their long journey they are learning so many lessons about what humans will do to achieve a more dignified existence. But so often, these lessons remain unspoken, just another of the many burdens of being a dreamer.
KRYPTONITE

August 10, 2014.

The day I confessed to my parents my intention of attending college they were rightfully afraid, especially my dad, concerned that such an action would reveal my status to school officials and jeopardize any chance our family would have at legalization under the Simpson-Mazzoli Bill. That bill became the Immigration Reform and Control Act of 1986, and with it my family and I gained amnesty and I a legitimate role as a college student.

In an effort to do the right thing, to make sure we all kept clean, my parents were willing to see me reject the acceptance letter Berkeley had sent me.

It was only when I argued that I would enroll in the Army if I was not permitted to attend college that mamá and papá agreed to let me go to Cal. In all likelihood, I wouldn't have been able to volunteer for military service without also revealing my undocumented status. That did not stop me from thinking about it, from hoping that such a gesture would earn me points as a potential patriot that I could use if I were ever caught.

"I'll help you as much as I can, but you have to pay for most of your education yourself," papá said the morning my confirmation of acceptance letter was due. As I sped through the rain-slicked streets of East Oakland up 82nd Avenue and down East 14th to the post office on 90th Avenue, I played George Benson's "On Broadway" on my father's car stereo at least five times. And yet, the terror I saw in mamá's and papá's eyes as I left, and every day that I attended Berkeley after that, told me that boot camp might have been an easier road to take. I saw that same terror in mamá's eyes fifteen years later when I told her I was leaving my academic position to pursue the life of a writer. She looked at me from where she had been standing in front of the kitchen sink. She turned off the faucet, straightened up after wringing her towel, and wiped her hands on her apron.

"Pero mi'jo, why would anyone ever want to read stories about our lives? We are little people just struggling to make it from one day to the next." She smiled when she sat on the chair next to mine.

We spoke for almost an hour; she asked questions and nodded as I tried to explain. She never asked me not to write about what we had been through—the dozens of times we had almost gotten caught—she didn't have to. I could see it on her face, in the subtlety of her frown, and the way she crossed her arms, as if that self-embrace was the only thing keeping her from collapsing mere inches in front of her first-born son. She seemed anxious about what I had in mind, worried about the kinds of secrets I might expose in my stories. Still, she said nothing and merely sat tense, quiet, looking at me as if I were a puzzle she would never learn how to solve.

It reminded me of the way she had sat in the passenger seat of papá's green station wagon in the summer of 1976 as we rode home after a hot day at the San Jose Flea Market. Papá had bought a box full of strawberries—big, luscious, perfectly ripe fruit. On the way home, as we moved slowly through the Sunday afternoon traffic on the Nimitz Freeway, papá, really all of us, had one of those moments where we forgot about our status. A coworker had told him about a park not far from the highway we were now stuck on. It had a lake, dozens of pine trees, and a picnic area where we could enjoy our strawberries. As soon as he saw an off-ramp, papá exited the freeway and headed towards the area his friend had told him about. As we looked for a place to park, papá found himself driving the opposite way into

the City of Fremont Police Department's parking lot, just as a police cruiser was exiting.

"It is a common mistake," the officer said to my sister Silvia as he pointed towards the right entrance to the park. Mamá remained quiet in the passenger seat, her eyes towards the front, a subtle frown on her face and her arms wound tightly across her torso. That's the way she stayed all the way home. And, that's the way she sat as I told her I would no longer be a college professor, that I would instead write our family stories.

Maybe I learned my own fear from mamá. More precisely, the main lesson I learned from her was to protect family at all costs, that the needs of the many must always outweigh the wishes of the few. This, after all, is the way she has always led her life, the reason that she ventured to the United States with her children in tow to find her husband. This also seemed to be the reason for her concern about my writing and why she silenced her terror so many years ago in that Fremont Police Department parking lot.

Today, the family needs have changed. I am no longer hunted. Today, I am a Mexican American citizen of the United States. Safety is no longer contingent on remaining silent and invisible. And every endangered community eventually learns that silence equals death. If I want my citizenship to matter, I must learn how to speak to the Jim Garcias of the world. If I want my people to know their worth, I must learn how to speak for the immigrants in the United States who cannot yet speak for themselves.

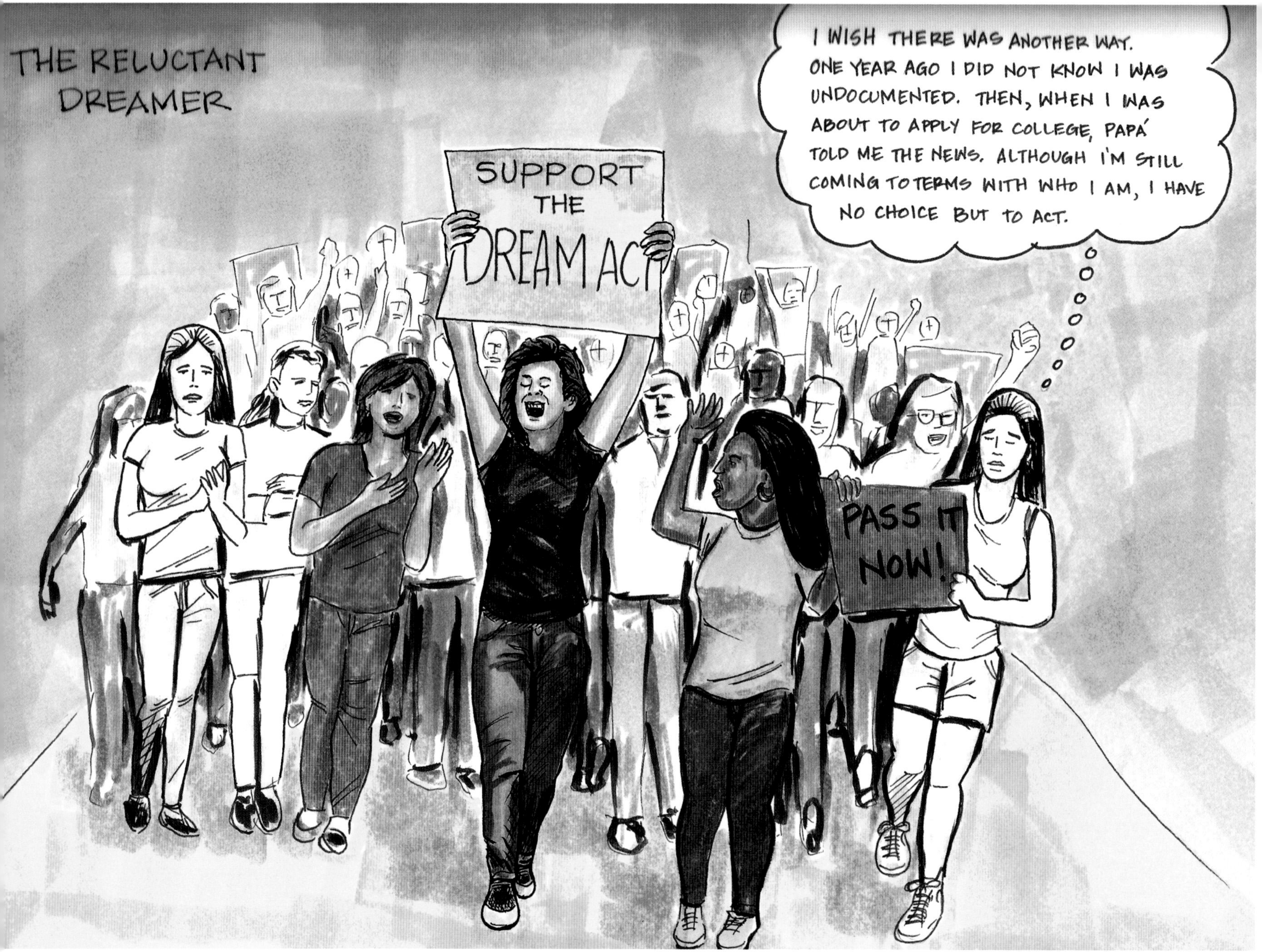
THE RELUCTANT DREAMER
I WISH THERE WAS ANOTHER WAY. ONE YEAR AGO I DID NOT KNOW I WAS UNDOCUMENTED. THEN, WHEN I WAS ABOUT TO APPLY FOR COLLEGE, PAPÁ TOLD ME THE NEWS. ALTHOUGH I'M STILL COMING TO TERMS WITH WHO I AM, I HAVE NO CHOICE BUT TO ACT.
SUPPORT THE DREAM ACT
PASS IT NOW!

November 11, 2013.

CHAPTER 5

ASSISTING THE RELUCTANT DREAMER

"Good news, Alberto!" Carlos waved his right arm aloft when he crossed Bancroft Avenue, his smile glowing as he ran towards me.

"We finally met him and I actually told him all about my situation!"

He beamed when he spoke, clearly giddy from what had seemingly been a life-transforming event.

"Met who?" I asked and smiled, not expecting the specific detail of what he was about to say in his response.

"The Chancellor, man." He pushed his slipping glasses back up the bridge of his nose with his index finger and swung his overstuffed backpack from one shoulder to the other. "I'll stop by your office to tell you all about it later. Right now I'm late for class."

I could not finish the half Caesar salad I was having for lunch on that late September day of 2007. "What had happened?" I wondered. Who had been there? What exactly had been discussed? Questions multiplied in my mind as I hunted for bits of crispy grilled chicken in a sea of overdressed romaine. I finished eating and hurried to catch the green light so I could cross Telegraph Avenue and get back to campus. All the while I tried to grasp the enormity of what Carlos had just shared with me: How was it that he had managed to confess his undocumented status to the Chancellor without experiencing any immediate repercussion? How was it that he was walking around Berkeley as if everything were still okay? I came back to my office earlier than usual. And yet, though I waited for him to come by, that blustery day seemed to last forever. It took Carlos almost a week before he finally stopped by my door and told me exactly what had transpired. I could hardly believe it.

Although Carlos and the other student that Katherine Gin had arranged to meet with Chancellor Robert Birgeneu had taken a personal risk in confessing their undocumented status, what they had done also affected me deeply. I was shocked by their boldness, stunned by the matter-of-factness with which they had interacted with our campus's highest-ranked administrative officer. I had never thought to be that direct, always assumed that if any progress were to be made at Berkeley on supporting our increasing number of undocumented students, it would have to be made incrementally, through a gradual shift in the overall narrative about immigration. Now I was presented with the power of direct action, of raw honesty, of an unembellished story standing on its own, unadorned by rhetorical flourishes or appeals to syrupy emotion.

Now that I reflect on it, I realize that what Carlos, Katherine, and the other student who accompanied them did stands as a watershed moment in immigrant student activism and advocacy at the Berkeley campus. That specific act, according to various interviews Chancellor Birgeneau has granted since on the issue, went farther in informing his own ethical and political stance on undocumented immigration, than any of the treatises and briefs he had read on the subject. In many ways, that act also brought attention to the years of advocacy work that many of us had already spent doing on behalf of undocumented students on campus. Following the Chancellor's lead, other top administrators at Berkeley suddenly opened up to hearing more about our insights into the plight of undocumented students. All at once, the Immigrant Students Issues Coalition (ISIC), an ad-hoc staff organization to which I belonged, commanded the increased attention of other campus stakeholders. However, as support for undocumented students became a cause célèbre at Berkeley, the eagerness of well-meaning allies to do something also presented a dilemma for that segment of the undocumented student population that was not ready to come out publicly.

And so lured by the promise of a great job in the land of milk and honey, Pancho Pooh and his best friend, Cuco el tigere tonto, cross into the Vast Unknown as undocumented immigrants...

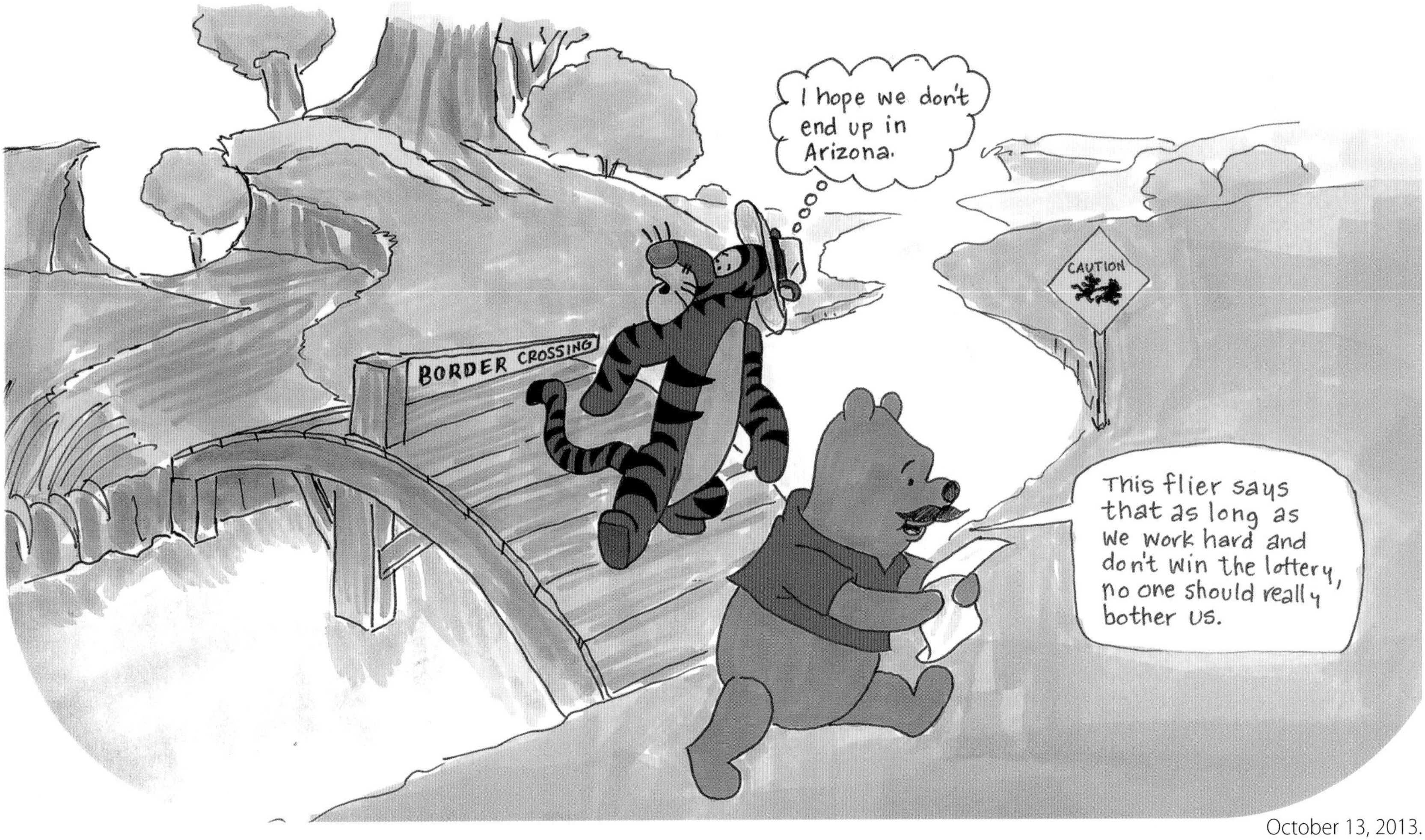

I hope we don't end up in Arizona.
CAUTION
BORDER CROSSING
This flier says that as long as we work hard and don't win the lottery, no one should really bother us.

October 13, 2013.

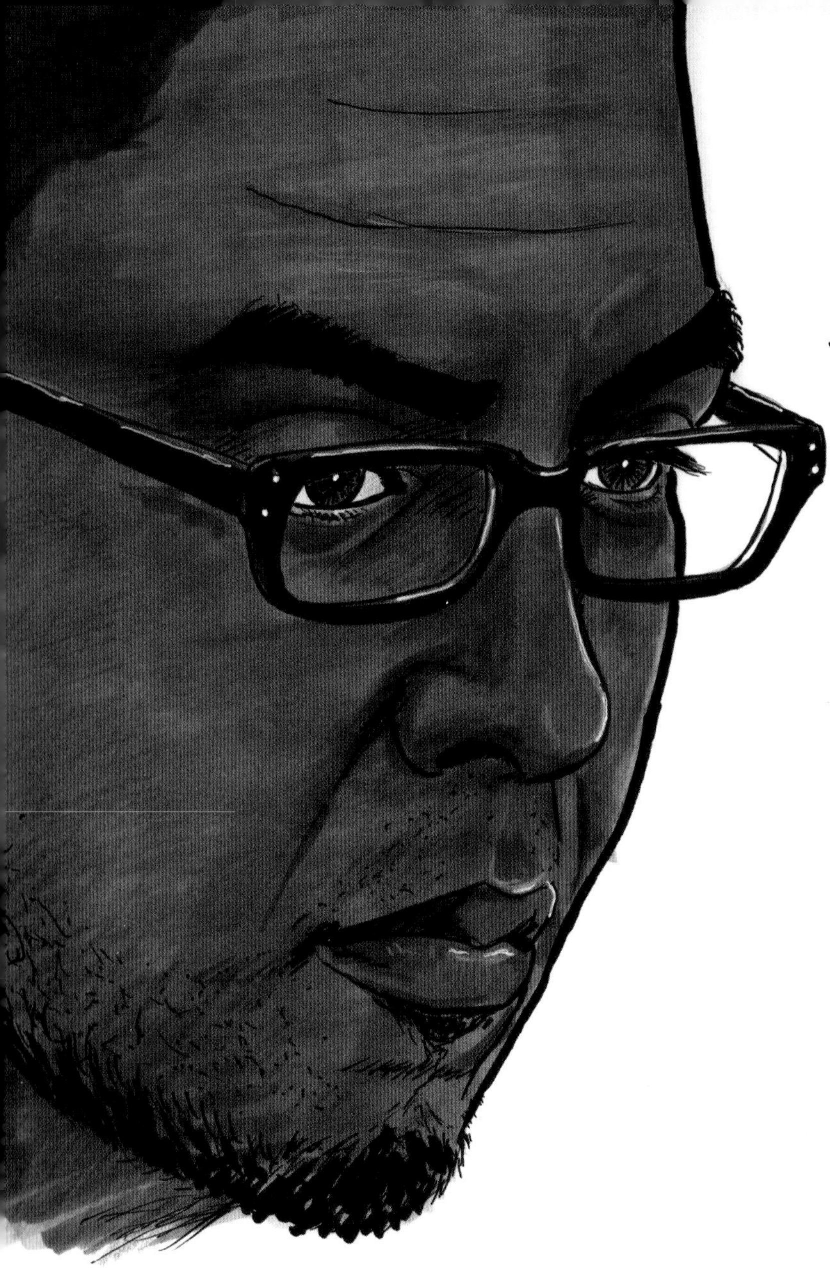

Sometimes I worry that my luck will run out, that my dream to graduate from this place will finally be shattered. Though I have many friends who are also undocumented and hard-working, they have been in the US longer and seem to struggle less with having to play the "brilliant while undocumented" role. Unlike them, it seems that I am always on the cusp—always so close to running out of money or not doing well in my courses. The truth is that I am a founding member of "The Bad Dreamers Club."

September 21, 2013.

For many of us in ISIC, it became clear that with the emergence of support for undocumented immigrant students on campus came a subtle, but unrelenting, pressure for these students to confess who they were via ever-increasingly gut-wrenching stories. As financial resources and access to other support services became available, a validation of these resources was increasingly accompanied by testimonials of appreciation by students who had already survived and transcended what seemed like a ubiquitous pattern of hellish experiences. These students, "Dreamers," as they came to be known, suddenly became a new kind of model minority. It was not enough for students to publicly declare that they were, in fact, undocumented; now they needed to accompany that confession with what seemed like a pre-packaged ode to their own talents for survival.

To be sure, whether or not to encourage undocumented students to come out and share their stories as a way to appeal for empathy and support was a hotly debated subject within ISIC long before Carlos and his friends stepped into the Chancellor's Conference Room. Though our organization had had several undocumented students sharing their experiences in the context of larger staff presentations, we had facilitated soon after California's Assembly Bill 540 had passed, we had initially encouraged our students to use pseudonyms because we were convinced that Berkeley was not that "safe" a campus yet.

"This is not the kind of genie that you can put back in the bottle if you change your mind," I had argued from the first moments when one of our other members had suggested that it would be a good idea for our students to just come out and declare themselves as undocumented.

"These students are heroes," my colleague would often assert. "We need to recognize and reward their persistence!"

Though I never disagreed with his call for action, I also thought that achieving it was a complicated task.

"Sometimes it feels as if the only 'guaranteed' right undocumented students seem to have is 'the right to remain silent.' Why give that up so easily when we are not sure what people will do with it?" I was adamant in my conviction, convinced as I was that not everyone would see undocumented student experiences as heroic. After all, there was the Bradford Decision, a ruling issued by the California high court in 1995 that had undone all of the benefits of the 1985 undocumented-friendly Leticia A decision. What was significant about that judicial act was that a staff member at UCLA, Bradford, had initiated it. When he had refused to implement the Leticia A policy, Bradford had been fired, and so he had chosen to sue the university as a result of it. "How can we assume that we have no Bradfords at Berkeley?" I often asked.

I grappled consistently with a mix of emotions as undocumented students began to be presented with a modest but increasing array of sources of support. I learned from colleagues working in the financial aid office that a handful of private donors were now interested in helping undocumented students specifically. Suddenly, scholarships that had previously required proof of citizenship did not. Internships in local non-profit organizations opened up. Even those students who had had the most difficult time in finding ways to pay for their education seemed to have new options. Given my own frustrations with finding support when I was an undocumented student in the mid 1980s, and given all the individual crises of the dozens of undocumented students who visited my office regularly, I should have been ecstatic, but something about the way that students spoke about their undocumented experience felt jarring.

It was soon after my chance meeting with Carlos that another student came to visit me at my office to talk about how much difficulty she was having with writing an essay. Because many students on campus had found out that I was active in ISIC and that I had once been undocumented, they often visited me to solicit advice. This is what she wanted.

"They have this new scholarship application at the business school that is designed for immigrant students and it does not require proof of citizenship. I just don't know what to say. Nobody at Berkeley knows I'm undocumented and my parents have always discouraged me from even talking about it."

The agony in her face as she sat in front of me, her arms holding her red notebook tightly as she tried to tell me what she was trying to write, was a familiar one to me. Talking about being undocumented is not something that was encouraged in my own family. In fact, the only time "our situation" was mentioned was when my father wanted to warn me about letting anyone know about our status.

"Do you think that being undocumented matters to the kind of work you want to do at the business school?" I asked, hoping that she would have reflected more on the uniqueness of her situation than I had at her age.

"Yes, absolutely! I want to be a success in business so that I can help my family and my community. I have noticed that most of the business in my hometown seem to ignore undocumented consumers."

"Say that!" I smiled. "Say it with confidence. Let them know that you are bringing a resourcefulness and perspective to the school that they don't already have." Her face brightened as she seemed to realize that sacrificing her secret

was a fair cost for the opportunity she would be given. She then thanked me and left.

Then again, there was also that rally on Sproul Plaza that I had attended in the spring of 2009. It had been on a crystal clear day in late March that several of us in ISIC had gone to support a rally attended by a few of our students. Though we had only expected a handful of people to show up, the crowd that had gathered as we made our way towards the steps in front of the administration building had already numbered in the hundreds. It was clear that many of the protesters had arrived from off campus, including dozens of high school students who were huddling around large cardboard signs calling for the passage of the Dream Act. I noticed a cameraman from Univision who was setting up his equipment a few steps from where we were standing. Then I saw Professor Carlos Muñoz, Jr. approaching two women who were standing by the main microphone. One was holding a clipboard, while the other was pointing to various people in the crowd below. Carlos waved at me. He was wearing the same Panama fedora that he had worn when he had arrived to my doctoral oral exam in 1992. A boy of sixteen or seventeen stepped up to the microphone and grabbed it. He was dressed in a navy blue graduation gown and matching mortar board cap, a placard with the word "Dreamer" hanging around his neck.

"No matter how hard I've worked to become an A student. No matter how many thousands of lawns my father has cut or thousands of houses my mother has cleaned, we are all regarded as nothing more than criminals!"

I don't know why I stepped back from where I was standig with my ISIC colleagues. All I remember at that moment was the ring of the boy's voice echoing across the quad, the raw power of his indignation and anger thumping in my chest. It was an anger that resonated with me, an indignation that I absorbed like the nectar of that rarest of fruits. I felt inspired, my heart racing as he spoke about his experience. But it was also too much. It was all too sudden. I felt a surge of terror every time the boy looked towards where we were standing in the front row, afraid that he would ask me to step up to the mike and offer up my own testimony. And I wanted to. But I was afraid at the same time. Suddenly I felt the urge to flee, to curl up like one of those roly poly bugs I used to hunt as a kid. I stepped away slowly, a feeling of yearning overflowing my heart as speaker after speaker called for action, as the crowd continued to grow, and as fists sprouted in the air like flowers in a field.

Allan, one of my colleagues in ISIC, quietly walked to where I had moved.

"Are you okay?" he asked, his hand resting lightly on my shoulder.

"I don't know." I felt a bead of sweat running down my cheek. And I left.

Grappling with the emotions of being undocumented, even for someone who has now spent decades enjoying the benefits of naturalized citizenship, is no easy matter. It requires coming to terms with an identity that is too often shunned by the same families one is trying to help. It is an exercise in exorcising contradictions, in sharing the most vulnerable of secrets. But grappling with these emotions is what we precisely ask every undocumented student who enters the university to do. Their solicitation of help is based on how well (read dramatically) they can convey their experience. Indeed, surveys and individual meetings with the many dozens of students we had worked with over several years convinced many of us in ISIC that there has always been a large number of undocumented students who have been generally reluctant to publicly declare their undocumented identities in public. While for some of these students being undocumented has not always been a source of pride, for almost all of these students being undocumented has represented a new lens by which they have come to know the world, as their families have too often chosen to ignore reflecting on their experience from that epistemological vantage point.

University support of undocumented students is important, as is the advocacy necessary to making sure such support remains consistent. Still, as we celebrate the inclusion of undocumented immigrants within our university, it is important to recognize that many of these students are still processing the psychological repercussions of their identity. Requiring them to tell their story, in writing or in an oral presentation, as a condition for receiving support does not mean they have achieved a mature understanding of their experience. Maybe such a requirement should be optional? Maybe we should first ask them to embrace their undocumentedness slowly, with self-compassion and a good amount of oxygen?

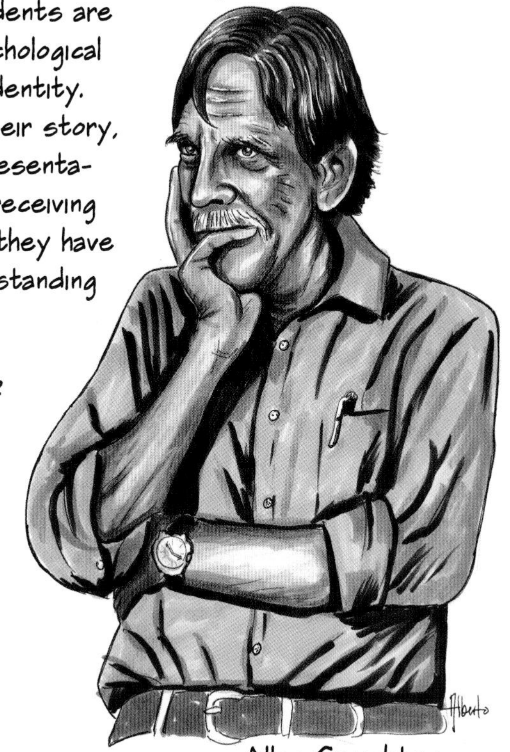

Alberto

Allan Creighton

Long before the Dream Act Movement came into being, J.P Bone's novel, Illegals, presented the compelling story of a small group of undocumented immigrant shoe factory workers who risked deportation in order to demand better treatment as workers. Told in a sequence of taut vignettes, the novel chronicles the genesis of a group's collective coming to courage at a time when most undocumented immigrants remained silent about the abuses they experienced. In this way, the book is prophetic and revealing. It provides excellent background reading for anyone looking to understand why today's undocumented immigrant community is asserting itself politically. The book was also ahead of its time in the way that it depicted a pan-Latino and cross-ethnic coalition of workers striving towards a common goal. Readers will enjoy the story as much as the characters. And, in the end, they will gain an important new perspective that remains, in spite of the decades since it was first published, as elusive as ever.

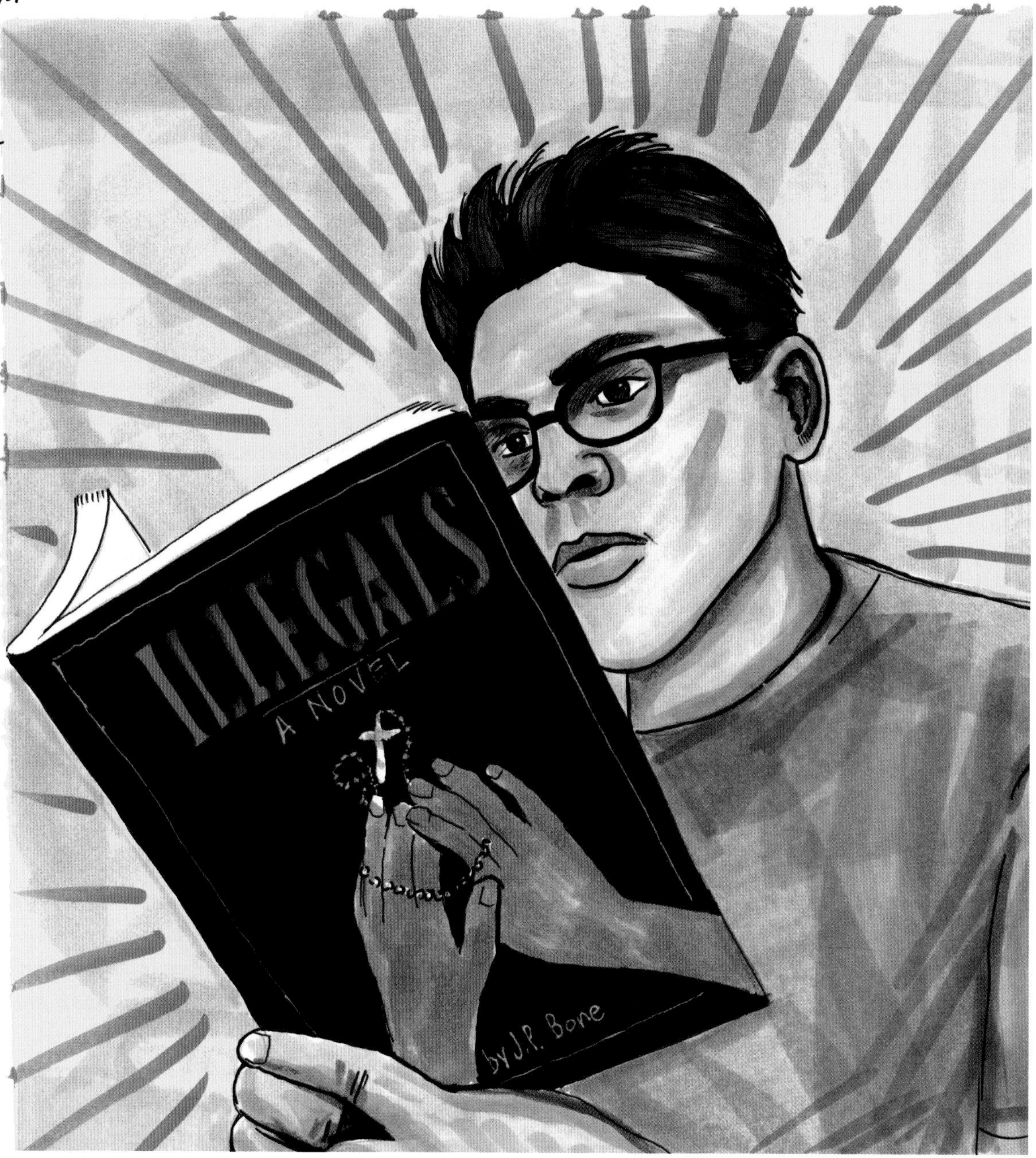
ILLEGALS
A NOVEL
by J.P. Bone

October 8, 2013.

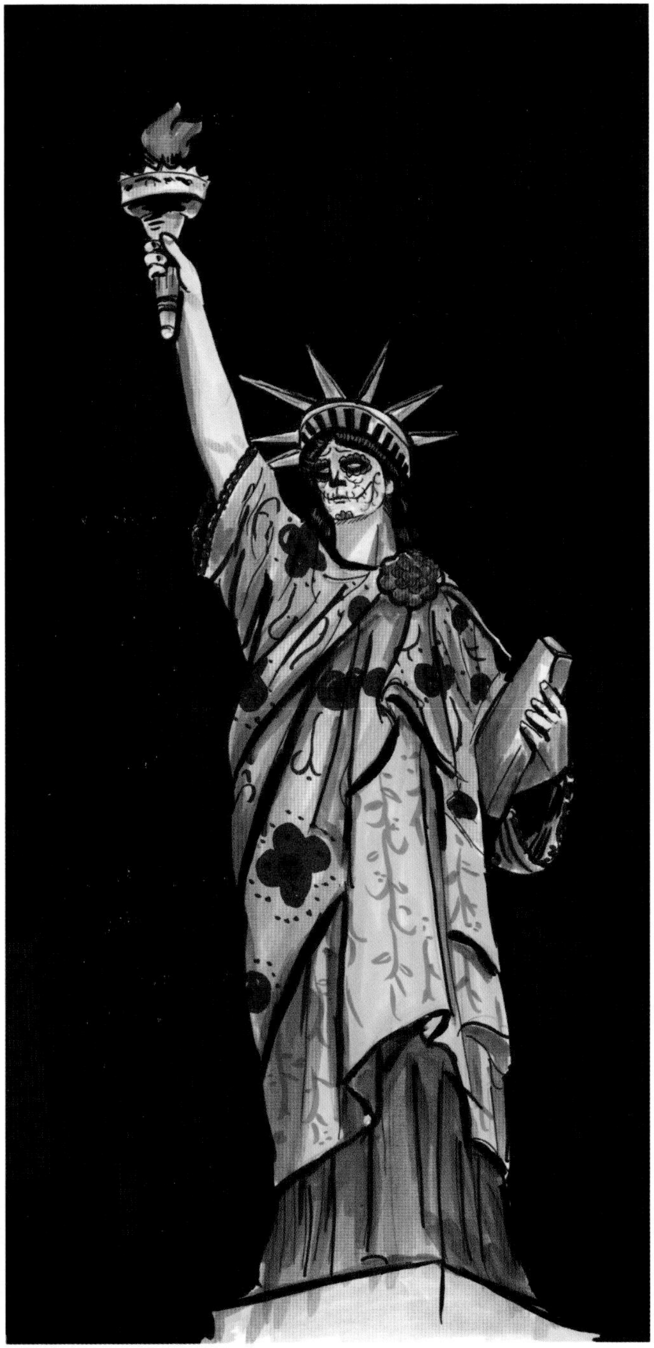

"Calaca-liberty." October 19, 2013.

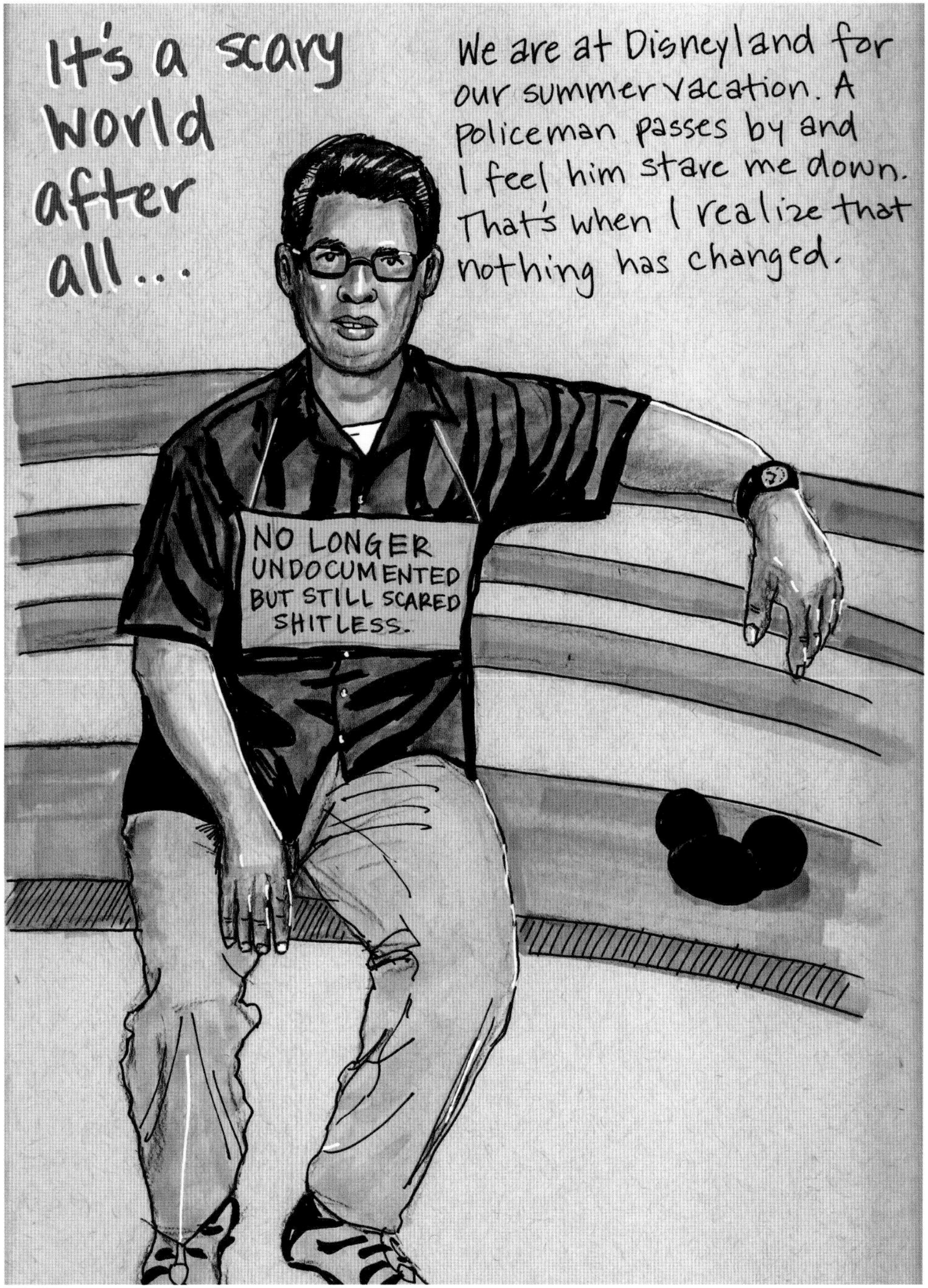
It's a scary world after all...
We are at Disneyland for our summer vacation. A policeman passes by and I feel him stare me down. That's when I realize that nothing has changed.
NO LONGER UNDOCUMENTED BUT STILL SCARED SHITLESS.

March 18, 2013.

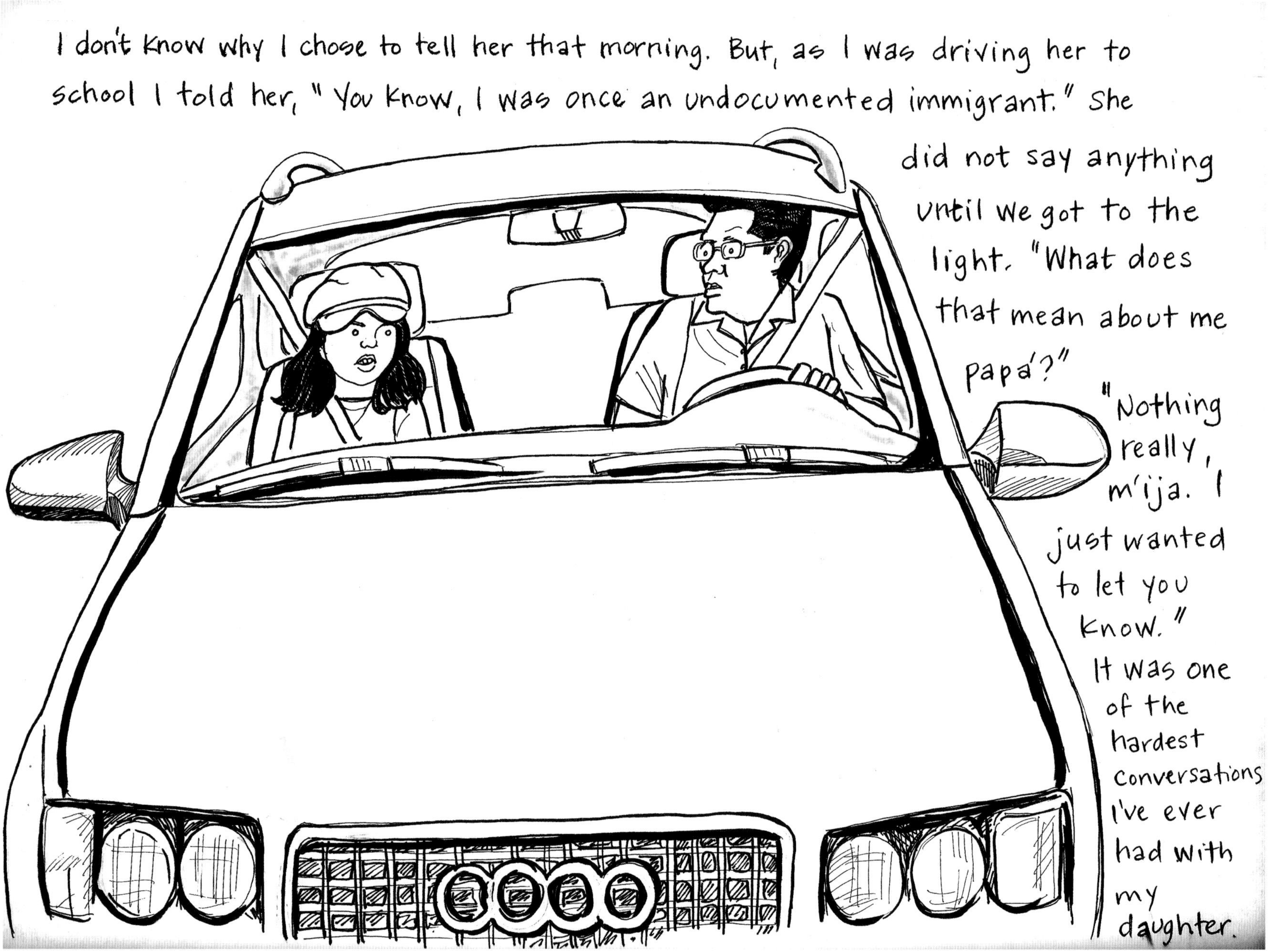
I don't know why I chose to tell her that morning. But, as I was driving her to school I told her, "You know, I was once an undocumented immigrant." She did not say anything until we got to the light. "What does that mean about me papá?"
"Nothing really, m'ija. I just wanted to let you know."
It was one of the hardest conversations I've ever had with my daughter.
September 7, 2015.

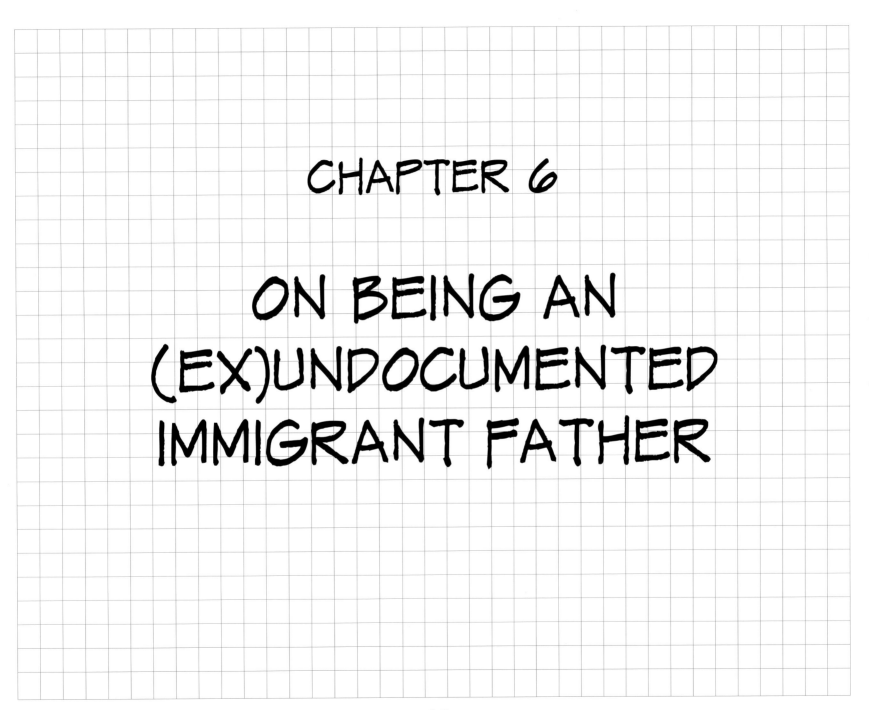

CHAPTER 6

ON BEING AN (EX)UNDOCUMENTED IMMIGRANT FATHER

Sofia and I had been making that left turn at Redwood Road and Castro Valley Boulevard since we had moved to Castro Valley five years before. In all that time, the Wednesday protestors at that corner had become an easy example I could point to of the way politics worked in the United States. Each time, after I picked her up from her after-school childcare at abuelita's house, we waited for the arrow to turn green while we read banners and heard the protesters chanting over the whirr of the traffic. Each time, Sofia would turn to me.

"What does 'Impeach Bush' mean, papá?" She had asked me that question when she was in the third grade, on an evening when she had apparently noticed a protester holding a poster of George W. Bush behind bars. Dozens of car horns had beeped in agreement. "You beep too, papá!" she had implored when our turn came to cross.

A few years later, soon after Barack Obama had been sworn in, she wondered, "Why do they still want to 'End the War'? Didn't President Obama say it was over?" That night, as we were surrounded by the sound of car brakes screeching and the roar of engines revving forward, I tried to explain what I understood about the way politics works, that foreign policies shift slowly between administrations. She listened in silence as we made our way home, nodding as we passed strip malls and gas stations and I told her that American laws were shaped as much by our economic interest as by the personality of our leaders. She made only one comment.

"Do you mean that the people on the corner are now going to protest against Obama?"

Those protestors provoked Sofia to ask all sorts of questions about the economy, funding for schools, gay rights, health care.

Through their picket signs and placards, Sofia came to know names like Hilary Clinton, Dick Cheney, John McCain, and Sarah Palin. But I could have never guessed what she would ask me that first Wednesday in October of 2009.

It had been another hectic day at Berkeley. As I often did, I had picked her up late from my mother-in-law's house. "The 580 was packed. A red Tahoe overturned," I told her as she opened the passenger door and threw her backpack on the rear seat. "You're lucky I picked you up when I did."

As usual, she had remained quiet for a few blocks, saying nothing when we arrived at the intersection to wait for the turn. Instead, she had looked, as she always had, out the front passenger window towards the Safeway parking lot, to the protesters all dressed in similar black fleece jackets and blue jeans. They were now holding a "Beep for Peace!" canvas banner.

A moment passed. Cars began arriving behind us. Then she turned, looked at me intently, and asked, "Papá, what does it mean that you were once illegal?"

*   *   *

Ten years earlier, the doctor had discovered Sofia's umbilical cord twisted around her neck.

"Your wife and daughter are lucky." He had said when he placed Sofia's eight pound, six-ounce body on my arms. "Another ten minutes and I would have had to do a C-section."

Hers was a strange and yet familiar face, mostly cheeks and black hair.

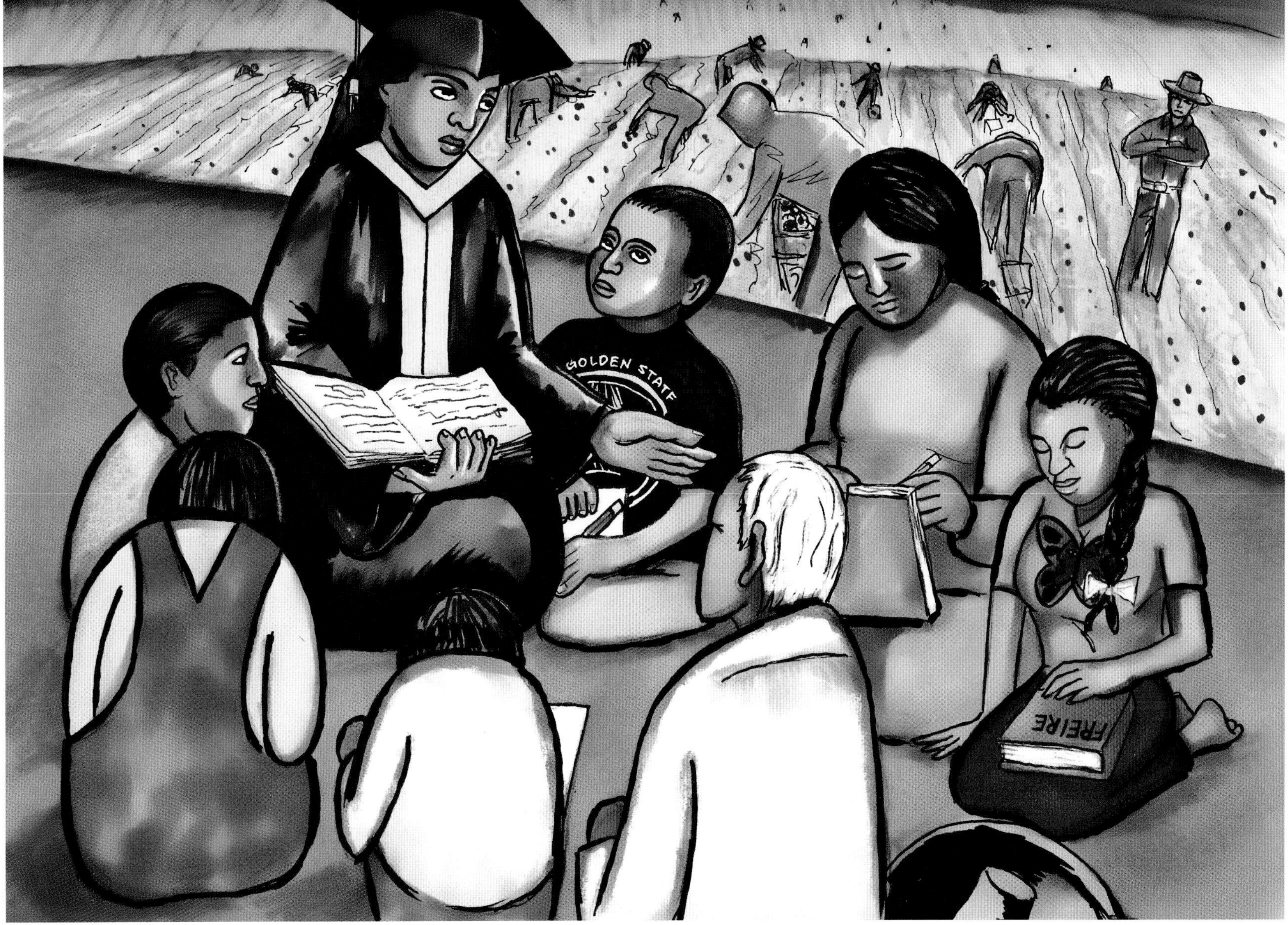
GOLDEN STATE
FREIRE
"One dreamer, many dreams." March 23, 2014.

It was then that I noticed the movement of Sofia's little jaw. It trembled, her mouth opening and closing, but no sound was coming out, only a faint wheezing when she inhaled.

"The cord." The nurse who came to take her from my arms said. "It must have put too much pressure around her throat."

Just like that my heart stopped. For a moment I imagined that I would never enjoy hearing her voice. That all I would ever hear being issued from her lips would be gasps of air. The nurse must have noticed my terror because almost immediately she spoke again.

"Don't worry, sir. After a while, your daughter will regain her voice. It happens all the time."

It took almost three days before Sofia's voice was no longer hoarse, three days that she and Leticia remained in the hospital so the doctors could monitor any complications from the tough birth. Those three days I struggled to hear my daughter's cry. And when it came, when I finally heard the splendor of her vocal cords ringing in my ears, it was a melody that thrilled as much as terrified me.

*   *   *

"What does it mean that you were once illegal?"

The only thing I can think of when my daughter asks me her question is of that Saturday afternoon in April of 1977 when papá drove us to Hayward in his new Ford station wagon. We are heading back home in the green 1969 Country Squire wagon that his buddy, Cheto, sold him the day before. My sisters, Silvia and María, and I are sitting in the back seat, enjoying the smooth ride back to Oakland, happy about the Spirograph drawing toy and Mother Goose potato chips papá bought us at the K-Mart. We are trying to find any Mexican grocery store along Hayward's Mission Boulevard. Mamá, who's sitting in the front seat holding my two-year-old brother, Julian, wants to cook us something special.

"Allí!" papá says as he points towards the Hayward hills. At first I can't tell what he's found, but he seems excited. He quickly turns the corner at Carlos Bee Boulevard, and the wagon begins to climb the steep road. Silvia, María, and I look at each other, seemingly puzzled, especially when papá parks in front of a lot that's been overrun by ivies and dandelions.

"Esperen aqui," he says with a smile and runs into the thick brush.

This is the first time we have travelled to this part of Hayward. Outside the station wagon we are surrounded by what appear to be recently built apartments, three- and four-story complexes made of beige-colored stucco and white-trimmed balconies all decorated with ferns. Now and then cars pass near us on their way up the hill. Mostly they seem to be newer model sedans, piloted by blondes wearing sunglasses.

Maybe because she is sensing our restlessness or because she is feeling restless herself, mamá asks us if we want to step outside and wait for papá under the shade of the lone oak tree closest to the curb. Julian loves it. He runs from one patch of grass to the other while mamá follows behind him, watching as he picks up a twig to bash the petals off of the lilies in front of him.

I am almost twelve years old. This should be fun for me. But all I want to do is run back to the wagon, to hide, especially when I notice that as each car whooshes by, as we hear the whine of their tires, all the drivers seem to be focusing on us. We are an oddity in this place—a Mexican family making its home among the weeds. We should just go back.

Close to an hour passes and mamá can't wait any longer. Julian is crying. The sun is making us thirsty even under the shade. Mamá has no choice but to call out to papá. "¡Viejo! ¡Ya es tiempo!" From somewhere behind the blackberry bushes and thistles, papá's voice screams back, "ya mero!" Almost. Another twenty minutes crawl by.

It is Silvia who finally spots the faded "No Trespassing" sign nailed high on a post. A barely legible cardboard placard that's been faded by countless days of direct exposure to the Hayward sun stares at us.

"¿Que quiere decir TRES-PASSIN?" Mamá asks, a blushed and sweaty Julian now asleep on her shoulder. Silvia is fourteen, almost in high school. As always, it is she who volunteers to do the translation for mamá. "Dice que no debemos estar aquí, que nos pueden meter a la carcel." Whatever Silvia means, mamá knows full well that we need to go.

"¡Viejo! ¡Ya vamonos!"

Finally, papá emerges from the bushes holding a mountain of cactus leaves on a piece of cardboard. He

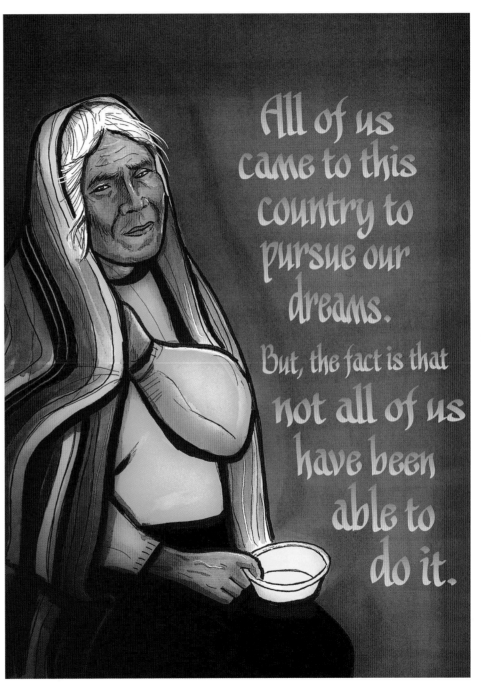

All of us came to this country to pursue our dreams. But, the fact is that not all of us have been able to do it.

March 16, 2014.

loads them in the back of the wagon and we are off. On our way home, I keep searching for papá's eyes in the rearview mirror. I am angry about the wait and the risk. I want to ask him why he stopped and disappeared into some strange person's land without telling us what he was going to do; but mamá is too busy talking about the chile con nopalitos y carne de puerco she will be cooking when we get home. It's been years since I had good cactus, she says and laughs, as if nothing has happened. Just wait and taste how tender the cactus is that your father picked.

I can't tell what Silvia or María are thinking because they, too, are slumped in the back seat of papá's new station wagon. So we travel down Mission Boulevard and onto East 14th Avenue never talking about what papá did. And that's how it remains for years, a fear and anger that can't find its words.

If I were a more responsible parent, Sofia wouldn't be sitting in the front seat of my new sedan. She would be in the back, with me taking only opportunistic glances through my rearview mirror to make sure she is okay. During the past year, however, I've become dependent on these little conversations we have when she is sitting by my side. There is no Nickelodeon, YouTube, DS, iPod, or her guinea pig, Tubby Tux, to distract us. There's only the twenty minutes of Castro Valley traffic from abuelita's house to our development in the Castro Valley hills near Hayward.

Except this time I'm the one who's quiet. I don't know how to answer Sofia's question. At least not without fearing that the line of inquiry will only lead to pain.

"I want you to get an education so that you don't have to break your back like me."

I glance towards her and notice that she is still upset about me picking her up late, that her brown eyes seem as tired as mine. I didn't think that it would be at ten years old that she would ask me that question. The red van in the next lane honks when I start drifting too close. I look at Sofía again and notice the wild mop of chocolate brown hair perfectly framing her round face. And I hope that whatever I say turns out well.

"You know, Sofía," I stutter while staring at the road ahead, "I was about your age when my dad asked my mom to bring us across the border."

Her eyes are focused on my lips as I try to explain.

"Things are complicated," I tell her. "At first we thought that we were just coming for the summer. Then it became a year. Then I graduated from high school and met your mom."

Now here we are, living in the same hills where my dad once stole cactus to celebrate buying his new car.

She is listening carefully, as if weighing the sincerity of each of my words. But I am lost.

"So where did you learn the word *illegal*?" I ask her as I focus on the road ahead.

"I dunno. Somewhere I guess." She answers the same way she does whenever she has done something wrong and knows that she will get reprimanded. I look at her and smile.

"*Illegal* is such a terrible word," I tell her. "Its only purpose is to make some people angry at other people without either understanding the true reasons for their anger."

I hear myself recounting only a few of the key events that happened when we crossed. All she hears is how María, Silvia, and I were smuggled in the back seat of some strange lady's red Camaro. How we pretended to sleep so that the border guard would not ask us questions as he reviewed someone else's birth certificate for each of us. I am not really explaining how I felt, how terrified I was about what we were doing.

I can tell that she is paying attention to my tone, to the inflection of each of my words.

"I really didn't have a choice," I tell her. And I am not sure if I believe it, am bothered because it almost sounds as if I am repudiating my parent's decision-making, as if I'm critiquing two people Sofía absolutely adores.

Ahead, just past the KFC next to CVS Drugs, a blonde teenager in baggy jeans and a beige bomber jacket is waiting to jaywalk. I slow down and let him pass. And I remember my own transgressions.

*   *   *

I am sixteen when papá and I have our first real argument about our immigration status. I want to get out of the house: To stroll down East 14th Avenue with my new friends, Sergio and Roberto, on Friday nights. To hang out with the homies at the Giant Burger on 38th Avenue watching their lowriders hopping by. To catch the midnight creature feature at the Grand Lake Theatre without worrying about what time I have to be home. But eight years after our arrival, we are still hiding, still living undocumented in the heart of East Oakland.

Papá doesn't seem to be in the mood for an argument. If not for the gig one of his pool hall buddies found him at the Pacific

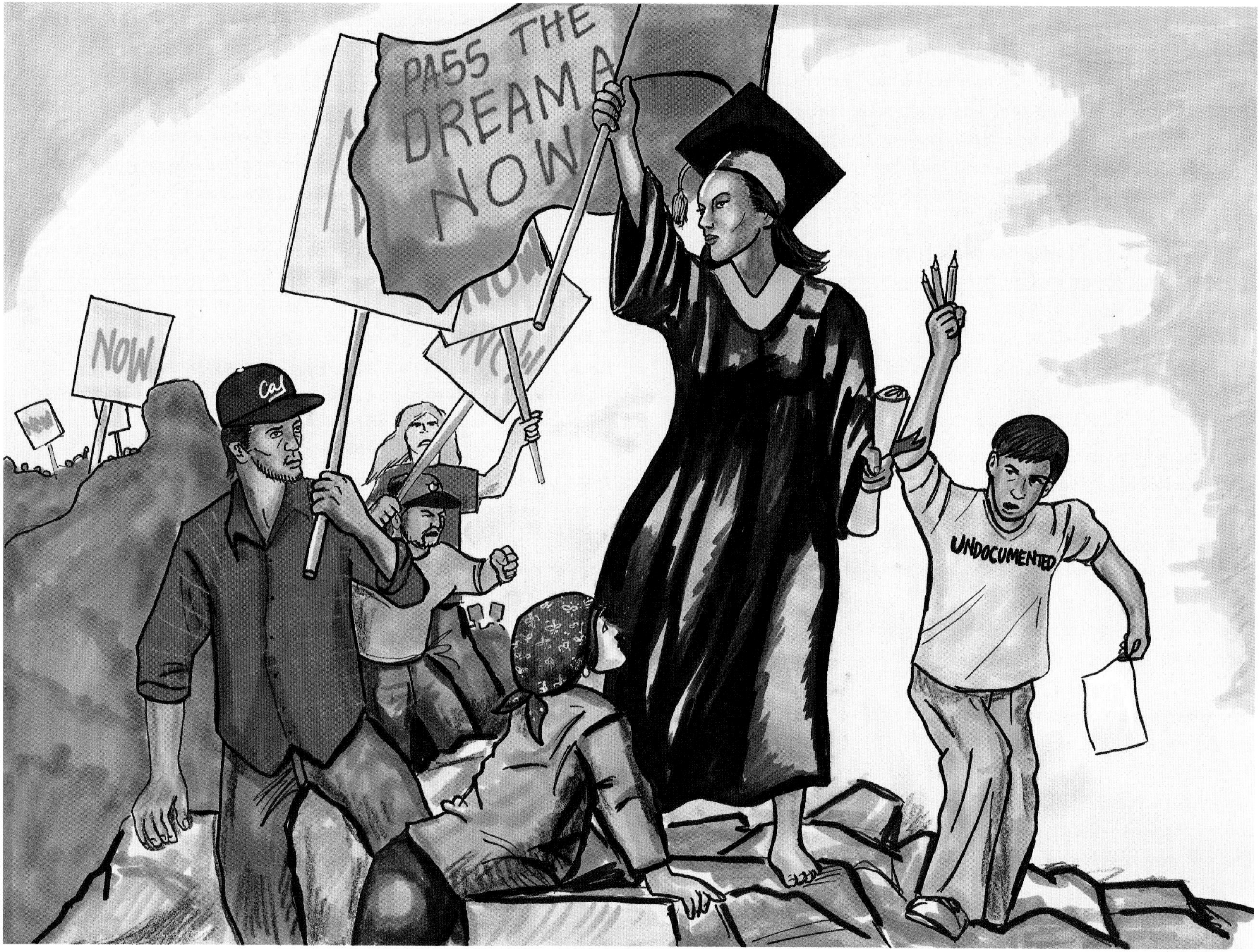
PASS THE DREAMA NOW
NOW
Cal
UNDOCUMENTED

"Educating the undocumented is a revolutionary act!" January 3, 2014.

Steel foundry in Albany, he would have already cut his losses and taken us back to Guadalajara. I am convinced of it. What has kept him in California is that he is the youngest in his family and his hermanos in Mexico are doing a little too well. He doesn't seem to want the humiliation of returning to Mexico empty-handed. Besides, it costs good money to transport a whole family to Jalisco. Money he doesn't have.

"No seas tonto." Don't be a fool, he tells me for the umpteenth time. There are things that you can't do "as long as you are ilegal," he says as he glares in my direction. "It doesn't matter how good you think your English is."

It's not fair. The only times we seem to get out are when we go to Los Mexicanos Market for the week's groceries. On Sundays we go to St. Louis Bertrand for the morning mass, maybe to the mall for Chinese food and strawberry Slurpees if the week's been good. We travel as a group, always within sight of each other. Mamá's greatest fear is that we will get lost, that someone will abandon her in the middle of JCPenney's just as the store is closing.

I've had enough of it. I am now in high school. I want to go places by myself, to explore this new world and the people in it, to be the kind of teenager that appears in a John Hughes movie.

That night, papá and I are sitting across each other at the kitchen table. He is drinking his Coors while I am toying with what is left of the chicken molé mamá served us for dinner. There's talk of more layoffs at the foundry. He is the low man on the totem pole. Mamá wrings her hands on her apron and tells him that, con el favor de Dios, everything's going to be alright.

If this were a different night, if it were a different event, I would think twice about what I'm about to do. But this is supposed to be my first high-school dance. I've been dressed for it since papá returned from the pool hall, my white shirt is still as pristine as on Sundays before we leave for church, in spite of the molé. And it's getting late. And Roberto and Sergio are already waiting for me inside the high-school gym. And papá is the only one who can give me a ride.

"I thought you were going to drop me off at school," I say. There is something about the way I'm looking at him that seems to offend him. He frowns, his unblinking eyes fixed on me as I plead.

"My friends are waiting for me. The dance has already started. I told you about it this morning."

He turns, pretends to ignore me, his eyes now focused on the television that's been left on in the other room, and he becomes absorbed by it. Except that we left it on channel 7 and he likes canal catorce.

"This is not right," I tell him. "You are keeping us locked up as if we were in prison."

He turns to face me and tells me that that's enough, that no one in this house is going anywhere tonight, that I'd better shut up and show some respect.

"Well, if you won't take me, I'll walk to the bus stop."

I see him getting up from his seat as if in slow motion. His brown irises are frozen on me and his jaw is tensed. Suddenly I feel the weight of his palm across my left cheek. It doesn't hurt. Really. There are no more words. Instead, he turns, stomps to the front room, and closes the door. All I feel is the sting of his rebuke.

67

An hour later, after I've locked myself in the back room, it is mamá who coaxes me out and walks me to papá's station wagon. He is waiting for me there, ready to take me to the dance, his jaw still tensed and his eyes still fixed forward. As always.

*   *   *

From the start, from the first moments of our immigrant life in East Oakland, I tried to make sense of the chaos by filling dozens of notebooks with drawings about what it felt like to be undocumented.

Even when he found them, papá did not seem to understand the deeper meaning in my drawings.

"Oye, m'ijo," he would smile when he found me at the kitchen table in the middle of the night sketching drawings with my pencil. "Ese sí se parece a mi y tu mamá." That really does look like me and your mother. But what's that other stuff? He would also ask.

It was a skill I perfected—the ability to draw seemingly surreal landscapes that, at first glance, had nothing to do with being undocumented. Almost nightly, I would hide in the back room of our house when I was in middle school to draw superheroes unlike any I read about in my Marvel comic books. It was my revolution. Mamá insisted that we say the rosary instead of letting us watch Monty Python on Channel 9, so I sat in my bed for hours, sketching under the light of the moon coming in through my open window. The following morning she would find my drawing on the kitchen table of Jesus playing soccer with the devil.

"Gol?" Mamá puzzled when she read my caption.

Angry about getting my money stolen by bullies at Havenscourt

Junior High, I would spend days drawing the story of Luis, a precocious immigrant kid who could always outsmart his enemies with clever riddles and putdowns.

"Go ahead, take my money," Luis said in the first panel.

"You're only making me work harder as a student," I would write in a thought bubble in the second.

"Some day, because of what you are doing, I will have much more than what you are taking from me now," I would finish in the third.

My journals were catalogues of a desired life. In them I recorded all the dreams I thought I could never achieve. In them, my father drove a big car, had bought us a futuristic mansion. In them, we had all the money in the world, we were healthy and without a worry that someone would want to deport us. Yet, just below the surface, in spite of my attempts at humor, my caricatures were lonely, sad, and existential figures lost in the corners of mostly blank pages. Gloomy eyes, frowns, and hunched backs. These have always been my specialties.

Not long after Sofia was born, I learned that I could always entertain her by drawing animals on the edges of my napkins while waiting for our meals at restaurants. She loved ponies, psychedelic monsters wearing sneakers, and Snoopy. Eventually, what began as a strategy to keep her from crying became a way of bonding with her. We looked forward to going to restaurants that took a long time to serve us. Sofia and I would sit together. I would pull out my pens, and away we went, drawing all sorts of images on napkin after napkin even when our meals arrived on time.

By the time she was six, Sofia had learned that each Friday

"Sofia." January 11, 2014.

she could always find me upstairs after dinner, hidden in my home office sketching cartoons in my art journal.

Each Friday I would hear the staccato of her short legs coming up the stairs. She never knocked on the door. She just darted in giggling, excited about what new picture I was working on. Usually I stopped working on my drawings. They were too complex, rife with painful images of my life as a kid. Instead, I would start new cartoons on fresh pieces of paper. Hamster World was her favorite. It was an idea we came up with together, an intricate landscape populated by anthropomorphic rodents doing all sorts of silly things. "Can you find the hamster escaping from hamster jail? Can you spot the hamster professor lecturing to his hamster students?" It was a three-dimensional world of hamsters riding roller coasters, emerging from tunnels and caves. She loved it.

I don't know when it happened exactly, but on one of the days when she darted into my office, I was too tired to work on another Hamster World.

"Is that abuelito?" She asked when she recognized the figure at the center of the page I was working on.

"Yes, m'ija," I said as I made two strokes to suggest the brim of my father's baseball cap.

"Why does he look angry?" The rectangles above his nose, thick strokes meant to represent his heavy bifocals, did not quite hide his eyes.

"He's not angry, m'ija," I responded. "I'm just not done with it." I don't know why I stopped hiding my drawings from her. At six years old she was too young to understand all the details I added in.

Soon, on Fridays, I found myself working on my sketches without worrying what she would see. She was bewildered by abuelita embracing a gigantic crucifix. Jesus wearing a sombrero and bandoleers. Karl Marx shaking hands with Frida Khalo. But she always stayed, her cheek pressed against my right arm as I inked caricature after caricature. Without fail, when I began coloring, she would grab a few pieces of printer paper to do her own masterpiece. It was the box of 120 Prismacolors that she loved most, pencils of every shade in the rainbow. "My artists," Leticia would say when she walked into my office to remind us that it was almost bedtime.

"Okay, mami," Sofia replied. And she would hurry to finish what she had started, the tip of her tongue peeking out of her pressed lips as she scribbled and scratched the last swaths of color on another bunny wearing glasses and riding roller skates.

"This one's for you, papi," she would then tell me. "You can hang it in your office at work."

At Berkeley, my walls are covered with Sofia's pictures. There was a pink fish one of my colleagues thought looked more like an iguana. The smiling red heart Sofia's teacher had laminated with Sofia's name across it, I had pinned it on the corkboard next to my desk.

Then, one Friday when I returned home, I found that Sofia had already finished dinner and had gone up to my office. She was kneeling on the seat of my chair, her torso laying on my desk, and her elbows resting by each corner of my opened journal when I walked in the room.

She looked up at me, seemingly afraid of what I would say. But I said nothing.

"Why are these kids hiding in the back of this car, papá?"

That had not been quite the way it had happened. Our crossing had been less dramatic. The car had not been that bright red and we had never been squeezed inside a trunk. But the little boy in the middle of two other bodies looked a little too much like the other cartoons I had drawn of me as a kid. The woman holding her kids looked a little too much like my mother. It was an image I hadn't wanted her to see. Not yet. "Where are they going?"

There was an outline of a guard tower in the horizon. There was a barbed-wire fence and soldiers. The car was speeding towards the soldiers.

I felt glad that I hadn't finished. That I hadn't drawn other bodies climbing over the fence. Bodies lying in pools of blood. She was only six, but already she knew that something in the image was not right. This was not Hamster World or Snoopy. There was something painful in the image. The eyes.

I recognized my mother's confusion in her face, that mixture of concern and fear that always precluded her questions. And I realized that she knew that something in the image had actually taken place, that this was the story of how we had gotten to the US.

"This is a drawing of what it was like when abuelita brought us across the border, m'ija."

"What's a border, papá?"

I didn't quite know what to say. Six-year-olds know so little about geo-politics. Where could I have started? Five hundred years ago? Or should I have gone ahead and told her of all the borders that still exist within my family? About grandpa's prohibition that we talk about what was really tearing us apart. That lack of communication, I remembered thinking as a kid, had been more impenetrable than any border we had ever faced. I didn't want to hurt her the way I felt I had been hurt.

"It's nothing, m'ija," I said.

At least twice a week, if not daily in certain weeks, papá would leave our house on 82nd Avenue for hours on end to visit the High Street Billiards. For years we were not sure what attracted him to that place. Routinely he would announce to mamá that he was just running out to get some leche, tortillas, or any other staple we seemed to be running low on. We would not see him until night. When he returned, he would usually be tipsy, drunk enough to have a temper but not enough that he couldn't walk a straight line.

After so many years of the same routine, of mamá imploring him to stay home, of Silvia, María, and I asking him if we could come along, the pool hall became synonymous with papá's desire to avoid pain. What he found at the pool hall was another Mexico. The pool hall was a place that offered him Coronas and carambola, the opportunity to talk to other men who were also escaping their own bracero misery. It was a sanctuary of sorts, a liminal space between a world in which he lived as a cog within the capitalist machine and a world where the male privilege he had left back in Guadalajara remained intact.

For the most part, the pool hall remained an exclusive refuge for him. Women and kids were not allowed in it—unless, of course, they were "those" kind of women or unless, of course, they were the kind of kids that stayed out of the way. In spite of this, there were a few rare moments when papá had no choice but to take us along. Usually, it was when mamá felt ill and, as a supposed gesture of goodwill, papá would take us to the grocery store. Inadvertently, we would always wind up at the pool hall, either waiting by the entrance as he played "just one game with a friend," or waiting in the station wagon with the windows rolled down.

It was this way that the pool hall came to life before our eyes. There, we witnessed papá among his friends. He was a different man. He smiled. His hazel eyes glimmered as he would slap another man's back and offer to buy him otra cerveza.

"Oye cabrón," one of his friends would often tease, "ya te traen de babysitter?"

"No chinges pendejo," papá would answer, "nomas los ando cuidando mientras que la costilla se recupera." I'm just taking care of them while the wife gets better.

He seemed a younger man in front of his friends, a boy prematurely saddled with the puzzle of being a parent.

"Oye Orejas!"—he referred to his friend as 'the ears'—"que noticias hay del terrenazo?" The pool hall was his CNN, his New York Times and San Francisco Chronicle all rolled into one, his link to what was taking place back home.

I've often wondered what our first years of living undocumented in East Oakland might have been like had papá never found the High Street Billiards. Would he have come home each night, tired from another day's work, kicked off his boots, and told us how the foreman at the foundry had screwed him again? Or, would he have spent more Saturday afternoons driving us to Robert's Park in the Oakland Hills, his soccer ball scuffed from too many kicks, and Julian, Maria, Silvia, and I exhausted from chasing him around? Not that he didn't do these things. He did. It's just that it was all too infrequent compared to his pool hall visits.

Sometimes, it appeared to me that mamá kept quiet about papá's trips to the pool hall just so she could force him to go to church on Sundays. Even when he came home drunk on Saturday nights, staggering as he did up the rickety back porch steps, even when he fell asleep in the front room or vomited on top of mamá's prized orchids, we would still find him behind the wheel of his station wagon on Sunday mornings, ready to take us to the early mass.

Weeks after Sofia had asked me her question, we visited my parents in East Oakland. Now retired, papá sat at the same table that had been there when I was Sofia's age. He had been watching las Chivas playing El America, drinking his cafecito as mamá boiled a pot of beans.

"She is so tall," he said as he hugged Sofia and looked towards Leticia and me.

"One of these days you are going to open your eyes and realize that she is all grown up."

It was while sitting at that table once again, while seeing mamá kissing Sofia as she asked her about school in Castro Valley, that I realized how much had changed in all the years since we had arrived from Mexico.

As kids, we always think that our parents have more power than they actually do. Undocumented immigrant kids are no exception. I never thought in those early years of being in the United States that mamá and papá were as desperate as I was to understand how to make sense of being undocumented. As a kid, I thought mamá and papá were in full control of their decisions, that it would be just as easy for papá to stop going to the pool hall and mamá to stop her infatuation with religious discipline as it would be to flip a switch. Now, a father, I am beginning to realize they were as lost as I was.

Truth be told, I don't know what I would have done had I been in my father's shoes. Mine, after all, is not the perspective of someone who was driven by a need to provide for his family and consciously chose to cross the border illegally—how I hate that word. I was brought over, like so many other kids who have had so many other fights with their own undocumented fathers and mothers about a condition no one really understands. One thing that I am convinced of, however, is that only through active communication will we be able to come to terms with the psychological ravages that being undocumented causes within families. This, after all, is what Sofia's question made me realize. It is better to share even those ambiguous moments of truth than keep her in the dark about a painful experience that has already profoundly shaped who I am and, by extension, who she is. My undocumented immigrant heritage is also hers, just like my father's anxieties are now mine. What matters is what I do with them. That's why she deserves to know. And that's also why every other kid whose parents have also experienced being undocumented in the United States deserve to know what their parents went through.

*   *   *

Eight months after Sofia asked me her question, her elementary school had its last open house of the year. The parking lot was already full by the time I arrived, late from work again. I parked at the Pigilly Wigilly across the street. It was a long enough walk that Leticia had to call to ask where I was, to say that the teacher was already addressing the parents. I hurried.

My own elementary school—and Leticia's for that matter—was never as nice as Sofia's. Manicured lawns, flat-screen computer monitors, new books, and pristine blackboards. We moved to Castro Valley so that she could have what we never had. Then again, this is exactly what my own parents must have thought when they first visited my own elementary school. They had never gone past the third grade in Mexico, had brought their kids across a dangerous border, to East Oakland, so that we could have a better life. When they had enrolled us in our own elementary school, it must have appeared to them as luxurious an opportunity as Sofia's school now appeared to me. Maybe even more.

"It's been a pleasure to teach your children this year," Sofia's teacher was finishing her comments when I walked in the door. She was young, still enthusiastic about her work, in spite of what state budgets portended.

"Please have a look around. See what your kids have created. And please take all your child's work home when you leave."

Parents struggled to stand up from the minuscule chairs. Soon we were brushing past each other, examining the plethora of projects students had produced for this exact event. There were posters covering every inch of the walls. Students had drawn their portraits on them. There was a large, rectangular table at the back of the room with three portraits of George Washington Carver painted using peanut butter.

Sofia directed us to her desk.

"This is what I did," she said as she picked up a stack of papers. That's when I saw it. It was a laminated roll of paper as wide as a strip of toilet tissue. She had recorded all the major events in her life and projected what she hoped to experience up until 2020. She called it "Sofia's Life Line."

There was a cartoon of a baby swaddled in a pink blanket for the first event. Under it she had written, "I am born. San Francisco, 1999." Above the cartoon she had also written the words, "Yay! It's a girl!"

I don't know why, but seeing her images moved me. There was an innocence to them. They seemed uninhibited by limits, as if she had enjoyed drawing each of them, as if she had taken her time to sketch each one and gently elbowed her friends so they could see what clever things she had drawn. I smiled, proud of the voice she had captured in each stroke of her pencil.

I unfurled the timeline and read each event. She had recorded the many times we had moved since she had been born, first, from San Francisco to San Lorenzo, then, from San Lorenzo to Alameda. She had drawn our move to Castro Valley, a tiny U-Haul truck with smoke coming out of its tailpipe meant to represent the constant motion. She had also drawn events in my own life that we had discussed in our rides from abuelita's house; I was a smiley face stick-figure with glasses and buck-teeth holding a magazine with the following caption, "After five tries, papá's story finally gets published." Yet, what made my eyes tear up most, what made me look at her and feel the urge to pick her up and hug her in front of all her friends—something she passionately dislikes—was the last item of her timeline. In 2020, Sofia wants to publish her own book. And, if my work continues to inspire her, I will keep writing forever, though I may never publish another word.

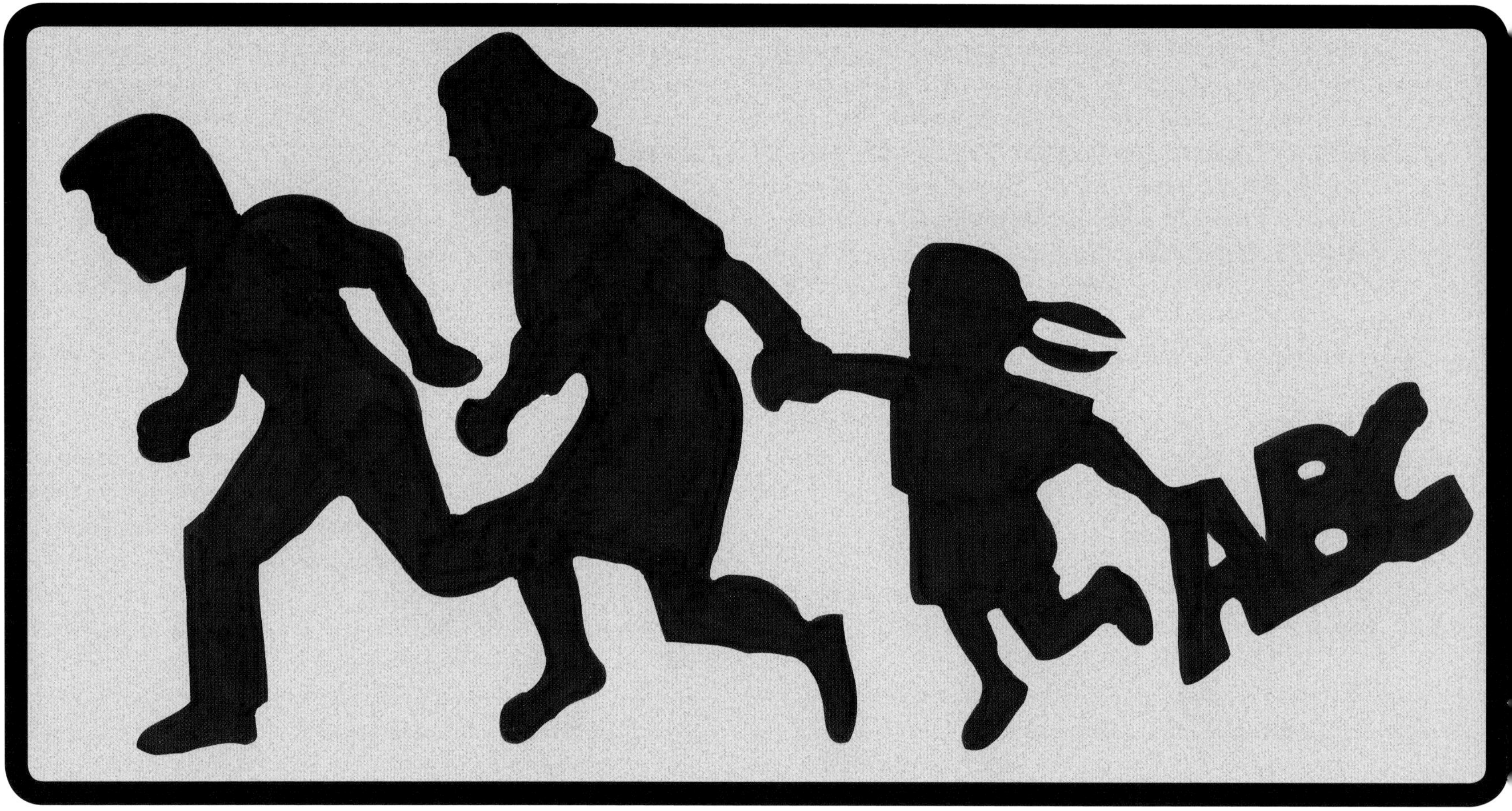
ABC

CHAPTER 7

THE UNDOCUMENTED ALPHABET

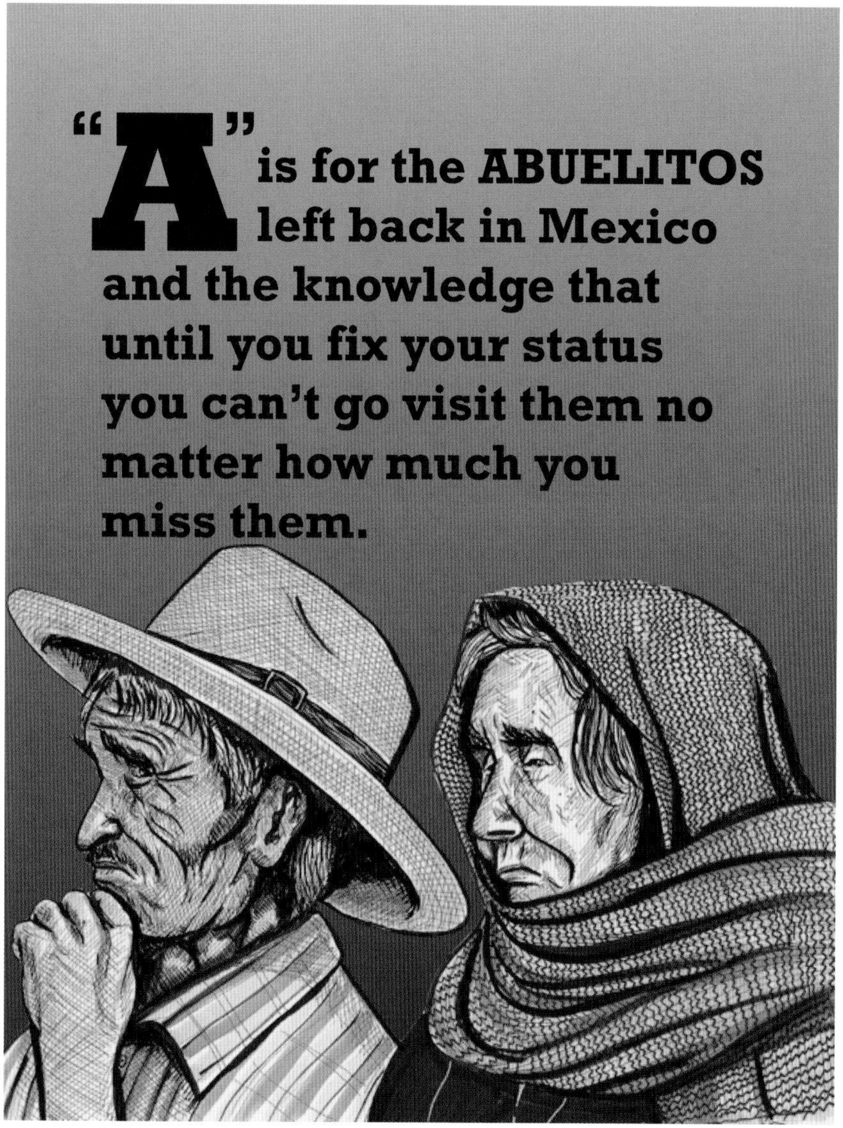
"A" is for the ABUELITOS left back in Mexico and the knowledge that until you fix your status you can't go visit them no matter how much you miss them.

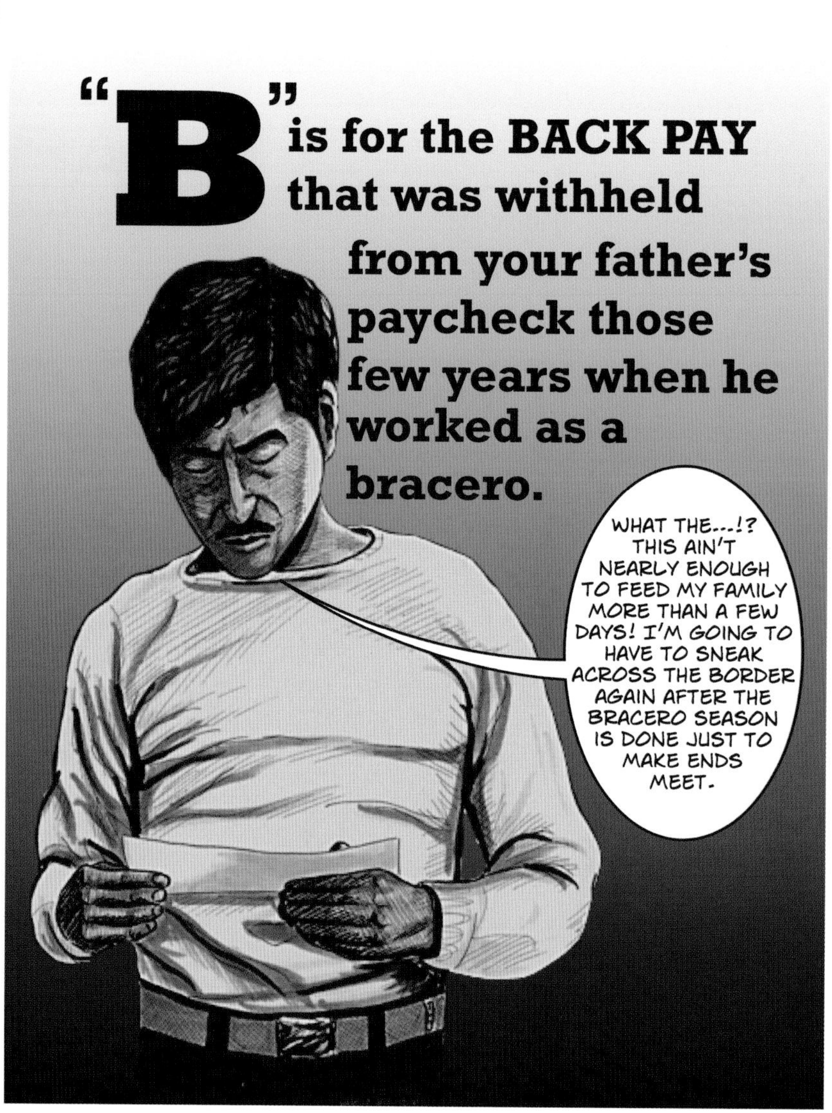
"B" is for the BACK PAY that was withheld from your father's paycheck those few years when he worked as a bracero.
WHAT THE...!? THIS AIN'T NEARLY ENOUGH TO FEED MY FAMILY MORE THAN A FEW DAYS! I'M GOING TO HAVE TO SNEAK ACROSS THE BORDER AGAIN AFTER THE BRACERO SEASON IS DONE JUST TO MAKE ENDS MEET.

“**C**” is for the **COYOTE** who almost got your father killed when he crossed the border in Arizona.

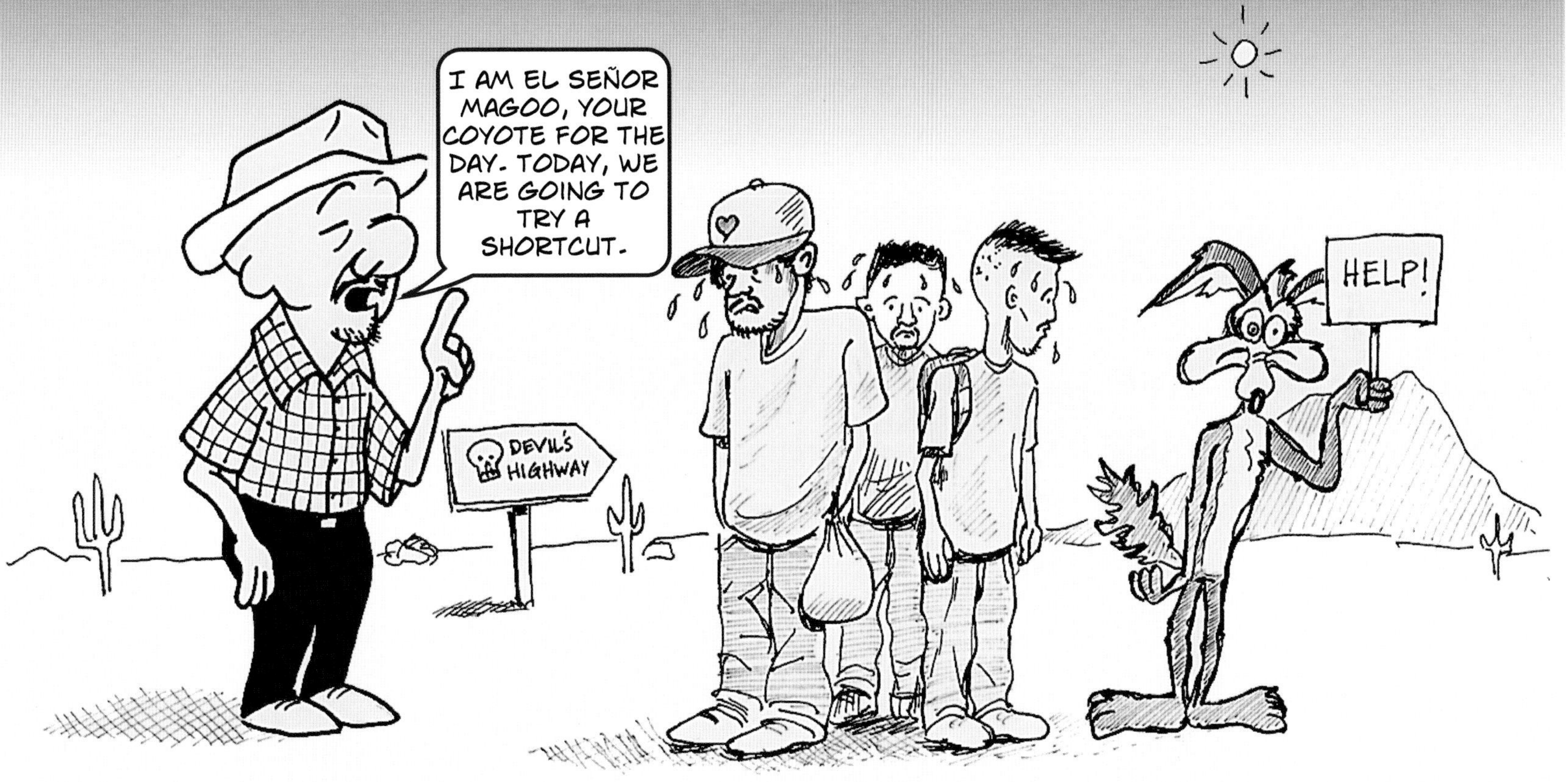
I AM EL SEÑOR MAGOO, YOUR COYOTE FOR THE DAY. TODAY, WE ARE GOING TO TRY A SHORTCUT.
DEVIL'S HIGHWAY
HELP!

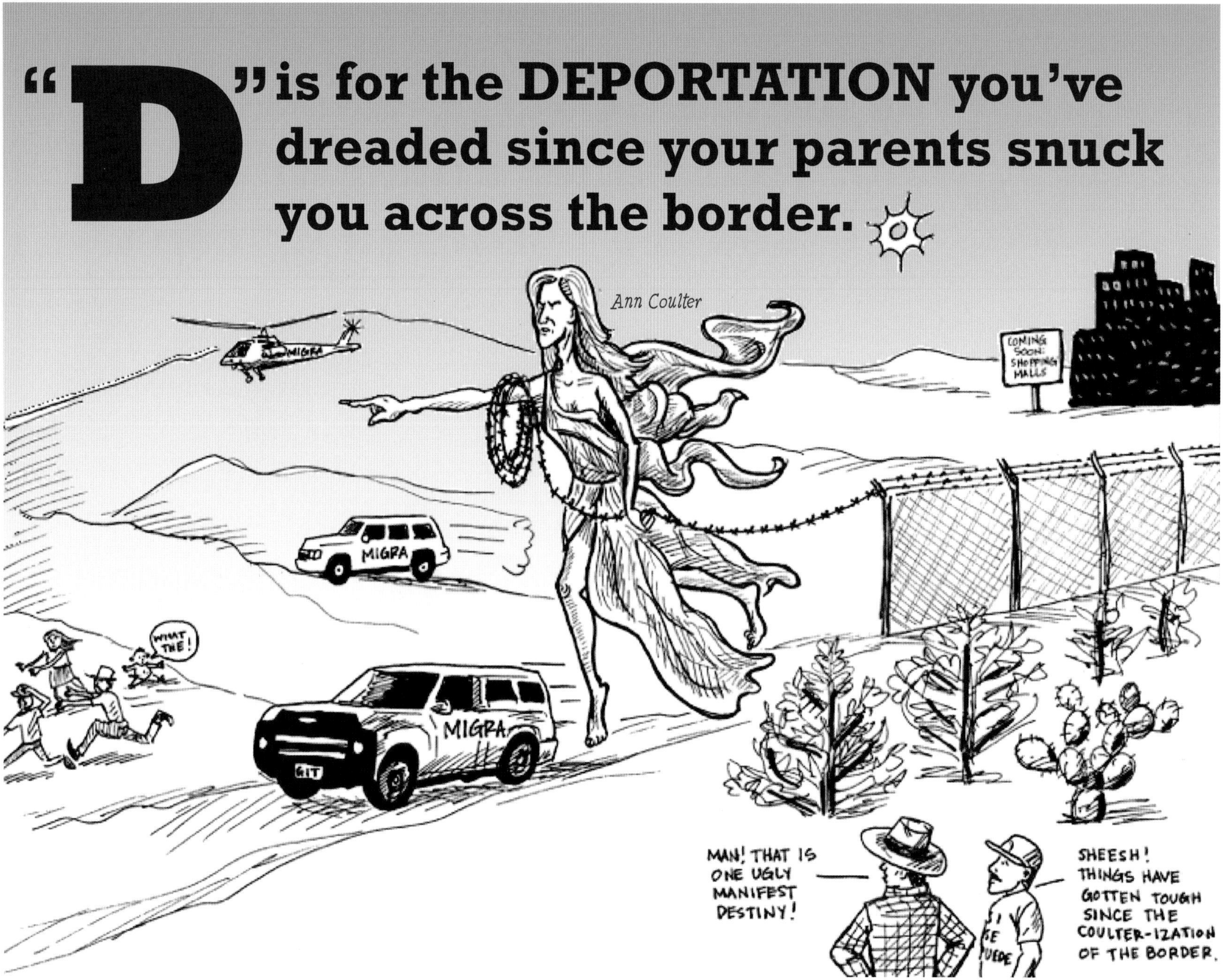
"D" is for the DEPORTATION you've dreaded since your parents snuck you across the border.
Ann Coulter
MIGRA
COMING SOON: SHOPPING MALLS
MIGRA
WHAT THE!
MIGRA
GIT
MAN! THAT IS ONE UGLY MANIFEST DESTINY!
SHEESH! THINGS HAVE GOTTEN TOUGH SINCE THE COULTER-IZATION OF THE BORDER.

"E" is for the EDUCATION your mother asked you to get so that you wouldn't end up working at the same garment factory she did.

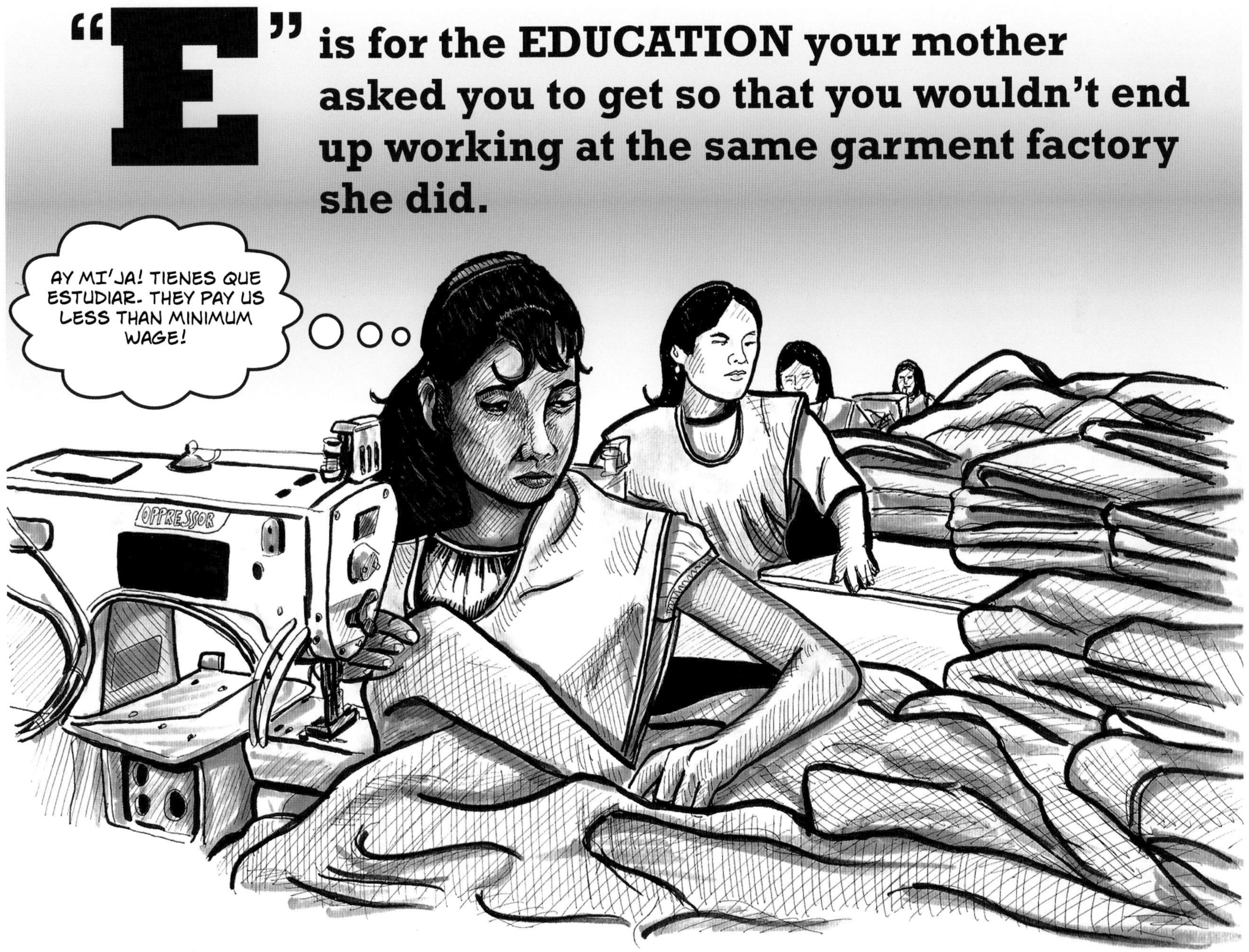
AY MI'JA! TIENES QUE ESTUDIAR. THEY PAY US LESS THAN MINIMUM WAGE!
OPPRESSOR

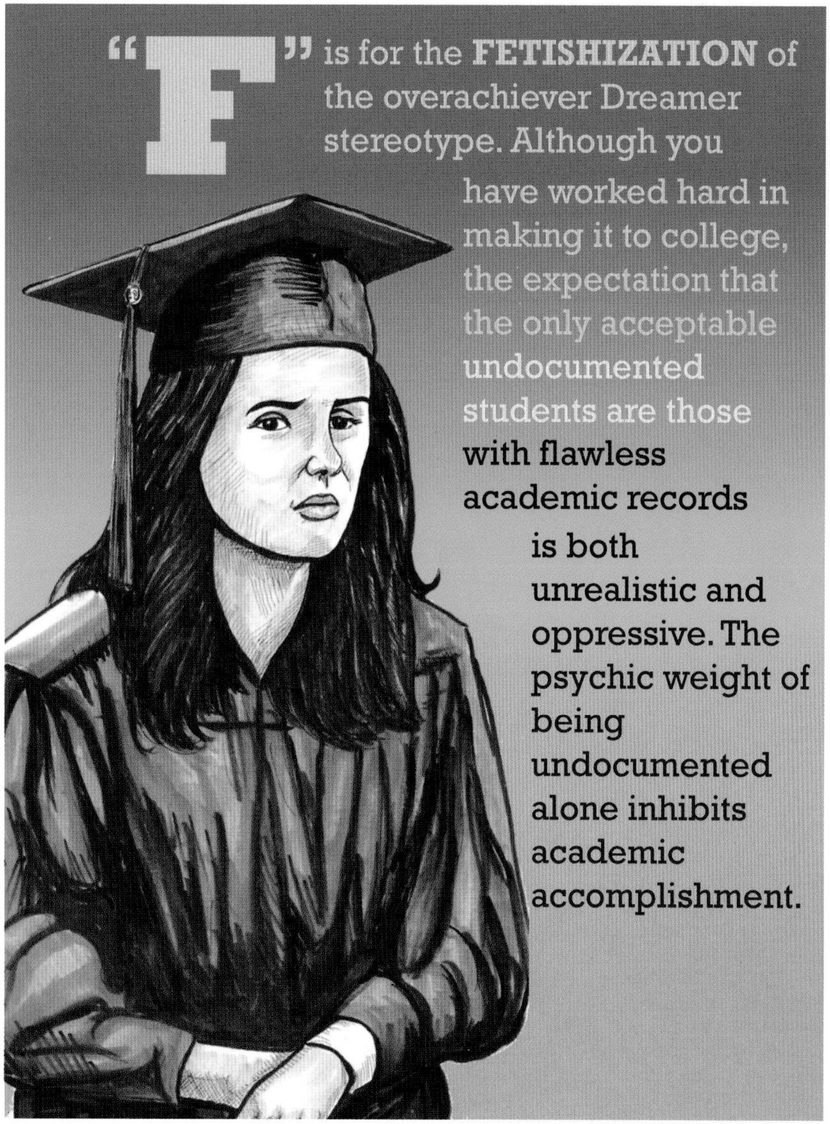
"F" is for the **FETISHIZATION** of the overachiever Dreamer stereotype. Although you have worked hard in making it to college, the expectation that the only acceptable undocumented students are those with flawless academic records is both unrealistic and oppressive. The psychic weight of being undocumented alone inhibits academic accomplishment.

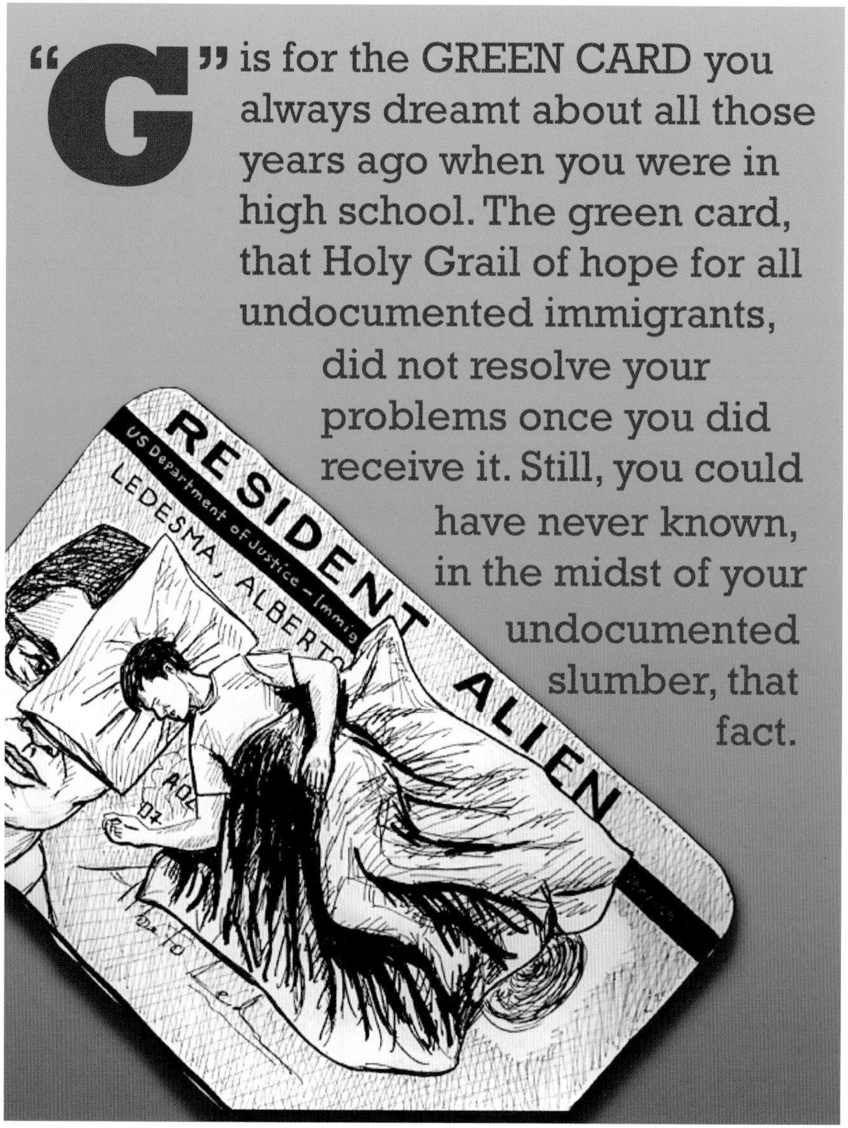
"G" is for the GREEN CARD you always dreamt about all those years ago when you were in high school. The green card, that Holy Grail of hope for all undocumented immigrants, did not resolve your problems once you did receive it. Still, you could have never known, in the midst of your undocumented slumber, that fact.
RESIDENT ALIEN
US Department of Justice – Immig
LEDESMA, ALBERTO

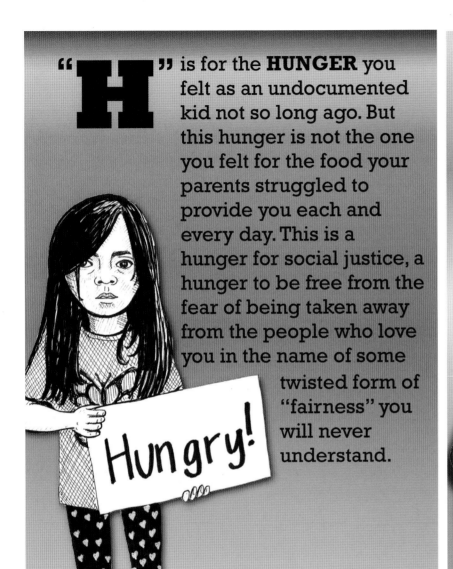

"**H**" is for the **HUNGER** you felt as an undocumented kid not so long ago. But this hunger is not the one you felt for the food your parents struggled to provide you each and every day. This is a hunger for social justice, a hunger to be free from the fear of being taken away from the people who love you in the name of some twisted form of "fairness" you will never understand.

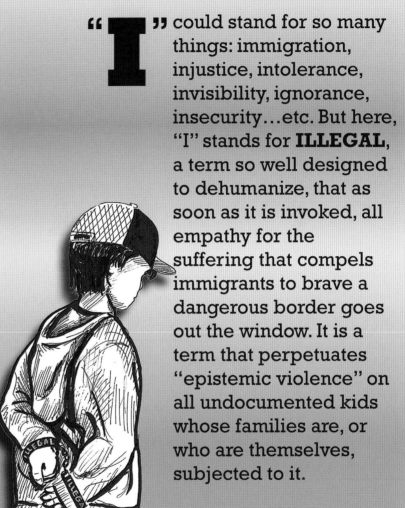

"**I**" could stand for so many things: immigration, injustice, intolerance, invisibility, ignorance, insecurity…etc. But here, "I" stands for **ILLEGAL**, a term so well designed to dehumanize, that as soon as it is invoked, all empathy for the suffering that compels immigrants to brave a dangerous border goes out the window. It is a term that perpetuates "epistemic violence" on all undocumented kids whose families are, or who are themselves, subjected to it.

"**J**" is for the **JOY** you felt when you were finally reunited with your mother across the border.

Suddenly, all those days you spent traveling from Guadalajara to Tijuana felt like seconds.

“**K**” is for undocumented **KNOWING**. Sure we live in a magical society that often offers numerous opportunities to those who work hard. But, this society can also be cruel in the way that it denies basic dignity to a whole class of people. And only members of these “disposable” communities who are denied the chance to improve their lives know the pain of this denial, for theirs is the epistemology—the knowing—of always being rejected.

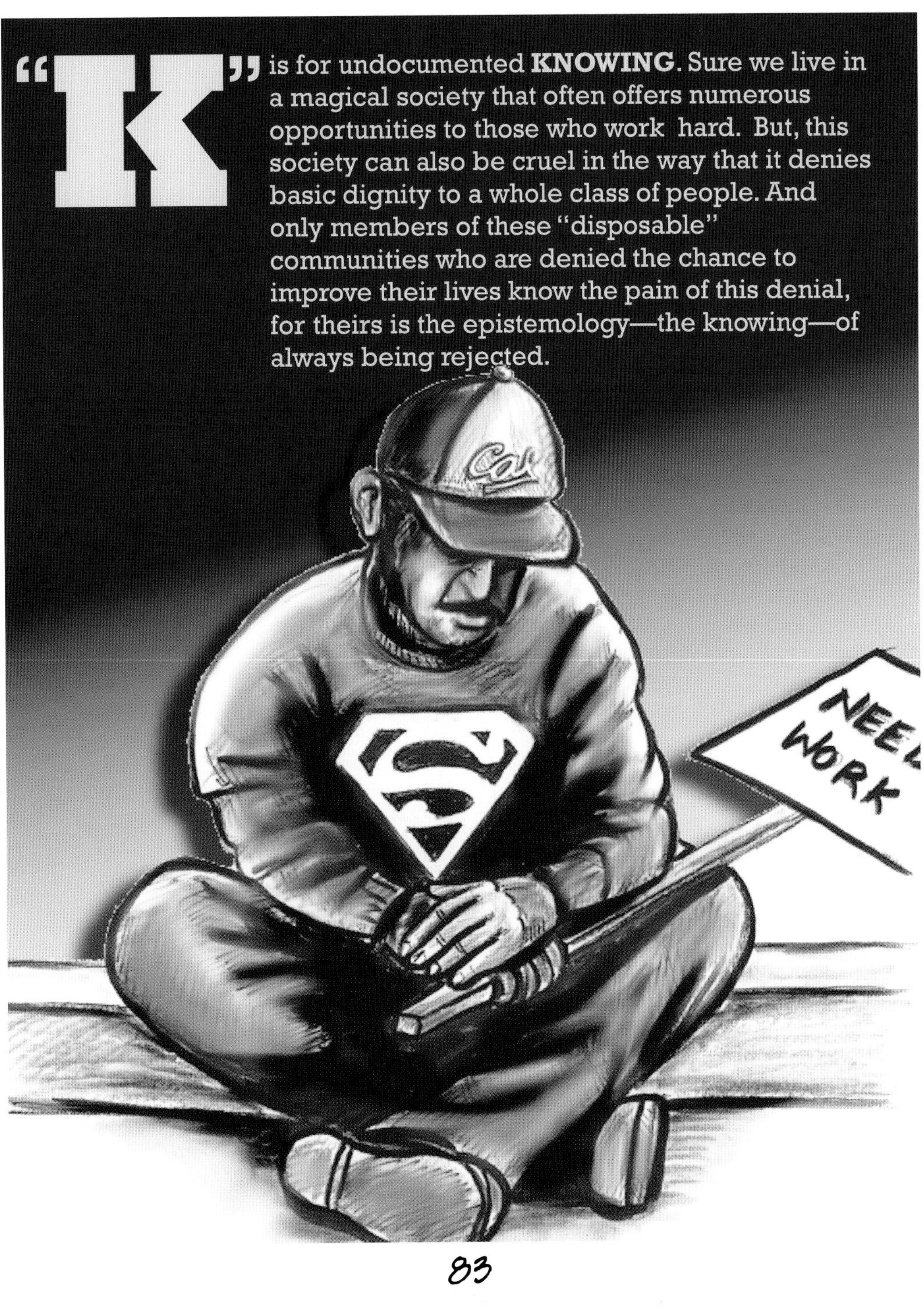
NEE
WORK

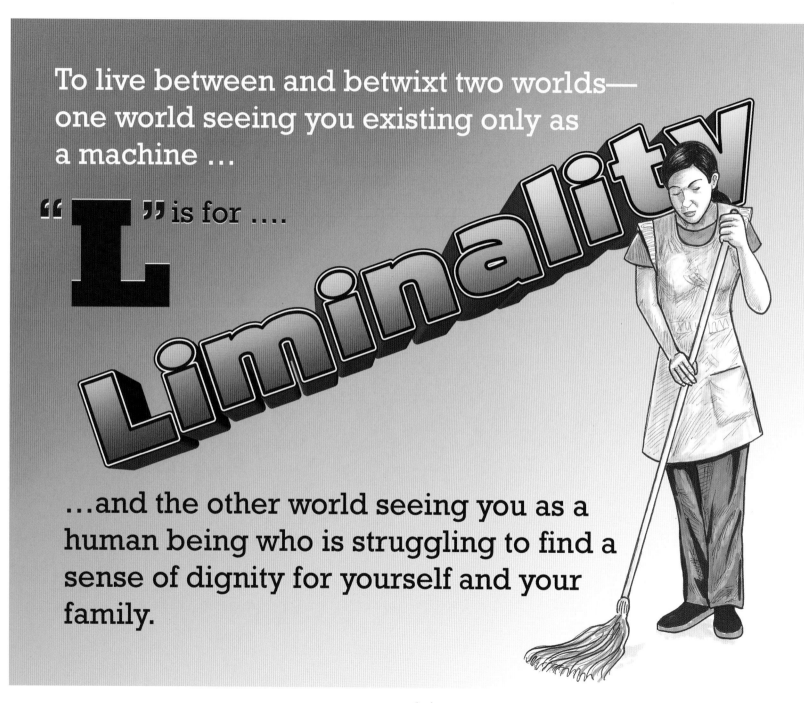

To live between and betwixt two worlds—
one world seeing you existing only as
a machine ...

"**L**" is for ....

Liminality

...and the other world seeing you as a
human being who is struggling to find a
sense of dignity for yourself and your
family.

“M” is for **MACHINE,** the inevitable result of an immigrant worker’s metamorphosis from human being to mechanical instrument. Such is the transformation that countless immigrants experience where their repetitive effort produces profit for someone else. In an effort to survive within the system, these workers must function as part of a cold, metallic organism that has all but forgotten the joy it once felt in its ancestral home, becoming in the process an iron tool so dedicated to its labor that it ignores the exuberance it once felt as a kid.

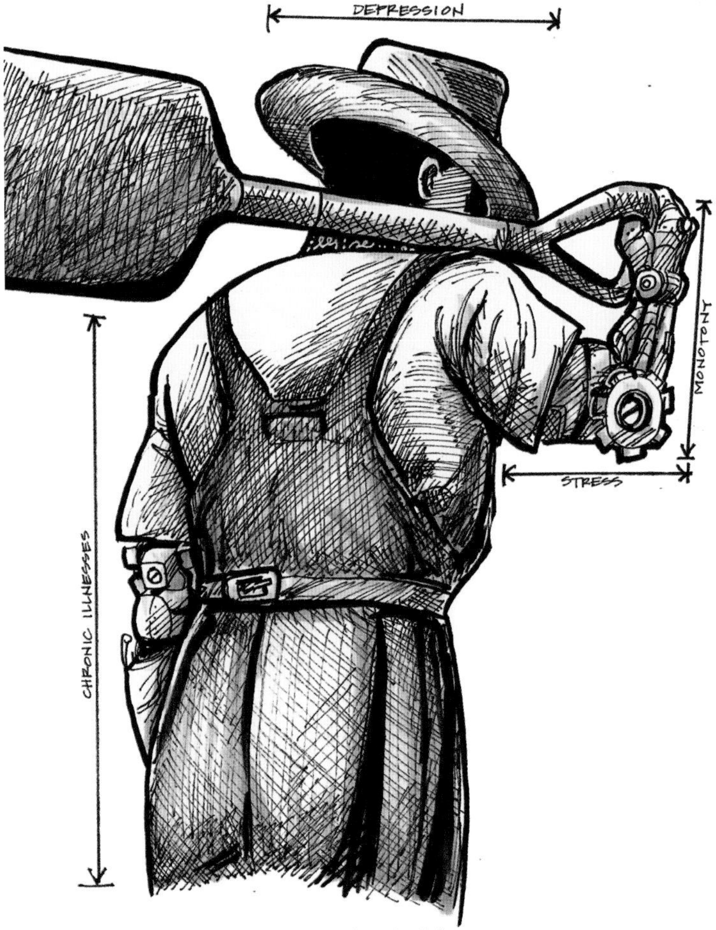
DEPRESSION
MONOTONY
STRESS
CHRONIC ILLNESSES

I CAME NORTH TO GIVE THEM MY ARMS AND THEY TOOK MY SOUL.

"N" is for NATIVISM— that angry feeling experienced by "righteous and patriotic" native-born Americans who are convinced that immigrants are encroaching on their rights.

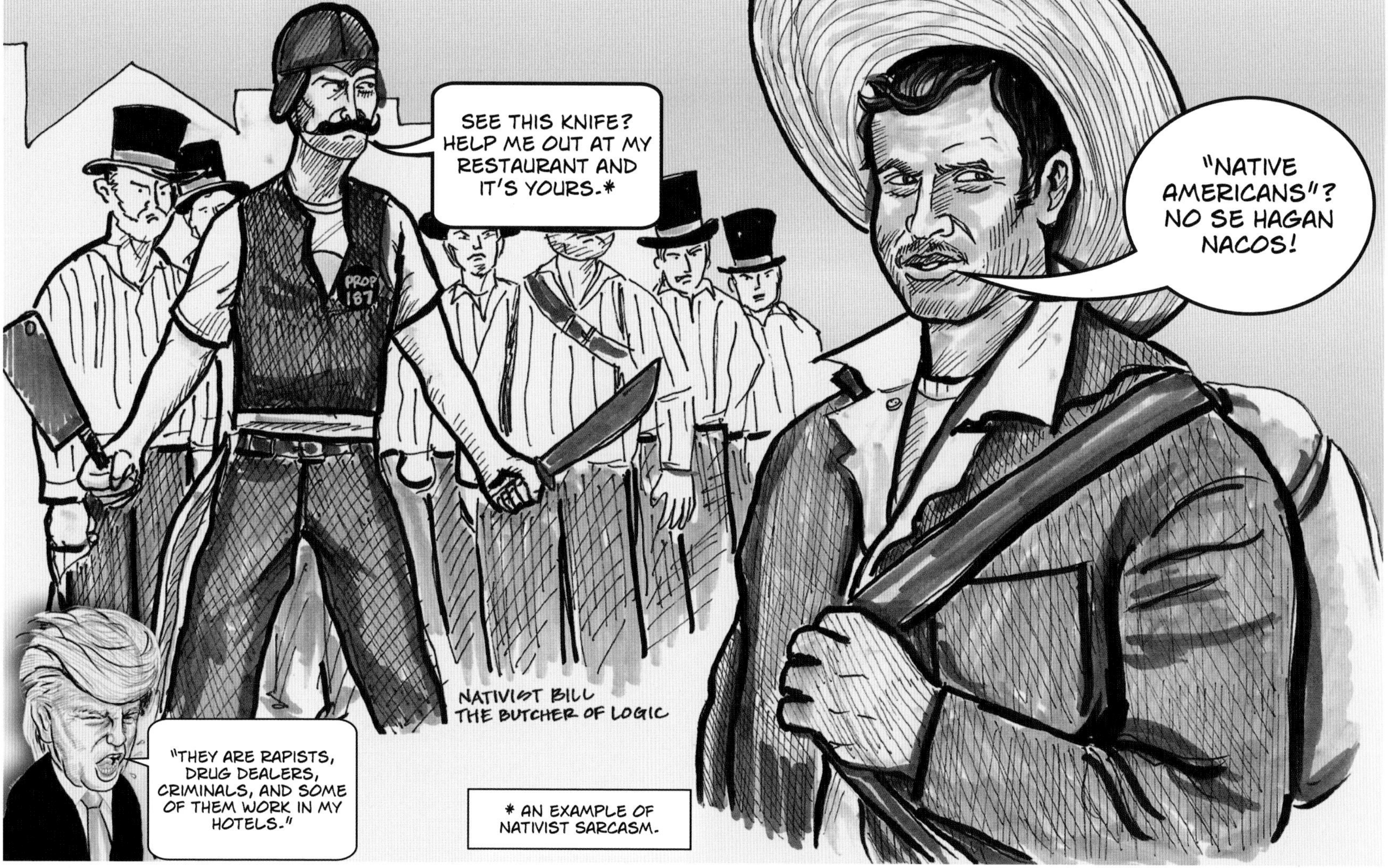
SEE THIS KNIFE? HELP ME OUT AT MY RESTAURANT AND IT'S YOURS.*
"NATIVE AMERICANS"? NO SE HAGAN NACOS!
PROP 187
NATIVIST BILL THE BUTCHER OF LOGIC
"THEY ARE RAPISTS, DRUG DEALERS, CRIMINALS, AND SOME OF THEM WORK IN MY HOTELS."
* AN EXAMPLE OF NATIVIST SARCASM.

"O" is for **OBFUSCATION**—the art of creating narrative confusion through the rapid use of non-sequiturs and references to irrelevant topics. This is a skill that undocumented immigrants often use to avoid being found out.

"Where are you from?" an interlocutor might ask an undocumented bumpkin.

The obfuscating response would be thus:

"Pos mira Chato, it's so great that you asked about my youth. Those were the best years of my life. But life, what is it really? What is its real purpose if not to suffer? Right? Indeed, I did most of my youthful suffering close to my dear mother while I was growing up somewhere near Los Angeles. Or was it Texas? Now that's real suffering. Let me tell you about it…"

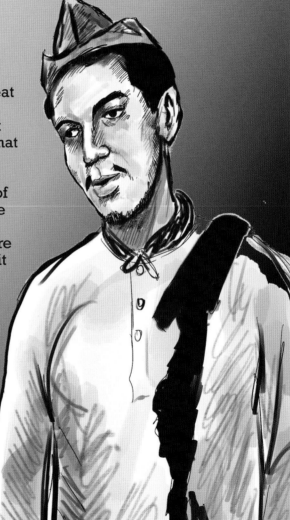

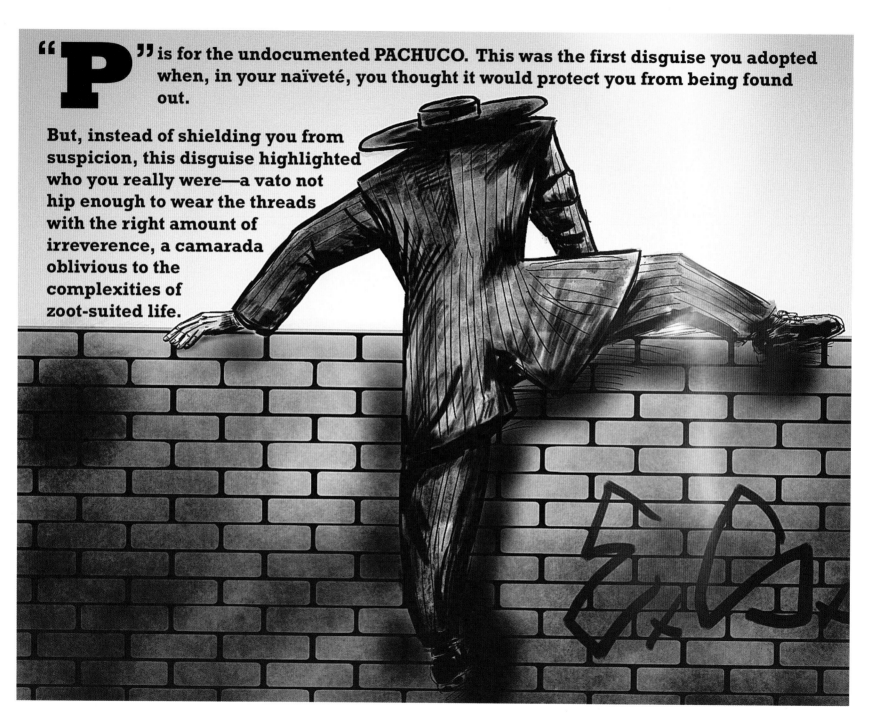

"P" is for the undocumented **PACHUCO**. This was the first disguise you adopted when, in your naïveté, you thought it would protect you from being found out.

But, instead of shielding you from suspicion, this disguise highlighted who you really were—a vato not hip enough to wear the threads with the right amount of irreverence, a camarada oblivious to the complexities of zoot-suited life.

**"Q"** is for the undocumented immigrant **QUEST.** You may think that the main reason I left my country was to look for a better life. To some degree, you would be right.

After years of being hungry all the time, of having no work to do that did not involve having to thank some unscrupulous patrón for treating me as his slave, my family and I had to abandon everything we knew. What we discovered after crossing the border was a new version of ourselves, a new adventure in which we are trying to overcome the challenges of a new patrón.

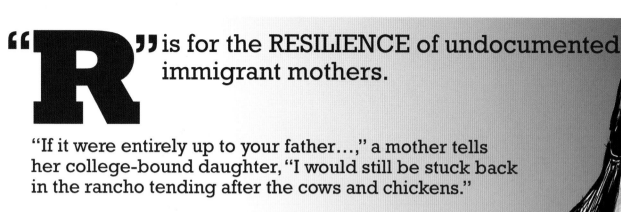

"R" is for the RESILIENCE of undocumented immigrant mothers.

"If it were entirely up to your father…," a mother tells her college-bound daughter, "I would still be stuck back in the rancho tending after the cows and chickens."

"It's been fifteen years since he left us," the daughter thinks as she opens a book on her desk.

"The man mamá chased across the border because he wasn't sending us money. I never really knew him."

"Believe me," the mother sighs as she gets ready for work, "the best thing that man ever did was to force me to come north."

"She is strong," the daughter thinks as she smiles at her mother. "The rock upon which I have built all my hopes and dreams."

But when the daughter looks into her mother's eyes, she sees a melancholy that makes her wonder about all that she has lost.

"It is for her that I will persevere. For her that I work as hard as I always do."

98

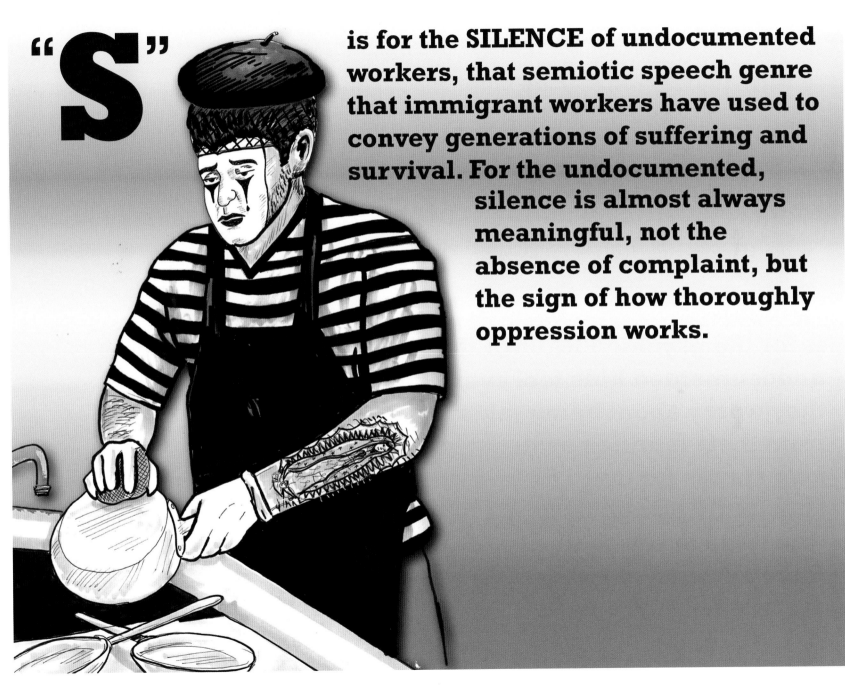

"S" is for the SILENCE of undocumented workers, that semiotic speech genre that immigrant workers have used to convey generations of suffering and survival. For the undocumented, silence is almost always meaningful, not the absence of complaint, but the sign of how thoroughly oppression works.

"T"

is for the psychic **TRAUMA** that undocumented kids feel every day as they worry about being taken away from their families by deportation. It also stands for that **TERROR** that constantly hovers close by, that threatens to separate parents from their kids and crush their collective dreams for a better life.

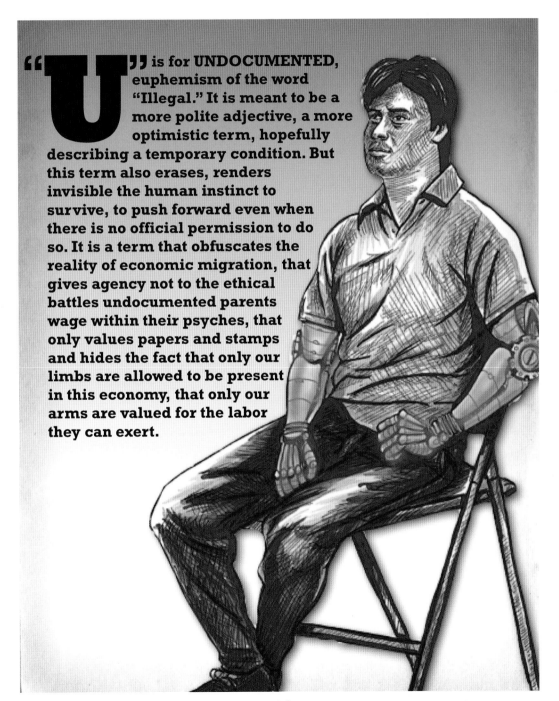

"U" is for UNDOCUMENTED, euphemism of the word "Illegal." It is meant to be a more polite adjective, a more optimistic term, hopefully describing a temporary condition. But this term also erases, renders invisible the human instinct to survive, to push forward even when there is no official permission to do so. It is a term that obfuscates the reality of economic migration, that gives agency not to the ethical battles undocumented parents wage within their psyches, that only values papers and stamps and hides the fact that only our limbs are allowed to be present in this economy, that only our arms are valued for the labor they can exert.

“V” is for parents who downplay their own heroic efforts to survive the challenges of undocumented immigrant life, only to live (and here’s our word) VICARIOUSLY through the many accomplishments of their overachieving children.

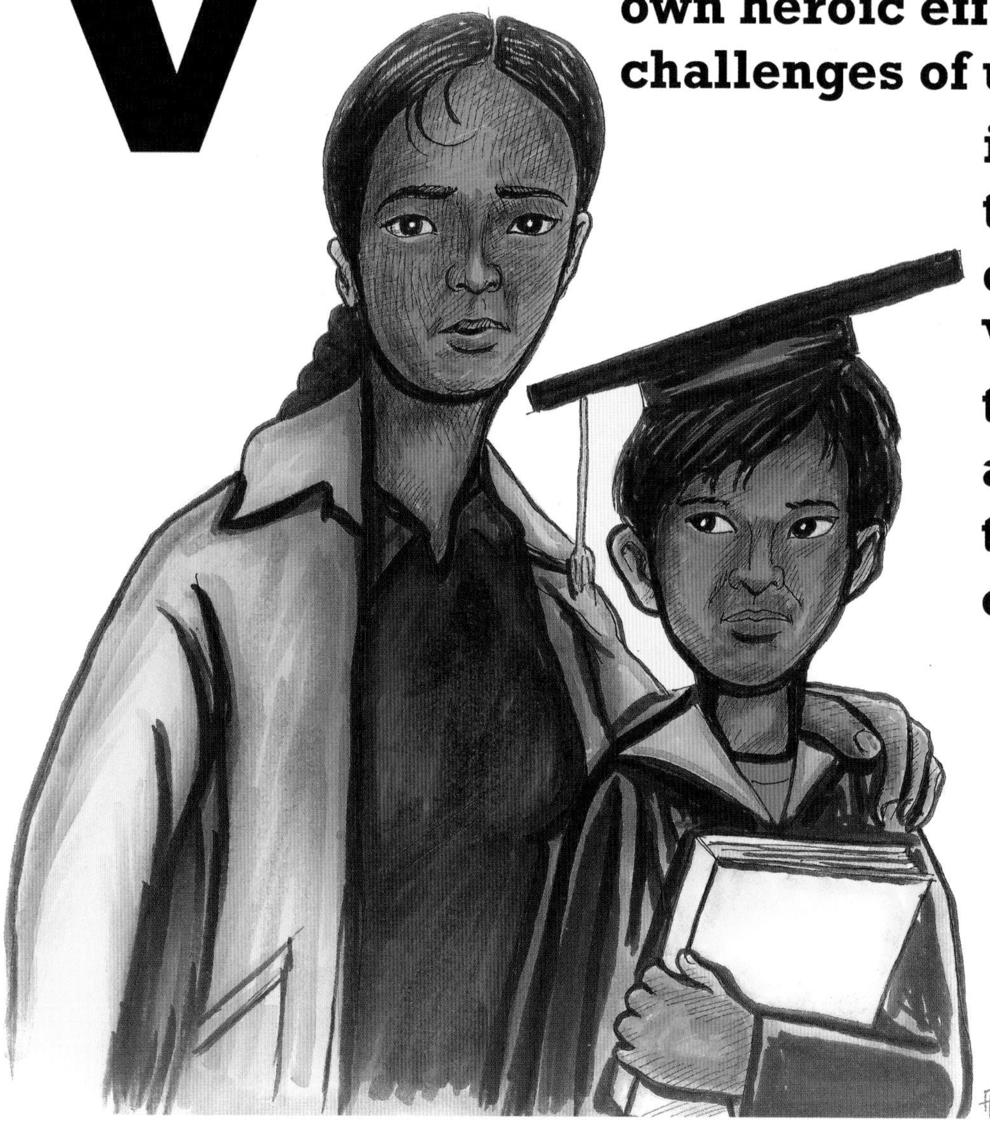

"W" is for WAITING, the waiting of young Mexican girls expecting their fathers to return from their undocumented sojourn, the waiting of undocumented sons who have not been able to return to their parents in El Salvador because their papers are not in order, and the waiting of so many undocumented kids hoping that a humane and sensible immigration law will soon be adopted.

But, this waiting is not done in vain. It is corrosive, a stress that eats at our psyches and freezes us in a liminal state of perpetual torture.

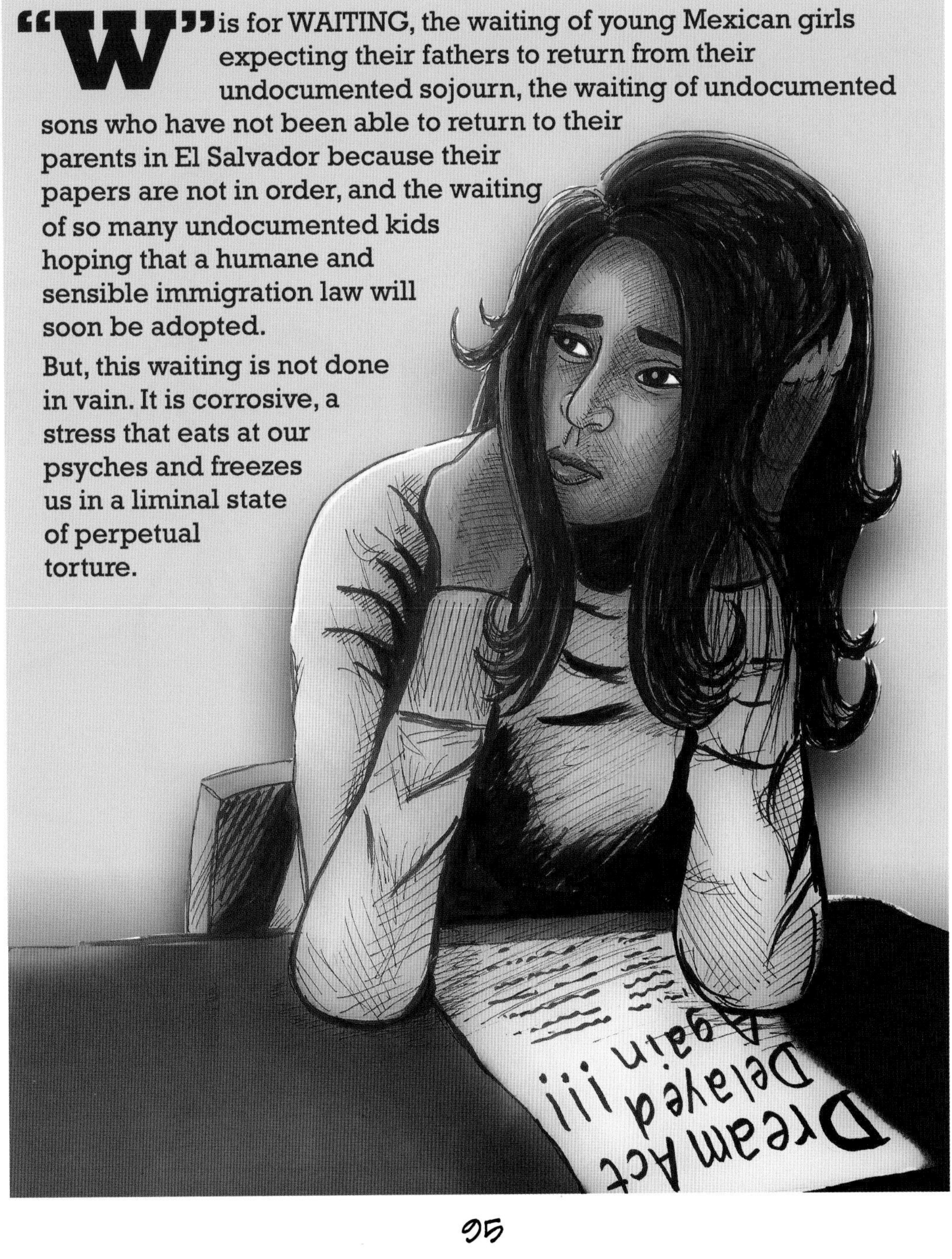

Dream Act
Delayed !!!
Again

"X" is for the word "Xenophobia," the fear of those who come from different ethnicities and races. Undocumented immigrants know much about xenophobia. It is a fear that has been marshalled against them for decades, an anxiety manipulated by the masters of society to foster division among other working people; it is an obstacle—and maybe the biggest one—that prevents the formation of an effective labor movement.

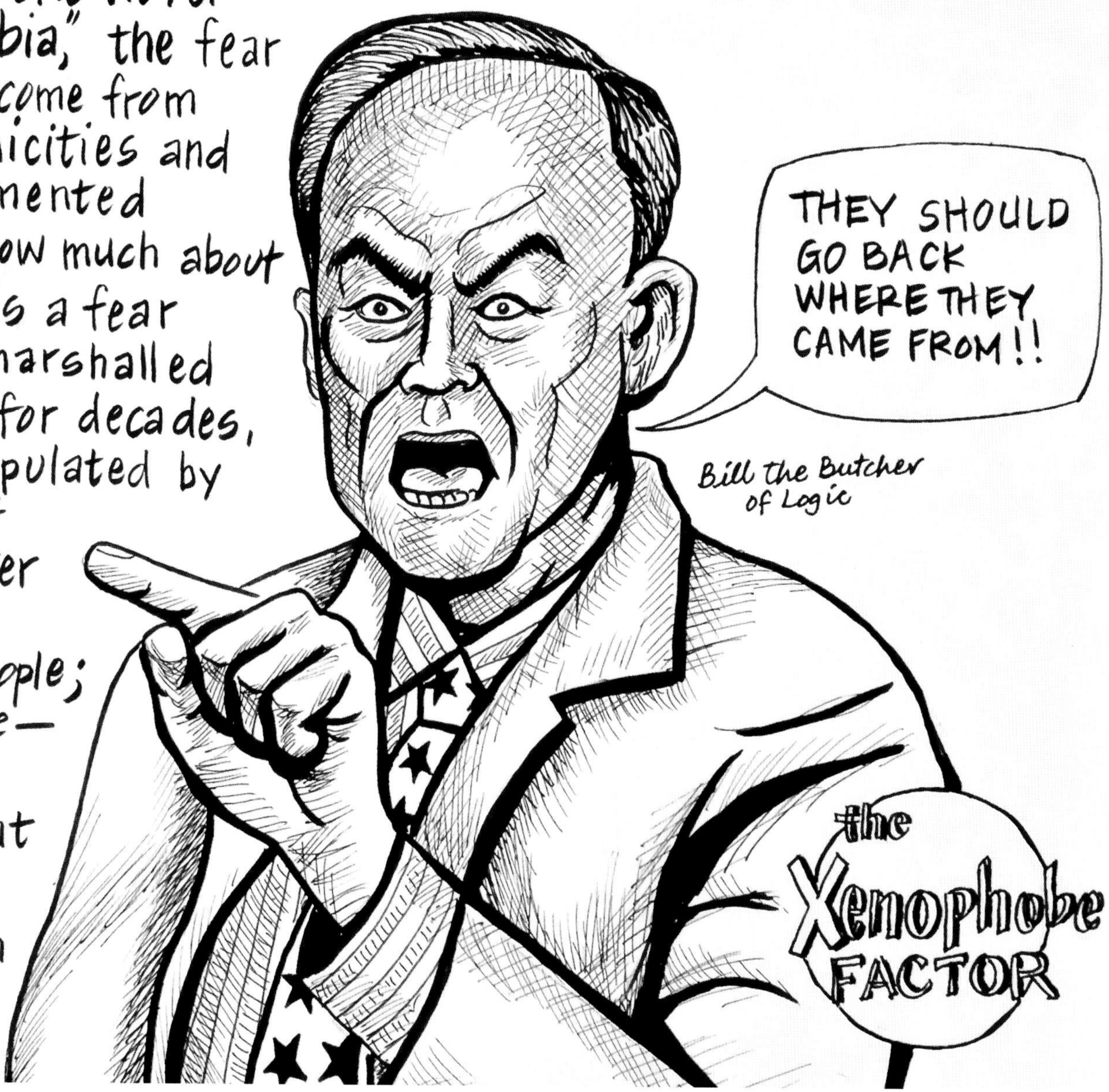
THEY SHOULD GO BACK WHERE THEY CAME FROM!!
Bill the Butcher of Logic
the Xenophobe FACTOR

"**Y**" is for the word "yearning", that intense longing that all undocumented immigrants feel for a more just world where their suffering and hard work might be rewarded. It is a desperate hope that if you work hard enough you can actually change your life. But, this yearning is fickle, often dissipating into the nihilistic realization that no matter how much you may want it or how much you may work for it, that divine justice you are hoping for is just an illusion.

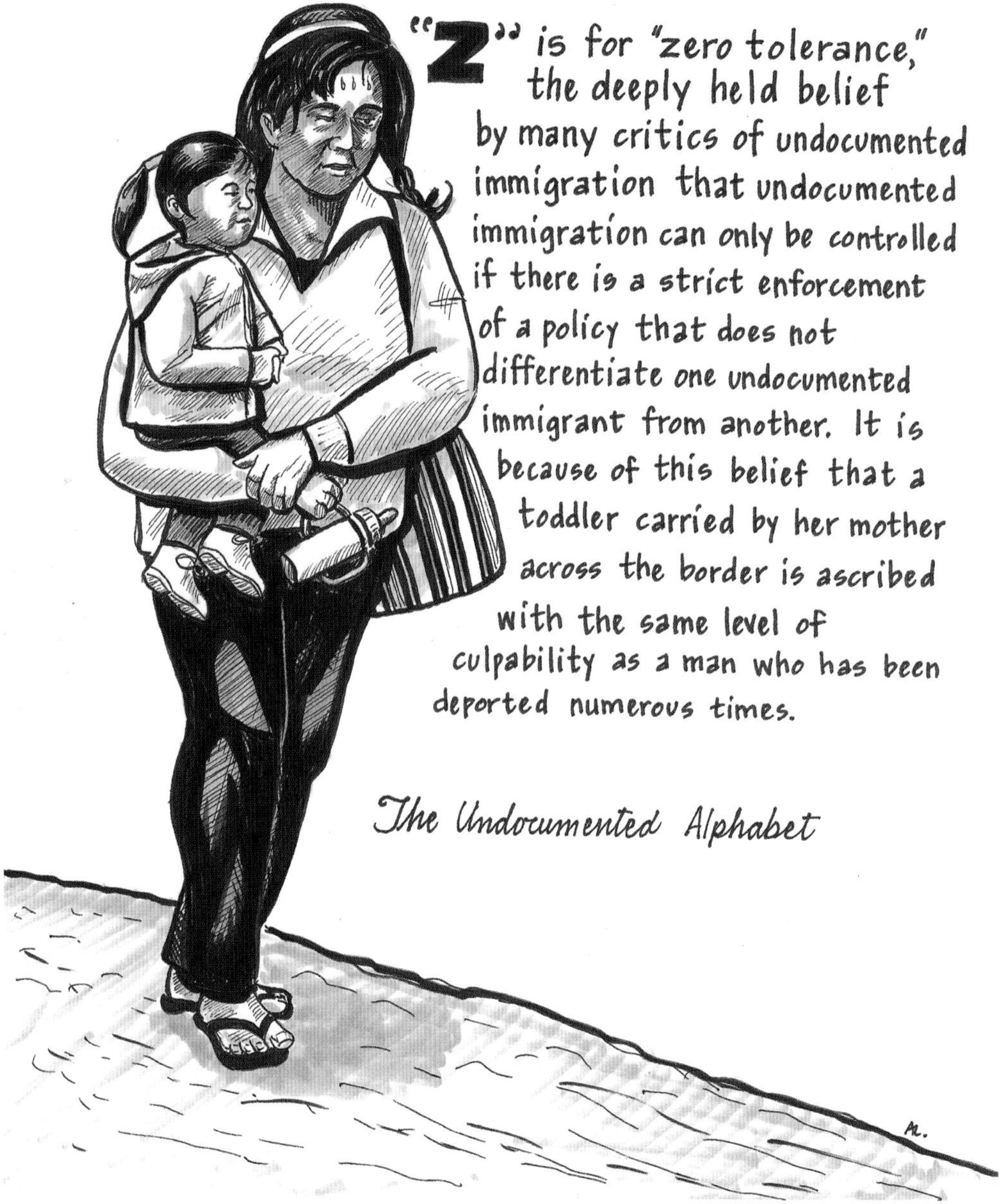
"Z" is for "zero tolerance," the deeply held belief by many critics of undocumented immigration that undocumented immigration can only be controlled if there is a strict enforcement of a policy that does not differentiate one undocumented immigrant from another. It is because of this belief that a toddler carried by her mother across the border is ascribed with the same level of culpability as a man who has been deported numerous times.
The Undocumented Alphabet
AL.

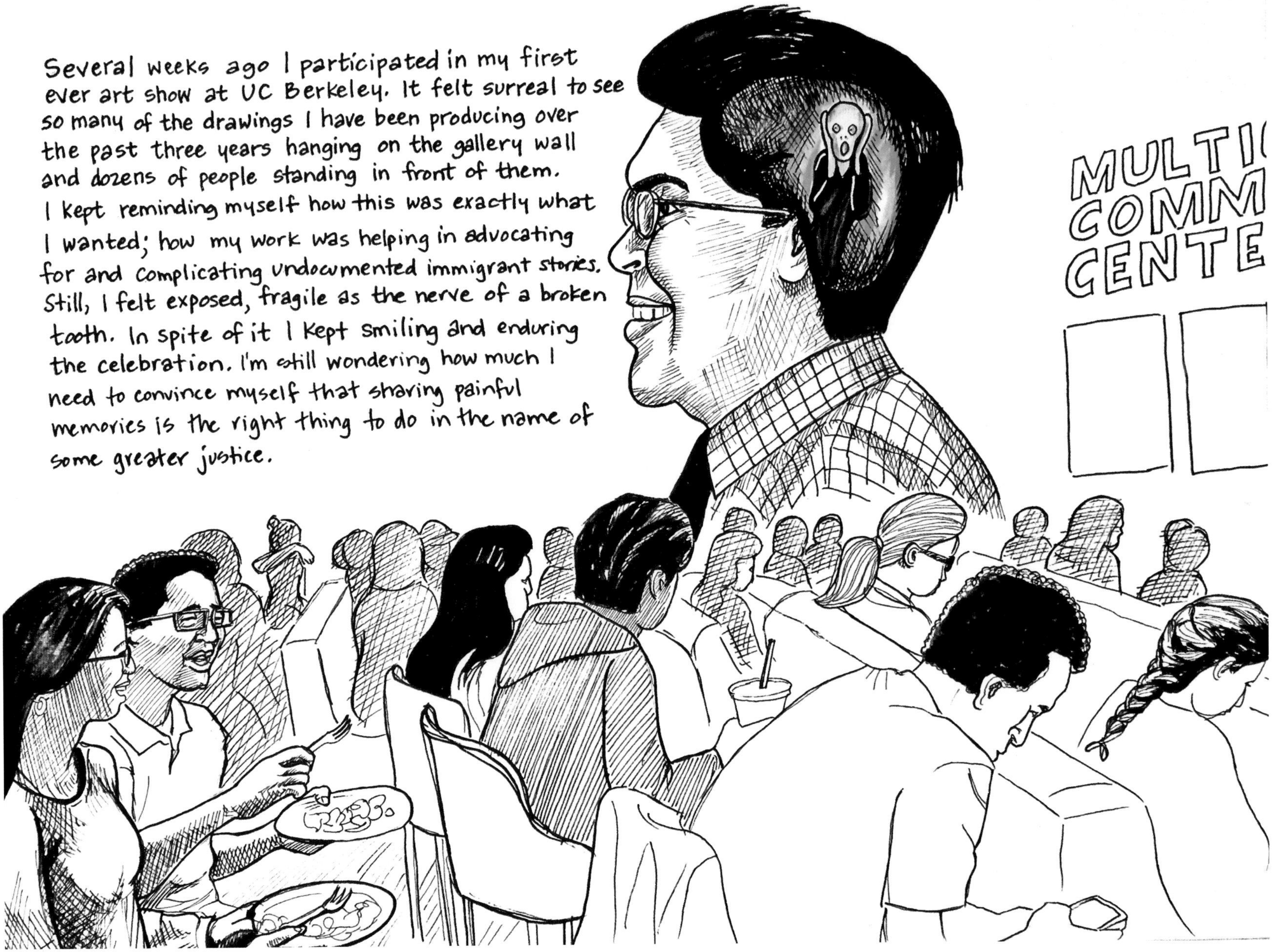
Several weeks ago I participated in my first ever art show at UC Berkeley. It felt surreal to see so many of the drawings I have been producing over the past three years hanging on the gallery wall and dozens of people standing in front of them. I kept reminding myself how this was exactly what I wanted; how my work was helping in advocating for and complicating undocumented immigrant stories. Still, I felt exposed, fragile as the nerve of a broken tooth. In spite of it I kept smiling and enduring the celebration. I'm still wondering how much I need to convince myself that sharing painful memories is the right thing to do in the name of some greater justice.

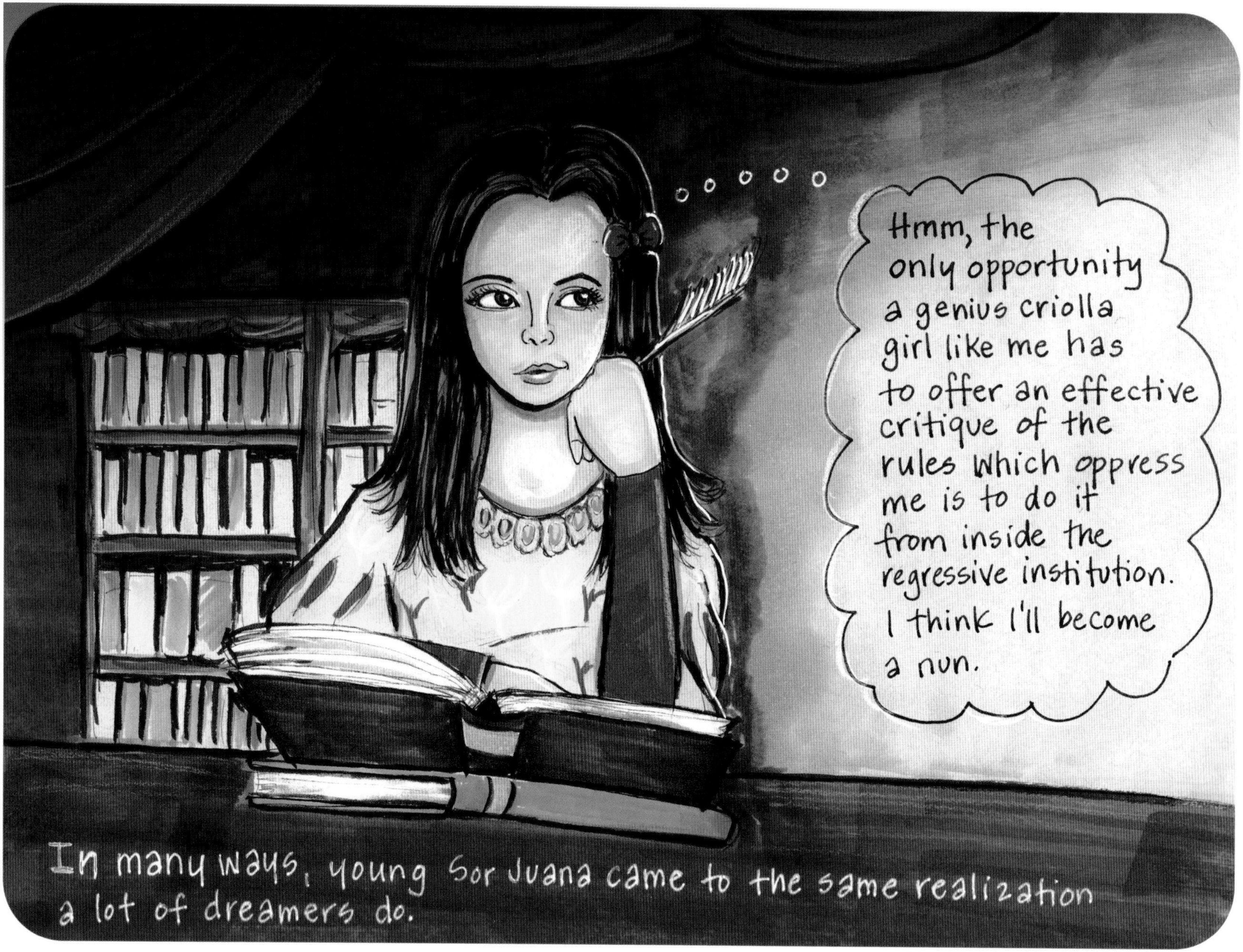
Hmm, the only opportunity a genius criolla girl like me has to offer an effective critique of the rules which oppress me is to do it from inside the regressive institution. I think I'll become a nun.
In many ways, young Sor Juana came to the same realization a lot of dreamers do.

CHAPTER 8

ON THE NEED FOR SELF-AMNESTY

Speech Delivered at UC Berkeley's Chicano/Latino Alumni Association Scholarship Brunch on October of 2013

It is really nice to be here, spending this gorgeous Sunday morning with all of you. I want to thank Lupe Gallegos-Díaz and the Chicano/Latino Alumni Association for inviting me to this wonderful brunch. I am particularly humbled because I know of so many colleagues at Berkeley who could have just as easily been here, talking with you about the amazing work they are doing with AB540 students. I am absolutely honored to be sharing these words with you.

To tell you the truth, speaking in front of a group like this one is something that I thought would never happen. Though I do have to admit that I have dreamt about it since I was in high school (and that is a really long time), I never thought I would actually be able to share my undocumented experience in public, even after my family and I were granted Amnesty.

Though a part of me thought that it would never happen, I often dreamt of standing at a podium like this one, addressing a roomful of brilliant students who have experienced the same things I had—the trials and tribulations of being an undocumented student at a major American university. It wasn't until about a decade ago, that I thought this speech might even be possible. Before that, I knew of few other students who had gone through the same things I had.

All of us have dreams that we hope will someday come true. This is what defines the best parts of human ambition and optimism, the reason we work hard and endure sacrifices. The scary thing is that sometimes we subvert the few chances we have at achieving our dreams because we become too accustomed to the stress of the pursuit and too fearful of what succeeding would actually mean for our lives. Today, I want to talk to you about how this almost happened to me, and what it was that I learned from the experience.

I entered UC Berkeley in 1984 as an undocumented student. The truth is that there was nothing radical about what I did; it was the logical next step. As a smarter than average student at Oakland's Fremont High School, I had been encouraged to pursue a college education by all my teachers. It was my high school counselor, however, who took the tear-soaked application I had left on his desk that Friday afternoon when I had confessed my undocumented situation, and he submitted it, without me knowing it, to Berkeley. Suddenly, I found myself at Cal in 1984, unsure about how I would negotiate this new world, and almost as terrified about it as my parents.

As I'm sure some of you know, in order to survive Berkeley's competitive academic environment, particularly when one enters from an under-resourced high school, one must often pretend to be better prepared than one is. This is the way I came in; I was an affirmative action kid, a poor kid from a poorly-performing district. Add being undocumented to that and what you got was a student who became a master at feigning being smart, who quickly learned how to deliver well-placed and assertive "howevers" and "therefores" in order to hide the fact that I had hardly understood the material I had read. Inside, of course, I was always terrified and worried that I would be caught. In class after class I learned to adapt, paid attention to the phrases the smartest kids used when they participated in class, and I pretended I was one of them. In a way, I felt like Cantinflas trying to fool the world; but, unlike Cantinflas, I did not feel that mischievous joy about my linguistic or rhetorical cleverness.

Being an undocumented student at this prestigious university often provoked bouts of extreme insecurity and perfectionism in me. It wasn't just that I was always fearful of being caught and causing my entire family to be deported. I was also

My fountain Pen

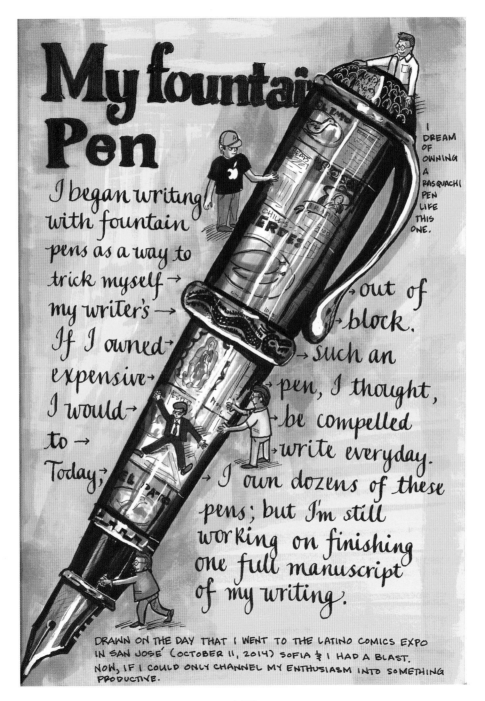

I DREAM OF OWNING A RASQUACHI PEN LIKE THIS ONE.

I began writing with fountain pens as a way to trick myself → out of → block. my writer's → If I owned → such an expensive → pen, I thought, I would → be compelled to → write everyday. Today; → I own dozens of these pens; but I'm still working on finishing one full manuscript of my writing.

DRAWN ON THE DAY THAT I WENT TO THE LATINO COMICS EXPO IN SAN JOSÉ (OCTOBER 11, 2014) SOFIA & I HAD A BLAST. NOW, IF I COULD ONLY CHANNEL MY ENTHUSIASM INTO SOMETHING PRODUCTIVE.

convinced that if I had advanced, it was only because I had tricked the system and figured out a way to move forward without really being tested. This is the way I felt when I received my bachelors in the late 1980s, my masters in the early 1990s, and my PhD in 1996. No matter how many awards and accolades I collected, I never felt that I was good enough.

Even in those early years when my academic work was being published and I was presenting invited work at international conferences, I still felt as if I did not belong. I would step up to podiums like this one to read my work, always afraid that someone in the audience would raise their hand to say that I had gotten it wrong, always nervous even when I was the only one who had done research in that subject. Confidence is the result of a process that must be nurtured from a young age.

My process always involved filtering my experience through an undocumented epistemology. How could I feel good about who I was in public when no one really knew the critical essence of who I really was in private? The fact is that being undocumented often inoculates us from acknowledging our resourcefulness and perseverance as talents; rather, we learn to see these skills as the necessary tools required for survival.

And yet, about ten years ago something magical happened that gave me a new perspective. An immigrant rights movement erupted across the nation at about the same time that I joined the Immigrant Students Issues Coalition. Suddenly, there was a space on campus where I could productively share my experience and where I could discuss, along with my colleagues in ISIC, the experiences of the hundreds of undocumented students who were now enrolling at Berkeley.

In ISIC I witnessed how my colleagues, Lupe Gallegos-Díaz, Allan Creighton, Jere Takahashi, Luisa Giulianetti, Nora Sandoval, Fab-

rizio Mejia, and Margi Wald, among many others, grappled with the challenge of supporting students who, like me, would often keep their needs hidden. We moved from merely proposing tweaks to current immigrant student services and policies, to asserting that, if the university was going to consciously continue admitting undocumented immigrant students to this campus, it bore a responsibility to create the structural changes needed to address the unique circumstances these students presented. It was ISIC's proposal for an Undocumented Student Resource Center that the University eventually adopted a few years ago.

For me, working in ISIC allowed me to understand myself better. Suddenly, all those years of academic preparation, all the research I had conducted on immigrant narratives, had a clear purpose. But, if I actually wanted to make a concrete difference, there was still another step I needed to take. Buoyed by the support I had received in ISIC, and many months before the "Undocumented and Unafraid" student movement took off, I decided to publish an essay which I titled, "Embracing My Undocumented Immigrant Identity," (You can still find it in Colorlines). In it, I argued for undocumented immigrant assertiveness and self-compassion, a recognition that being undocumented was not a cultural choice, but a material reality that profoundly shaped who we are and how we see the world.

I had decided to publish my essay in spite of the terrible things I felt that doing so would trigger. But not publishing it meant something worse—it meant keeping inside a story that could be immediately helpful to the emerging undocumented student movement, something I could not accept. So I did it, and I braced for the worst.

In those days that followed the publication of my essay, I learned an important lesson about trusting people's better natures; instead of vehemence, what I received as result of my writing was support from hundreds of people across the US who, like me, had been keeping their undocumented immigrant experience locked up inside. College administrators, doctors, lawyers, and many many students contacted me via Facebook to say, "Hey, I also went through that. Thank you for writing your piece. I thought I was the only one." A year later I wrote another essay that focused on being an "Ex-undocumented Immigrant Parent," and I received just as many positive responses. Finally, all those years of working in solitude were beginning to pay off.

More recently, instead of essays, I have been drawing visual vignettes that focus on what growing up as an undocumented kid meant for me. Because these vignettes, cartoons really, are able to communicate complex moments much more efficiently and effectively, compared to long essays, I have been able to explore a wider spectrum of my undocumented experience, everything from romantic relationships to the terror of seeking financial aid. As Lupe Gallegos-Díaz once said to me, "I like your drawings because in trying to grapple with your own experience, you actually help others heal. Besides, sometimes they are funny." Similar to the essays, the dozens and dozens of cartoons I have shared on Facebook have elicited a positive response, and, like the essays, they have now become the raw material for a book I hope to publish in the very near future.

All of this, I guess, has taught me the essential lesson I want to share with you today. That is, I have learned that entering a university like Berkeley as an undocumented student is not a radical act. It is where smart, resourceful kids belong, where we are training ourselves for a brighter and more inclusive future. What is radical is not being ashamed or vindictive about our experience, but generous in sharing the higher consciousness about human perseverance that the experience has taught us.

It is this generosity that has begun to change the politics of immigration in this country. As more and more stories come out about what being undocumented entails, more and more allies are joining our effort to better define what being undocumented is about. Allies are generous in the way they offer their energy and resources so that we may find our own voices. And we are generous when we offer our experience without needing to castigate those who, in their apathy, have accepted oppressive laws as the natural order of things.

But the greatest generosity is that which we practice with ourselves. I believe that only by communicating the triumphs and stresses of our experience without self-judgment, only by initiating a public dialogue about what being undocumented means that is free from self-accusation, will our society finally accept that having been undocumented is just another kind of American experience.

I am so proud that you selected me as your speaker.

"Diego Rivera on Facebook."

In my world
the Border Patrol
would greet
immigrants with
flowers and say,
"Thank you for
helping us with
our labor needs.
The least we
could do is offer
you a free education."

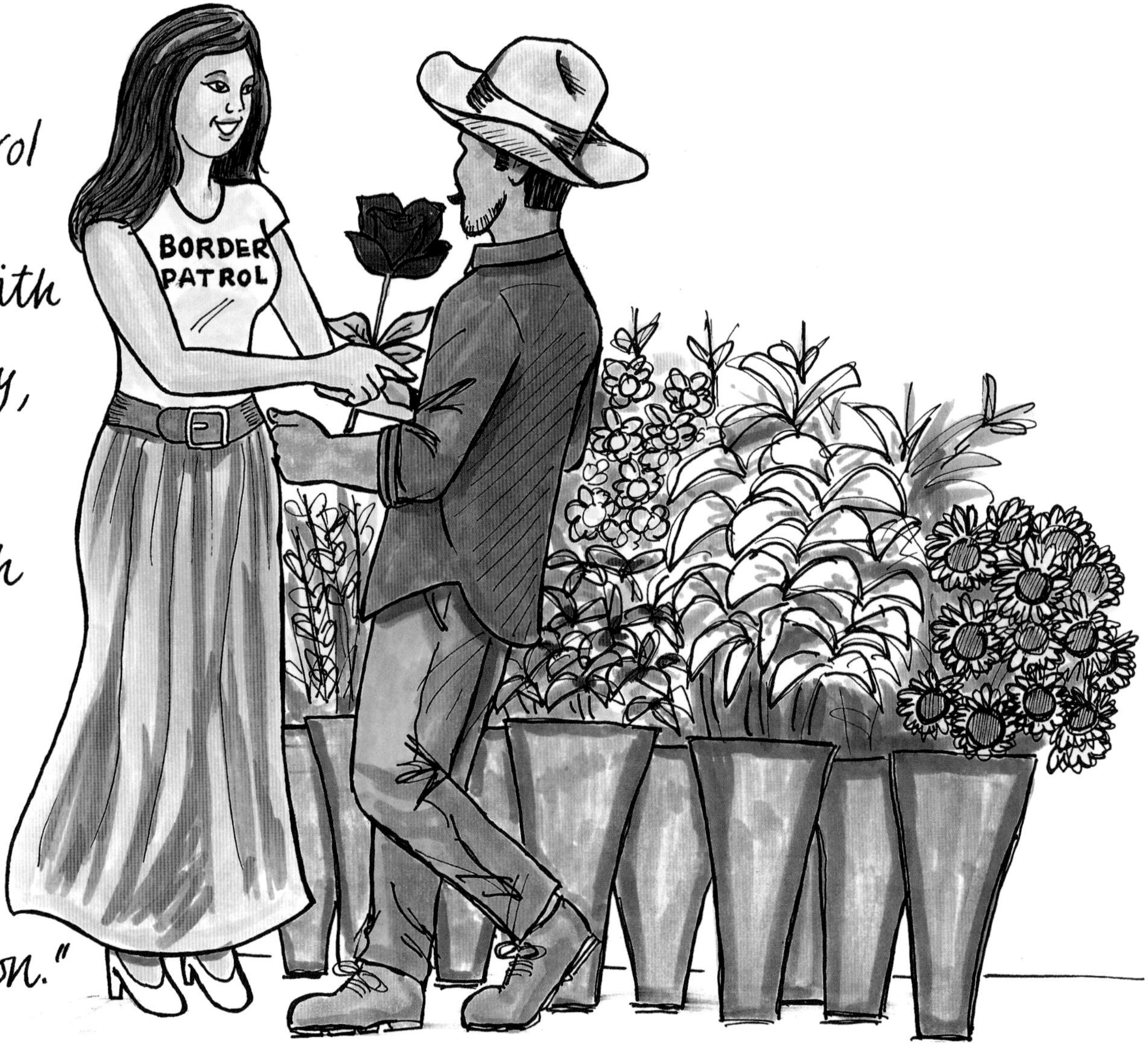
BORDER
PATROL

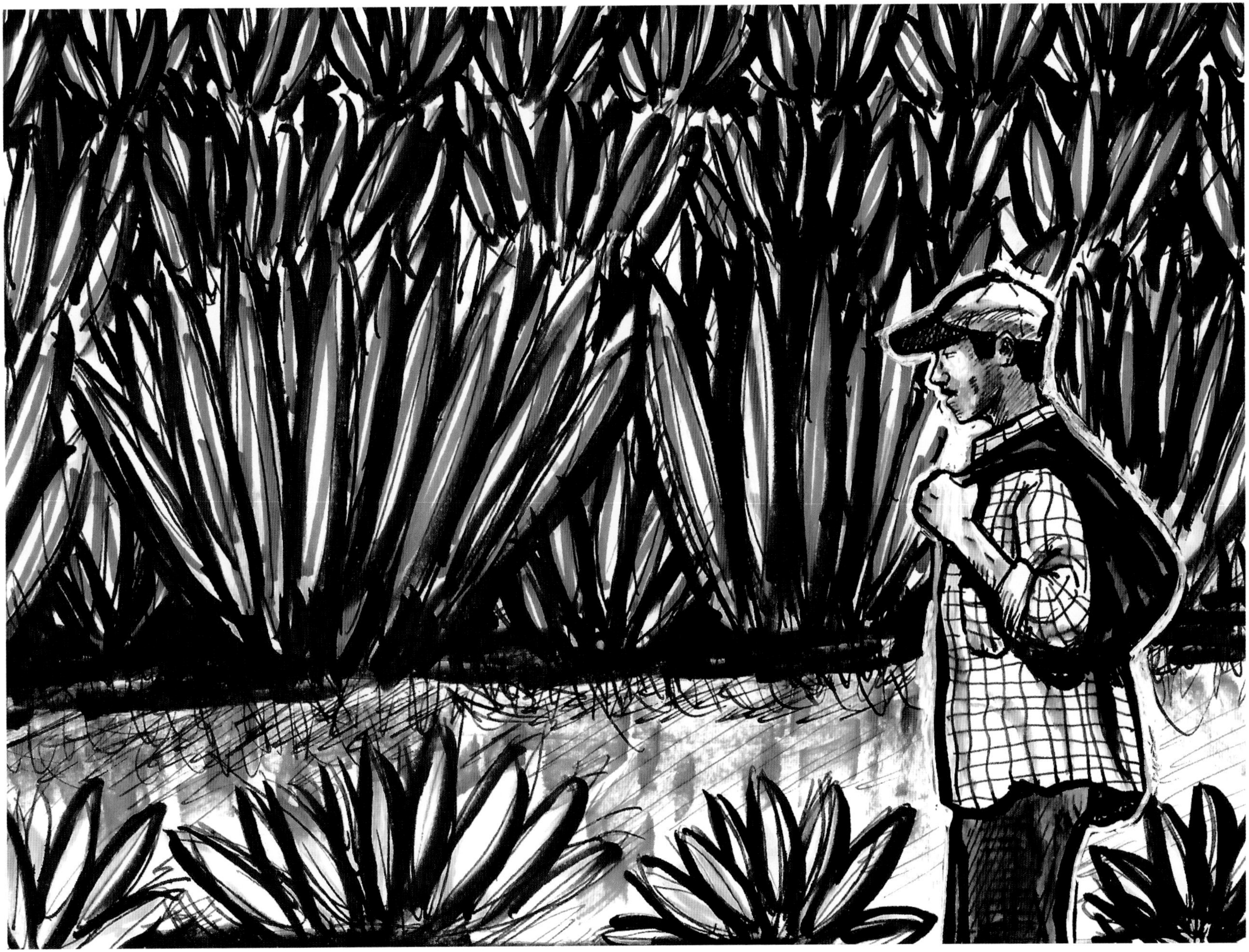

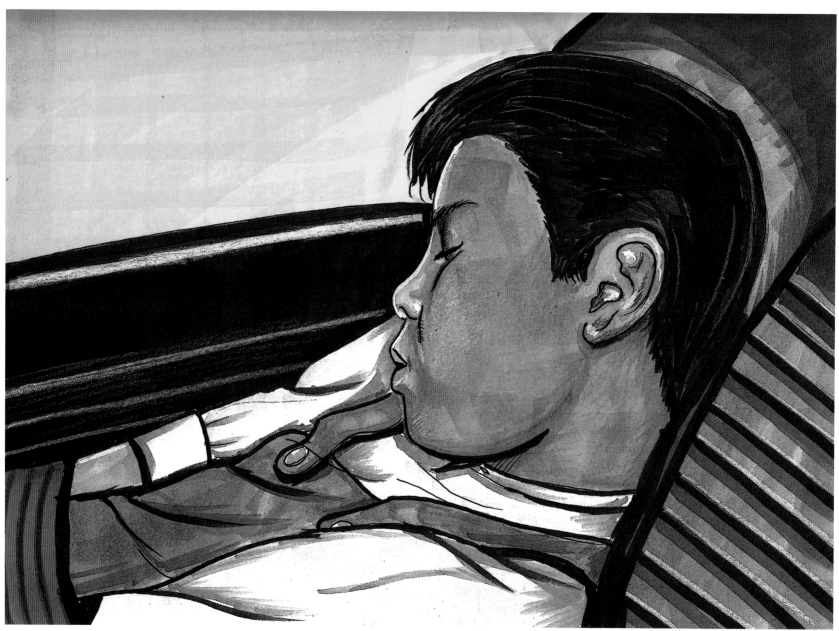
"Pretending to sleep as I crossed the border."

CONCLUSION

DECONSTRUCTING THE DREAMER

One of the foundational myths at the heart of American meritocracy is the idea that through hard work any achievement is possible. I used to think this way, believed that if I had indeed overcome the obstacles in my undocumented past it was because I had worked hard. The truth is, however, that while I did work hard, that while I took all sorts of odd jobs during my first years at Berkeley and spent too many all-nighters desperately preparing for next-day exams or presentations, I was also extremely lucky.

During those first years of our American adventure, after mamá had shepherded my two sisters and me to the Tijuana border, my father welcomed us to the United States in a very fortunate state. Unlike other undocumented men in our extended family at that time, he held a firm job that paid him a good hourly wage. This meant that mamá did not have to venture out into our strange new world in East Oakland to look for work, that she could stay in papá's rented home with her kids to help guide us as we adapted to a new language and a new set of customs. This also meant that, as the eldest son, I did not have to drop out of school once I reached my teen years to take on a job like some of my relatives had. Rather, I was left alone to dwell in the books I brought back from school and to doodle misanthropic hieroglyphics on the near-transparent leaves of paper papá bought us at the Embys on East 14th.

I was also lucky that when the time came for me to go to college, the Oakland Unified School District had already worked out an arrangement with UC Berkeley so that its higher performing students would get priority consideration during the admissions process. Thus, in 1984, out of the handful of undocumented students across the nation who were actually in a position to attend college, I had a rare opportunity. This deserves emphasis: I was admitted into one of the world's most prestigious universities that just so happened to be located a BART-

ride away from my home where my parents and my community could continue to support me. But, indeed, the most noteworthy development that allowed me to fulfill my academic goals and eventually realize my ambition of attaining my PhD was one that had to do with timing—Reagan's approval of the Federal Immigration and Control Act of 1986 and its amnesty provision took place while I was a sophomore at Berkeley.

I still remember that first line of the statement of purpose I wrote when I applied to graduate school: "Until recently I was an undocumented student in college," I started, strategically confessing my past so as to highlight my unique perspective. "I worked hard but could not earn better than a 3.0 GPA at Berkeley during my freshman and sophomore years; then, after I was accepted for amnesty, my GPA jumped to almost a 4.0! This is what I want to study: How does being an undocumented student affect our intellectual and literary development?"

I was lucky that I was accepted to grad school that year and that I received amnesty when I did and where I did. Indeed, as soon as we were able to, papá had us completing every immigration form, taking every test, and paying every fee so that we could normalize our status before the amnesty window could close. Then, in 1992, shortly before Pete Wilson put forth Proposition 187 with its threat to cut benefits to all undocumented immigrants and their American-born children, I became a citizen.

Of course, these transitions in my legal status did not pass in vain. Once, years after I had gotten my PhD, the stress of having made it past so many obstacles that had tripped and broken so many of my other undocumented friends and family compelled me to go see a therapist. There, as I slouched on her office chair and heard the squeak of the ancient leather cushion sticking to my legs, my therapist tapped the pink eraser of her yellow pencil on her bottom lip and casually observed, "I think that what you are suffering from is a form of survivor guilt."

"What is that?" I mumbled and leaned forward, the leather squealing as I shifted my weight.

"It is a psychological response most often associated with people who survived a terrible event. Think of people who survived the Holocaust."

The fact is that my story of survival as a hyperdocumented student is not the chronicle of someone who should be posited as a model of the ideal undocumented student. Instead, it is the story of someone who lucked out when, like Cantinflas, I was not kicked off the vaudevillian stage after I forgot my lines. I just kept going, helped along the way by well-meaning allies and mentors, improvising my way through all the chaos and confusion I was feeling inside, always working so as not to rouse suspicion among those policing the university to check for those who did not belong.

And yet, I know that every single undocumented student with whom I've met over the years has also attempted to improvise his and her own survival. All of them have worked hard to make it from one stage to another. They have all grappled with the same doubts and insecurities, overcoming their own impostor syndromes even as they have had to perform in the dark.

Too often, however, these students have acted in solitude, alone in their struggle. And so, without allies to assist them, they have been unceremoniously kicked off of the stage like the Saturday night acts that bomb on Amateur Night at the Apollo. Even today, after almost a decade of undocumented student activism and a sharp increase in undocumented support services for college students across the country, there are just too few of us who have actually made it all the way to doctoral positions.

Early on, when I began gathering pieces for this collection, I thought that the dreamer archetype was an accurate representation of my story. At its heart it evoked all the aspirations and hopes that attracted my parents and my siblings to the United States and it was the reason why we worked so hard to change our civic relationship to this country.

The dreamer reminded me of the hope Dr. Martin Luther King, Jr. envisioned when he delivered his iconic speech that August of 1963 in front of the Lincoln Memorial. But, the trouble with the dreamer archetype is that it paints all undocumented students with too broad a brush and suggests that the obstacles undocumented students routinely face are not real or substantial enough, that if they just work hard at it, they can do anything. It is because of this ideal that dreamers are expected to be flawless academics and emotionally impervious workers. That is precisely—so the story goes—the reason why they deserve to be protected from deportation, because we don't want to lose their exceptional talent as a nation. In this narrative of exceptionalism, there is no space for mediocrity. Excellence is the only commodity that will be accepted. And yet, the stresses that go along with being undocumented too often manifest as mundane mediocrities; and, thus, the flawless dreamer persona becomes an archetype that is just too difficult to achieve for the vast majority of undocumented students.

I do consider myself a type of dreamer because I still have hope that Dr. King's vision of a more just world can be achieved. But it is only because of that that I offer my experience as that of a "reluctant" dreamer.

Thank you so much for reading these pages.

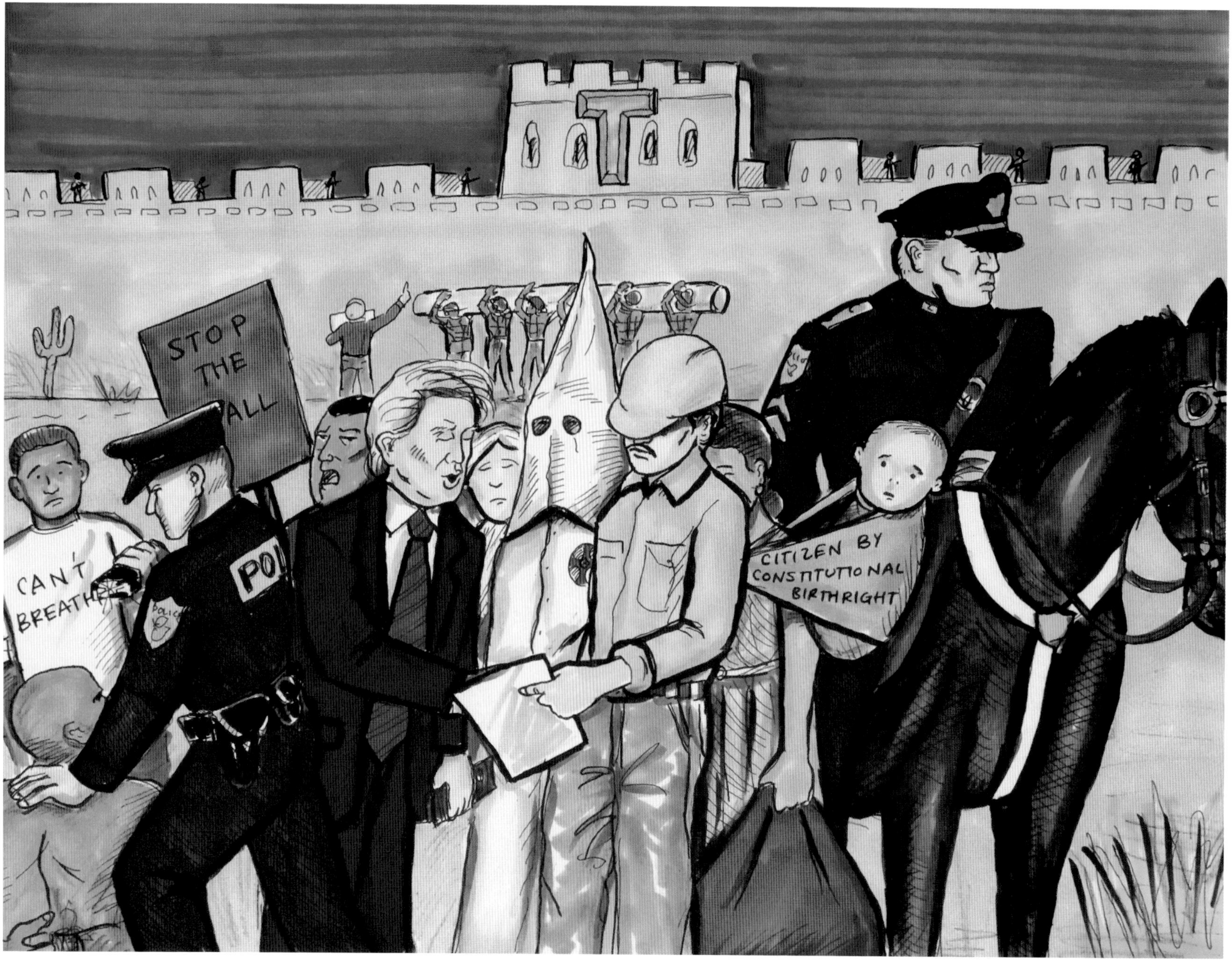
STOP THE ALL
CAN'T BREATHE
POL
POLICE
CITIZEN BY CONSTITUTIONAL BIRTHRIGHT

POSTCRIPT

ENTER TRUMP

Tonight I sat with my wife and daughter watching the election results, all of us in disbelief about the reassertion of a white America that seems to feel resentment about the browning of this country. "What does it mean for us?" my daughter asked as Trump's numbers continued to climb to their inevitable result. "Honestly, I wish I knew," I said as I massaged the throbbing contours of my forehead.

President Trump? Even thinking about the phrase feels as if I am uttering an uncouth incantation. He has stood in front of Weimar multitudes, ratcheting up jack-booted antagonisms targeted towards my people. My stomach churns with anxiety and disgust, as I don't know what tomorrow will bring. But I can't say that I am surprised by the complete removal of a veneer that has barely hidden such ugliness and division.

Though my first instinct is to be cautious, to stop assuming that all people agree with the stories I have been telling about undocumentedness being another kind of American experience, I remind myself that I need to keep articulating my experience in such a way that others may find some resonance with it. It is the only way that I know how to create communion—by exposing who I am and trusting that others will find some human connection with it.

Hope, in the end, is the only precious thing we truly own. The real tragedy would be if we give it up and descend into a nihilistic abyss. So I won't.

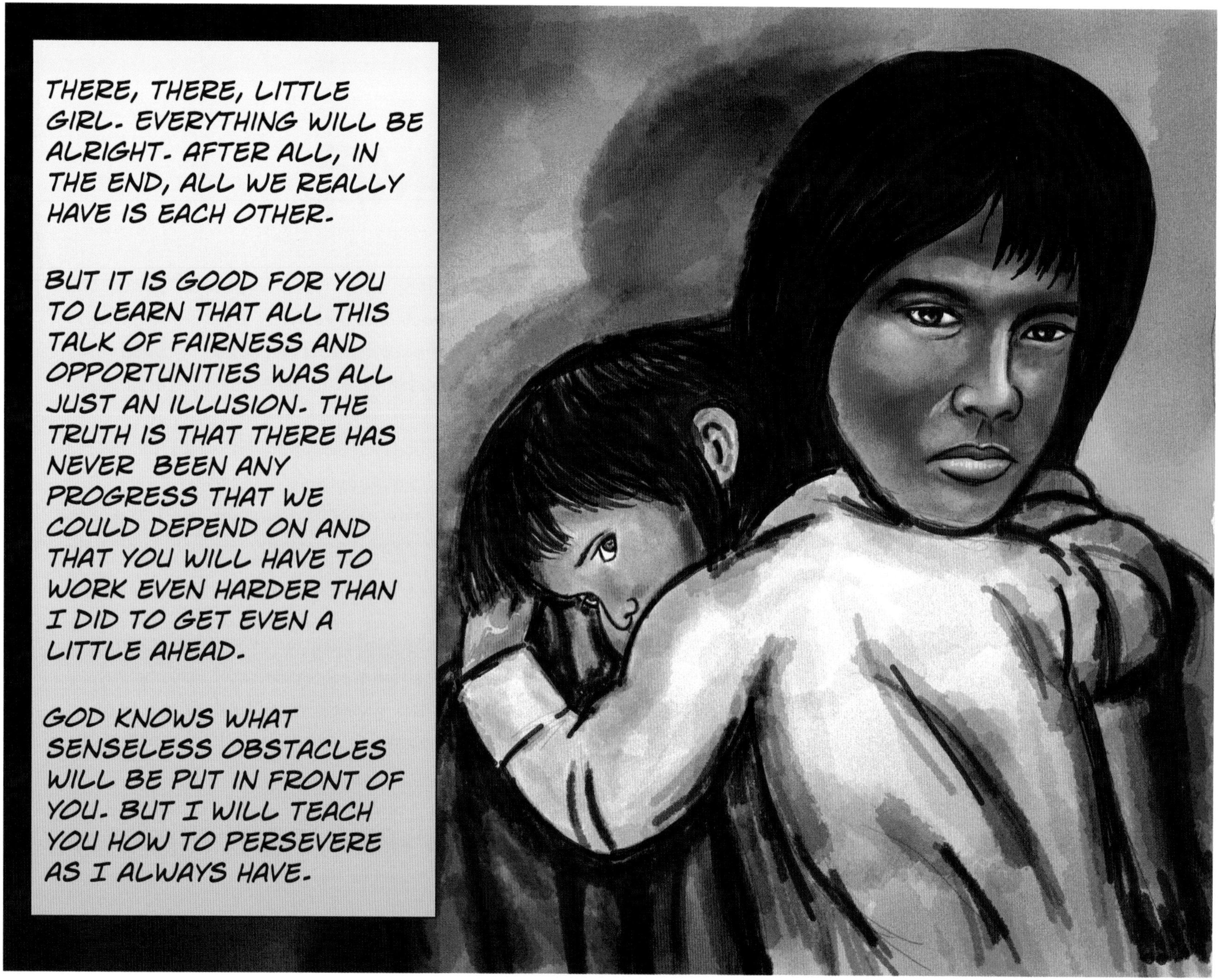
THERE, THERE, LITTLE GIRL. EVERYTHING WILL BE ALRIGHT. AFTER ALL, IN THE END, ALL WE REALLY HAVE IS EACH OTHER.
BUT IT IS GOOD FOR YOU TO LEARN THAT ALL THIS TALK OF FAIRNESS AND OPPORTUNITIES WAS ALL JUST AN ILLUSION. THE TRUTH IS THAT THERE HAS NEVER BEEN ANY PROGRESS THAT WE COULD DEPEND ON AND THAT YOU WILL HAVE TO WORK EVEN HARDER THAN I DID TO GET EVEN A LITTLE AHEAD.
GOD KNOWS WHAT SENSELESS OBSTACLES WILL BE PUT IN FRONT OF YOU. BUT I WILL TEACH YOU HOW TO PERSEVERE AS I ALWAYS HAVE.

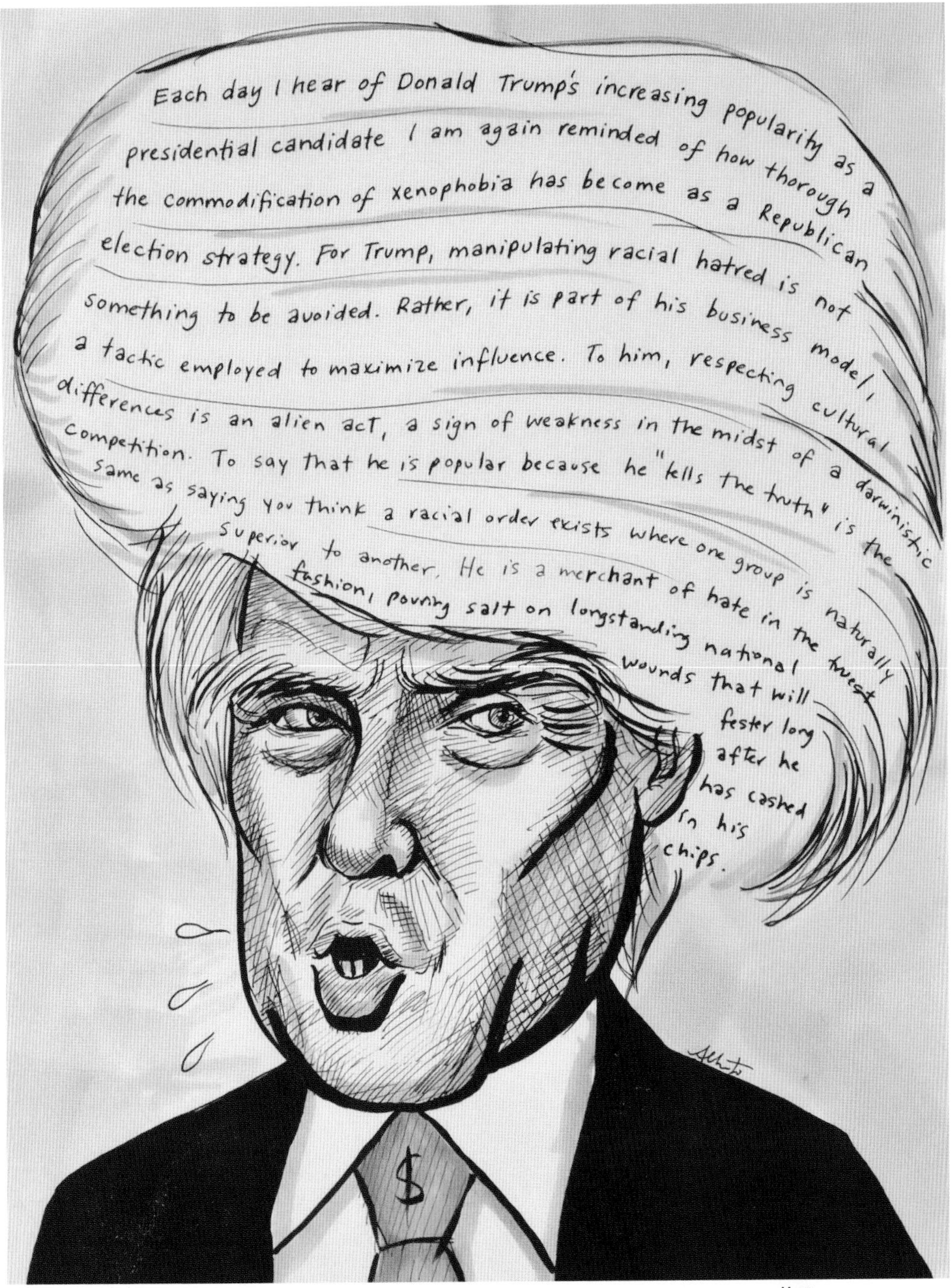
Each day I hear of Donald Trump's increasing popularity as a presidential candidate I am again reminded of how thorough the commodification of xenophobia has become as a Republican election strategy. For Trump, manipulating racial hatred is not something to be avoided. Rather, it is part of his business model, a tactic employed to maximize influence. To him, respecting cultural differences is an alien act, a sign of weakness in the midst of a darwinistic competition. To say that he is popular because he "tells the truth" is the same as saying you think a racial order exists where one group is naturally superior to another. He is a merchant of hate in the truest fashion, pouring salt on longstanding national wounds that will fester long after he has cashed in his chips.

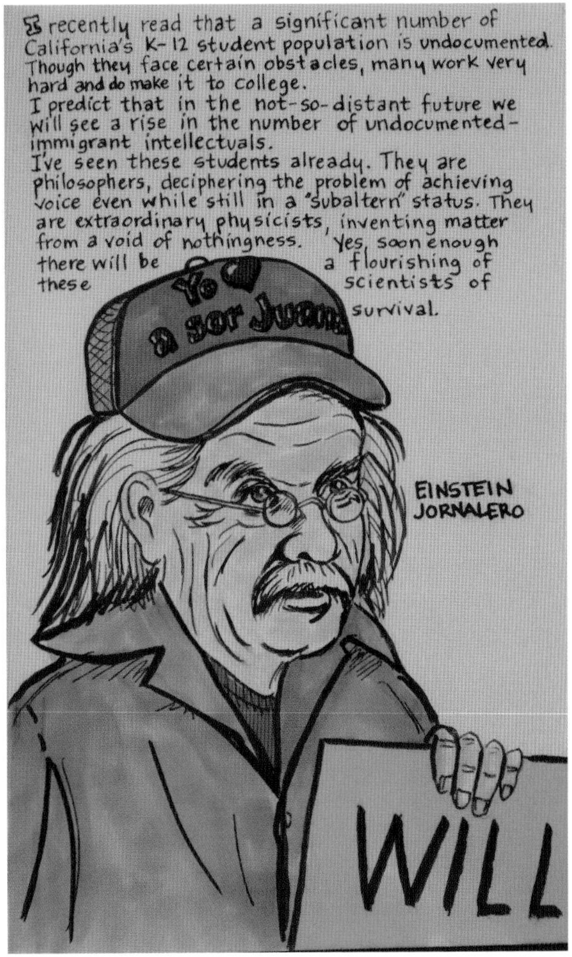
I recently read that a significant number of California's K-12 student population is undocumented. Though they face certain obstacles, many work very hard and do make it to college.
I predict that in the not-so-distant future we will see a rise in the number of undocumented-immigrant intellectuals.
I've seen these students already. They are philosophers, deciphering the problem of achieving voice even while still in a "subaltern" status. They are extraordinary physicists, inventing matter from a void of nothingness. Yes, soon enough there will be a flourishing of these scientists of survival.
EINSTEIN JORNALERO
WILL

ACKNOWLEDGMENTS

This little book took many years to come together. During the time that I labored to produce it, many people helped me with it. First and foremost, I would like to thank my wife and daughter, Leticia Aguilera-Ledesma and Sofia Ledesma, for bearing with me as I stayed up all night drawing and writing. A big thank you also goes to my parents and siblings, Adalberto and Josefina, Silvia, María, and Julian, for letting me chronicle the various mishaps that shaped our lives. To my colleagues at Berkeley, too many to name here, you have my gratitude for welcoming my creativity as an organic part of the work we do. And to my friends on Facebook, those countless people who encouraged me with your "likes" every step of the way, your comments were invaluable. Lastly, I want to thank Frederick Aldama and Kristen Elias Rowley at The Ohio State University Press for creating a venue for this work. Gracias a todos!

I would also like to acknowledge publishers who granted permission for me to reproduce versions of chapters 4 and 6. A version of "Embracing My Undocumented Immigrant Identity" first appeared online on February 5, 2010, in Colorlines Magazine. A version of "On Being an (Ex)Undocumented Immigrant Father" first appeared online on May 14, 2011, in New American Media.

LATINOGRAPHIX: THE OHIO STATE LATINX COMICS SERIES

Frederick Luis Aldama, Series Editor

This new series will showcase trade graphic and comic books—graphic novels, memoir, nonfiction, and more—by Latinx writers and artists. The series will be rich and complex, bringing on projects with any balance of text and visual narrative, from larger graphic narratives to collections of vignettes or serial comics, in color and black and white, both fiction and nonfiction. Projects in the series will take up themes of all kinds, exploring topics from immigration to family, education to identity. The series will provide a place for exploration and boundary pushing, and will celebrate hybridity, experimentation, and creativity. Projects will be produced with quality and care, and will exemplify the full breadth of creative visual work being created by today's Latinx artists.

Diary of a Reluctant Dreamer: Undocumented Vignettes from a Pre-American Life
ALBERTO LEDESMA